USUAL CRUELTY

THE COMPLICITY OF LAWYERS IN THE CRIMINAL INJUSTICE SYSTEM

ALEC KARAKATSANIS

THE
NEW
PRESS

NEW YORK
LONDON

Requests for permission to reproduce selections from this book should be made
through our website: https://thenewpress.com/contact.

"The Punishment Bureaucracy" first appeared in the *Yale Law Journal Forum*
in 2019. "The Human Lawyer" originally appeared in the *New York University
Review of Law and Social Change* in 2010. "Policing, Mass Imprisonment, and the
Failure of American Lawyers" originally appeared in the *Harvard Law Review
Forum* in 2015. The essays have been largely reproduced here in their original
form, with minor alterations for flow and consistency.

Published in the United States by The New Press, New York, 2019
Distributed by Two Rivers Distribution

ISBN 978-1-62097-527-5 (hc)
ISBN 978-1-62097-528-2 (ebook)
CIP data is available.

The New Press publishes books that promote and enrich public discussion and
understanding of the issues vital to our democracy and to a more equitable world.
These books are made possible by the enthusiasm of our readers; the support
of a committed group of donors, large and small; the collaboration of our many
partners in the independent media and the not-for-profit sector; booksellers, who
often hand-sell New Press books; librarians; and above all by our authors.

www.thenewpress.com

Book design and composition by Bookbright Media
This book was set in Janson Text and Redaction

Printed in the United States of America

10 9 8 7 6 5 4 3 2 1

For Tonya, Christy, Paula, and Cindy

We say your names with every breath

CONTENTS

Introduction

1

The Punishment Bureaucracy

13

The Human Lawyer

99

Policing, Mass Imprisonment, and the
Failure of American Lawyers

145

Author's Note

163

Notes

165

INTRODUCTION

WHEN I WAS A NEW LAWYER ALMOST TEN YEARS AGO, I WAS AT the jail in Montgomery, Alabama, one night with a client to prepare for court the next morning. As we discussed what would happen in his case, one of us made a joke, and we both laughed for a few seconds. Then, under his breath, he said, "I don't think anyone has smiled at me in a couple weeks."

I have been thinking a lot recently about what his words say about our society.

In the six years before my organization filed a constitutional civil rights lawsuit challenging the money bail system in Harris County, Texas, fifty-five human beings died in the local jail in downtown Houston because they were too poor to buy their release before trial. The American punishment system inflicts unspeakable cruelty every day, both in ways that make it into newspapers and viral videos and in ways that are only whispered about in jail cells late at night.

The essays in this book reflect on that everyday brutality. I wrote the three essays at different times in my career, and they're presented here with the most recent first. I wrote "The Human Lawyer" during my final year in law school and my first few months working in the legal system. At that time, I was particularly interested in legal education and how the culture of elite law schools produces professionals who tolerate a legal system that is profoundly unjust. I wrote "Policing, Mass Imprisonment, and the Failure of American Lawyers" when I transitioned to civil rights work after several years as a public defender in Alabama and Washington, DC, representing people accused of crimes who could not afford an attorney. By that time, after watching for years the senseless devastation of my clients and their families, I was focused on the moral and intellectual failures that led the American legal system to cage human beings at rates unprecedented in the modern recorded history of the world, without any evidence that it did any good. I examined the role of lawyers in crafting the doctrines that accomplish that transfer of bodies and explained how lawyers further this system each day by making choices about who they will represent. I wrote the most recent piece, "The Punishment Bureaucracy," in the months preceding the publication of this book, after five years of bringing civil rights cases across the country that are challenging widespread injustices in the punishment system. Writing that essay, I was surrounded by a new zeitgeist in the legal profession, and in our society more broadly, to "reform" the criminal system. But much of the "criminal justice reform" movement is superficial and deceptive. And it is therefore dangerous. It is designed to quell calls for genuine change while preserving the architecture of mass human caging. The essay talks about the nature and scope of the problem, because understanding why the punishment bureaucracy exists and who it benefits is vital to dismantling it.

The three essays are bound together by common threads.

First, I have long been interested in the chasm between how the law is written and how the law is lived. An enduring theme of my short career representing directly impacted people is the difference between how we advertise the law with beautiful inscriptions on our public monuments or lofty words in judicial opinions taught in law schools, and how we use the law to crush the bodies and minds of poor people and people of color in our streets, our prisons, and our courtrooms.

One afternoon, not long ago, I was observing a local courtroom in New Orleans, Louisiana. A black man was wearing an orange jumpsuit. He was fully restrained in metal chains as the court heard his case. He stood in between eight or nine other men—eight or nine other black bodies wearing eight or nine other orange jumpsuits bound in eight or nine other sets of chains. I thought of James Baldwin's letter to Angela Davis as she languished in a jail cell forty-eight years ago. "Dear Sister," he began. "One might have hoped that, by this hour, the very sight of chains on black flesh, or the very sight of chains, would be so intolerable a sight for the American people, and so unbearable a memory, that they would themselves spontaneously rise up and strike off the manacles. But, no, they appear to glory in their chains; now, more than ever, they appear to measure their safety in chains and corpses."

The question before the judge in New Orleans that afternoon was whether the man would be released back to his family before his trial. Because the man was very poor, if the court chose to require him to pay money for his release, he would likely be stuck in a jail cell until his case finished. If the judge released him with nonfinancial conditions of release, then the man could go back to his children, his spouse, his friends, his medical care—to all of the things, large and small, that give everyday life meaning. Because court cases can take a long time, this decision is a vital one. I had recently come across another man, in a different state, who had spent *three years* in jail on a drug possession charge because he could not pay $500 for his release while he waited for the state to run lab tests on the small amount of alleged drugs that led to his arrest. This is a pervasive problem, because almost half of American households cannot come up with $400 in an emergency.

In a hearing that lasted just a few seconds, the New Orleans judge required the man to pay $20,000 to be released from jail. Because the man could not pay, he would be locked inside the notorious New Orleans jail, which is under a federal consent decree due to the disgusting things that have been done for many years to the human beings who languish there. The court called the next case, and the man sat down. The man next to him stood up.

As a technical legal matter, the judge had done everything wrong. He violated the man's constitutional rights by jailing him without inquiring whether the man could afford to pay and without making any determination that jailing the presumptively innocent man prior to trial was necessary to serve any compelling government interest. Over thirty years ago, the Supreme Court explained in *United States v. Salerno* that, "In our society, liberty is the norm, and detention prior to or without trial is the carefully limited exception." In fact, my organization had just won a lawsuit in New Orleans declaring that, under the U.S. Constitution, the judge was not allowed to do what the judge did because it violates a person's rights to jail her solely because she cannot make a payment and without the government demonstrating that pretrial detention is absolutely necessary. Nonetheless, the judge did what judges in New Orleans and in over three thousand other cities and counties do every day: ignore the law on pretrial release. The man I saw had just become one of more than 500,000 human beings to be kept in a jail cell every night in the United States before being convicted of anything, most of them because they cannot pay money bail.

As I left the wood-paneled courtroom and walked up into the gorgeous nave lined with giant glass windows, I thought about how it is inside some of the grandest buildings that our society does some of its worst deeds. I thought about how hard it is to get courts to do what the law requires, especially in a place like New Orleans. After all, in Louisiana, it's not surprising that the judge would require as many people as possible to pay for their release from jail: the public defender who represented the man, the prosecutor who argued against the man, the sheriff who shackled the man, and the judge who ruled on the man's case all take a percentage cut of the money if the man pays for his release. If the man's family could pay the $2,600 that a for-profit bail company requires for a $20,000 bond, then these local officials would get $600 of that payment. (The for-profit company would keep $2,000.) Every year in New Orleans alone, this money amounts to about $250,000 each for the budgets of the public defender, district attorney, and sheriff, and about $1 million for the budget of the court controlled by the local judges. We had just won two federal civil rights lawsuits, in which the federal courts agreed that a

Louisiana judge's financial conflict of interest in collecting this bail money and in collecting a percentage of other fines and fees is unconstitutional. The local judges are currently appealing the two cases.

A few minutes later, I went outside and walked down the steps and across the street. I looked back at the courthouse. On top of the building, stretching for about a hundred feet on the marble façade, was carved this inscription: "The impartial administration of justice is the foundation of liberty."

A second related theme connects the three essays: all of us who work in the system have become desensitized to the pain that we inflict. When I went to Ferguson, Missouri, in 2014 in the wake of the murder of Michael Brown, my clients in Ferguson told me about how they were sleeping on top of each other on the floor in jail cells covered in feces and mold with no access to natural light or fresh air because they could not pay old tickets to the city. One client with serious physical disabilities explained that he had been jailed without a lawyer and without his medications because he could not pay a ticket he had received: police had searched his home without a warrant and without permission, found women's underwear, and arrested him for allowing a woman to sleep over in his home without getting an occupancy permit that the City of Ferguson required for friends, relatives, or romantic partners to stay overnight. Another client told me that she had spent forty-eight days in the jail without a shower, toothbrush, or any way to clean her menstrual bleeding because she could not pay traffic tickets. At the time we sued Ferguson and its neighbors—Jennings, St. Ann, and Velda City—St. Louis County itself had eighty-one different municipal courts, almost all of which appeared to be engaging in similar practices. And I have seen things like this over and over again around the country, in virtually every local courtroom and jail that I have observed.

My client Christy Dawn Varden was arrested in Clanton, Alabama, in 2015. When she found out that she could not go home to her children because she could not afford to pay a few hundred dollars in cash bail, she became anxious and panicked. She was taken to a corner of the jail outside the view of the hallway's security cameras. Christy was strapped to a chair and shocked repeatedly with electric current until she stopped crying and shouting. The prongs from the electric shock device burned open wounds all over her body that I photographed the next day.

One defining feature of America's punishment system is that it inflicts cruelty on such a scale that it no longer feels cruel. For three years, I worked as a public defender in Washington, DC. In the basement of the District of Columbia Superior Court, a few blocks from the National Mall, the DC government prosecutes children charged with juvenile delinquency. These cases are conducted in secret, closed to the public and to journalists. On my first day, I saw that the children in those closed courtrooms were fully restrained in metal chains, including their hands, feet, and waists. I saw tiny children as young as eight years old, children with severe intellectual disabilities, and children with histories of trauma, abuse, pervasive neglect, and mental illness. The children were routinely confused and disoriented because they could not move their limbs. Sometimes, children would be restrained for an entire day in court even though the DC government, consistent with what it recognized as pediatric consensus, considered it a special form of child abuse to shackle a child, even inside a children's jail, for longer than thirty minutes without medical attention. In three years, I never saw a white child in those courtrooms.

Until the public defender's office started objecting to indiscriminate child-shackling in 2011, I was told that no one had raised any problems with the practice in decades. After nearly three years of objecting to this treatment of our clients and trying to fight the issue, we finally managed to get an eleven-year-old child's case heard by the DC Court of Appeals. But after hundreds of pages of briefing and an oral argument in which the DC government did not even attempt to justify its practice of indiscriminate child-shackling, the court ruled that shackling children could not be challenged in the DC courts. The court explained its refusal to decide whether indiscriminate child-shackling was constitutional or not by arguing that, by the time any appeal could be heard months later, the child would no longer be shackled in court. In the words of the legal bureaucracy, the case was "moot." And, the court ruled in our case, indiscriminate shackling of children for a few hours was not important enough an issue for the court to use its discretion to create an exception to the local DC court's rules on "mootness."

We were later able to change some of the practices after an article in the *Washington Post* exposed this everyday brutality in the courthouse basement. (Instead of shackling one hundred percent of the detained children, they now shackle only about twenty percent of the detained children.) But I suspect that the judges, prosecutors, public defenders, and government employees who tolerated fully restraining vulnerable black children in secret courtrooms for years would have been outraged had they returned home from dinner to find that their babysitter had bound their children in metal chains, no matter how badly the children had misbehaved. They would have at least demanded justification for such treatment of their own children.

Brutality like this feels normal to many people who work in the punishment bureaucracy and to many people in our society—so normal that we can inflict it on a massive scale without needing any justification. This desensitization has led to a remarkable lack of intellectual rigor in every corner of the punishment bureaucracy: almost no one carrying out punishment in our legal system has any clue about whether what they are doing is leading to any good. They don't even know, for example, if locking people in jail cells actually increases or decreases the frequency of things that they call "crimes"—and a lot of evidence suggests that it makes communities *less* safe. They lack the most basic data, evidence, or rational explanations that one would expect from people before they cage millions of human beings in frightening conditions and separate tens of millions of families. The essays in this book explore how bureaucrats in the punishment system have allowed themselves to become desensitized to things that should shock them to the core.

A final theme is more forward-looking. I've always been interested, above all, in exploring what we can do about the senseless suffering caused by the punishment system. Each essay, in different ways, talks about how people might think about the moral obligations created by the American bureau-cracy of mass human caging. I talk about why personal deci-sions matter—how we spend our lives and careers, the work that we choose to do, who we stand next to and whose hand we hold, the way we spend precious time on earth, and how we decide to use the knowledge and energy that animate our bodies each day.

But these are also collective questions. I write about how to come together to organize with others to build the power nec-essary to demand a different way of doing things and about the language society uses to talk about the punishment system. After all, dismantling the system of mass human caging is not a legal battle for lawyers. It is, fundamentally, a political one. It is about power. And so we have to examine why the punish-ment system exists and how it has functioned throughout its history as a mechanism of preserving white supremacy and the distribution of economic wealth and social control. Its future depends on whether we can build enough power—on whether enough people organize together with enough urgency and clarity—to challenge the forces that created and benefit from the punishment system. Will we each go home every night thinking about how we can come together in solidarity with people whose bodies and minds and loved ones are on the line?

Dismantling mass incarceration is a deeply human project that requires a different cultural narrative about what the pun-ishment system is, why it looks the way it does, who it harms, and how it harms them. Because the success of the punishment system depends on erasing people and their stories, the suc-cess of a movement to undo it depends on a massive intentional effort to change the way society talks and thinks. This won't be easy, because it requires everyone—particularly people who are not directly impacted—to evaluate their own complicity in the criminal injustice system and to find creative ways to re-sensitize themselves and each other. It requires us to have open minds, to not be defensive, and to develop a new discourse. We must employ the language of life against the language of a bureaucracy—songs instead of shackles, poems instead of police reports.

THE PUNISHMENT BUREAUCRACY

How to Think About "Criminal Justice Reform"

[W]e do not expect people to be deeply moved by what is not unusual. That element of tragedy which lies in the very fact of frequency, has not yet wrought itself into the coarse emotion of mankind; and perhaps our frames could hardly bear much of it. If we had a keen vision and feeling of all ordinary human life, it would be like hearing the grass grow and the squirrel's heart beat, and we should die of that roar which lies on the other side of silence.

—Mary Ann Evans, *Middlemarch*[1]

I

On January 26, 2014, Sharnalle Mitchell was sitting on her couch with her one-year-old daughter on her lap and her four-year-old son to her side.[2] Armed government agents entered her home, put her in metal restraints, took her from her children, and brought her to the Montgomery City Jail. Jail staff told Sharnalle that she owed the city money for old traffic tickets. The city had privatized the collection of her debts to a for-profit "probation company," which had sought a warrant for her arrest. I happened to be sitting in the courtroom on the morning that Sharnalle was brought to court, along with dozens of other people who had been jailed because they owed the city money. The judge demanded that Sharnalle pay or stay in jail. If she could not pay, she would be kept in a cage until she "sat out" her debts at $50 per day, or at $75 per day if she agreed to clean the courthouse bathrooms and the feces, blood, and mucus from the jail walls. An hour later, in a windowless cell, Sharnalle told me that a jail guard had given her a pencil, and she showed me the crumpled court document on the back of which she had calculated how many more weeks of forced labor separated her from her children. That day, she became my first client as a civil rights lawyer.

II

Prisons do not disappear social problems, they disappear human beings.

—Angela Davis[3]

There are 2.2 million human beings confined in prison and jail cells in the United States tonight.[4] About 500,000 of those people are presumptively innocent people awaiting trial,[5] the vast majority of whom are confined by the government solely because they cannot pay enough money to buy their release.[6] This country has five percent of the world's population, but twenty-five percent of the world's prisoners—the highest rate of human caging of any society in the recorded history of the modern world.[7] At least another 4.5 million people are under government control through probation and parole "supervision."[8]

Between eighty and ninety percent of the people charged with crimes are so poor that they cannot afford a lawyer.[9] Twenty-five years into America's incarceration boom, black people were incarcerated at a rate six times that of South Africa during apartheid.[10] The incarceration rate for black people in the nation's capital, where I live, is nineteen times that of white people.[11]

I have traveled the country and seen nearly identical practices in every courtroom and every jail that I have visited. We have a legal system in which things like what happened to Sharnalle are simultaneously illegal and the norm.

III

*[T]he movement for reforming the prisons, for control-
ling their functioning is not a recent phenomenon. It does
not even seem to have originated in a recognition of failure. Prison "reform" is virtually contemporary with the
prison itself: it constitutes, as it were, its programme.*

—Michel Foucault[12]

A lot of people are talking about "criminal justice reform." Much of that talk is dangerous. The conventional wisdom is that there is an emerging consensus that the criminal legal system is "broken." But the system is "broken" only to the extent that one believes its purpose is to promote the well-being of all members of our society. If the function of the modern punishment system is to preserve racial and economic hierarchy through brutality and control, then its bureaucracy is performing well.

IV

> *Official language smitheryed to sanction ignorance and preserve privilege is a suit of armor polished to shocking glitter. . . . It is the language that drinks blood. . . .*

—Toni Morrison[13]

The emerging "criminal justice reform" consensus is superficial and deceptive. It is superficial because most proposed "reforms" would still leave the United States as the greatest incarcerator in the world. It is deceptive because those who want largely to preserve the current punishment bureaucracy—by making just enough tweaks to protect its perceived legitimacy—must obfuscate the difference between changes that will transform the system and tweaks that will curb only its most grotesque flourishes.

Nearly every prominent national politician and the vast majority of state and local officials talking and tweeting about "criminal justice reform" are, with varying levels of awareness and sophistication, furthering this deception. These "reform"-advancing bureaucrats are co-opting a movement toward profound change by convincing the public that the "law enforcement" system as we know it can operate in an objective, effective, and fair way based on the "rule of law." These punishment bureaucrats are dangerous because, in order to preserve the human caging apparatus that they control, they must disguise at the deepest level its core functions. As a result, they focus public conversation on the margins of the problem without confronting the structural issues at its heart. Theirs is the language that drinks blood.

It's useful to think about "criminal justice reform" by focusing on the concepts of "law enforcement" and the "rule of law." Both are invoked as central features of the American criminal system. For many prominent people advocating "reform," the punishment bureaucracy as we know it is the inevitable result of "law enforcement" responding to people "breaking the law." To them, the human caging bureaucracy is consistent with, and even required by, the "rule of law." This worldview—that the punishment bureaucracy is an attempt to promote social well-being and human flourishing under a dispassionate system of laws—shapes their ideas about how to "fix" the system.

But few ideas have caused more harm in our criminal system than the belief that America is governed by a neutral "rule of law." The content of our criminal laws—discussed in Part V—and how those laws are carried out—addressed in Part VI—are *choices* that reflect power. The common understanding of the "rule of law" and the widely accepted use of the term "law enforcement" to describe the process by which those in power accomplish unprecedented human caging are both delusions critical to justifying the punishment bureaucracy. This is why it is important to understand how they distort the truth.

I apply these arguments to explain why the current "criminal justice reform" discourse is so dangerous, focusing on several prominent national punishment bureaucrats and a new local wave of supposedly "progressive prosecutors." Finally, I discuss the new generation of directly impacted people, organizers, lawyers, faith leaders, and academics on the libertarian left and right who understand the punishment bureaucracy as a tool of power in service of white supremacy and profit. I explain why this growing movement must reject the "criminal justice reform" discourse of punishment bureaucrats and speak clearly about why the legal system looks the way that it does. I urge those interested in changing the punishment bureaucracy to ground every discussion that they have and every proposed reform that they evaluate in a set of guiding principles rooted in this movement's vision. I sketch some of those principles for their consideration below.

V

We are living in the era of premeditation and the perfect crime. Our criminals . . . have a perfect alibi: philosophy, which can be used for any purpose—even for transforming murderers into judges.

—Albert Camus[14]

What is a crime? The first step to understanding how we accomplish the imprisonment of millions of people's bodies is understanding what laws authorize government agents to take away a person's liberty.

A society makes choices about what acts or omissions to render worthy of different kinds of punishment. The decision to make something punishable by human caging authorizes the government to treat people in ways that otherwise would be abhorrent. For example, a person walking down the street smoking a cigarette cannot be searched by police. Even a police demand to stop walking or the probe of an officer's hand along the person's outer clothing would violate our Constitution's Bill of Rights.[15] But, in most of the country for the past fifty years, if that same person were smoking a cigarette containing a dried marijuana plant in addition to a dried tobacco plant, the person may be bound in metal chains, removed from the street, strip searched, placed in a cage, and held in solitary confinement with no human contact or natural light.[16] The person can be kept in that cage for decades.[17] The person can lose her right to vote, be removed from public housing and have her family removed from public housing, be kicked out of school, and be barred from employment.[18] She can also be deprived of basic human needs, such as hugging her child or having a sexual relationship with her spouse.[19] All of this treatment is allowed only because the person is a "criminal."

Criminal Laws Reflect and Legitimate the Environment in Which They Are Made

Choices about what is a crime and what is not are made by politicians and within the economic, social, and racial systems in which politicians exist. As a result, for better or worse, these choices reflect the logic of, promote the legitimacy of, and protect distributions of power within those systems.

Consider, for example, that it is a "crime" in most of America for the poor to wager in the streets over dice. Wagering over international currencies, entire cities' worth of mortgages, the global supply of wheat needed to avoid mass starvation,[20] or ownership of public corporations is accepted behavior.[21] Dice-wagerers become bodies to seize, search, confine, and shun.[22] Their private cash is "forfeited" to government ownership.[23] Wheat-wagerers become names on the wings of hospitals and museum galleries. Their cash makes them heroes, and charitable organizations providing legal services to low-income dice-wagerers in criminal prosecutions give them philanthropic awards at banquets.

This example is not a quirky outlier. Furthering and legitimating particular distributions of wealth and power are pervasive, defining functions of our criminal legal system—not minor, unintended byproducts.

These choices play out over the criminal law, from foundational laws criminalizing a physical breach of another person's private property to definitions of affirmative defenses like duress or necessity. (Poverty, for example, is not commonly accepted by American courts as a sufficient excuse for theft of subsistence goods.)[24] Our political choices answer questions like: Should it be a crime to beg for money? To charge high interest rates? To hoard wealth? To decide not to vote? To abuse a family dog? To abuse thousands of pigs to make higher profits from their flesh? To belong to a union? To decline to belong to a union? To refuse to grant mortgages to people of a certain race? To drill for oil? To seize land from indigenous people? To participate in a lynch mob? To enslave people? To refuse to pay reparations to people formerly enslaved on one's land? To spray carcinogenic chemicals into the ground to release natural gas? To hit one's child? To design political boundaries based on race? To run a bank for profit? To refuse to identify oneself to a police officer? To force sex upon a spouse? To search a person without probable cause? To grow tobacco? To have oral sex with another consenting adult? To hold profits offshore? To expose secret government misdeeds in the media? To dress a certain way? To possess a gun? To possess a hunting rifle ten years after a marijuana conviction? To donate to a foreign charity? To boycott apartheid? To terminate a pregnancy? To cross an imaginary boundary between two political jurisdictions to be reunited with one's child?

The standard narrative portrays "criminals" as a vast collection of individuals who have each made a choice to "break the law." Convictions and punishments are consequences that flow naturally from that bad choice: we must enforce the "rule of law." But these crimes are not chosen because of some assessment of the amount of harm prevented, and punishments are not selected because of demonstrated penological success. The difference in the way the bureaucracy treats someone using cocaine and someone using vodka has no empirical connection to the respective harm caused by those substances or to any analysis of how to prevent addiction to them. Instead, forces external to well-reasoned policy contribute to definitions of criminality and to decisions about appropriate punishment. The criminal law is not an inviolate repository of right and wrong, but—just like any other policy fashioned in a country as unequal as ours—a tool related to cultural, racial, and economic features of our society.[25]

Making it a crime to possess certain substances is a good example. The expansion and increase in severity of drug laws in the last forty years, as well as the lack of outrage over that punishment for many decades, has been shown to stem from a combination of conscious and subconscious biases and incentives.[26] It is now a federal and state crime in every American jurisdiction for any person to ingest a wide variety of substances into their own bodies.[27] And politicians have simultaneously decided that other harmful substances are *legal* to consume and to distribute for profit.[28] It was not always so. The history of drug prohibition was influenced by the desire to criminalize conduct associated with particular groups at specific historical moments.[29] And now, during what punishment bureaucrats call the "war on drugs," punishment bureaucrats make a choice to "fight" drug use (when it comes to *some* drugs when used in *some* neighborhoods) not as a public health issue but through armed agents and cages. No matter what one's views on drugs, there is one thing that all agree on: these laws were *never* based on empirical evidence about the best way to create a society with less use of harmful substances.[30]

Why does the evidence matter so little to the punishment bureaucracy? The punishment system would change overnight if the vast numbers of young, wealthy, and white drug criminals at private schools and famous universities were harassed and beaten by police in the streets, had their family homes raided at night, were sexually and physically assaulted in prisons, and were confined to live and die in cages. The human costs of the bureaucracy would be evaluated differently if drug searches by undercover police and SWAT teams were as common at

Yale University as they are down the street in the low-income neighborhoods of New Haven. The brutality of separating tens of millions of families from their loved ones—with no empirical evidence of a benefit—would not be tolerated if it were happening to different people. Our culture would see it as widespread violence in need of serious justification, if not a human rights crisis demanding urgent and immediate action, rather than as a vague and impersonal aspect of the need for "law enforcement."

And so the knowledge that laws will be enforced in particular ways against particular people changes what laws powerful people create. Elites need not worry about creating crimes with harsh punishments if they know that the laws will not be enforced against them.

While many of these choices reflect background social, racial, and economic forces, other choices in the criminal law are more obvious political calculations. For example, while politicians decided to make insider trading a crime for ordinary people and private investors, they had also decided, until recently, that insider trading should be *legal* for members of Congress. This meant that elite politicians could make millions of dollars based on inside information that they learned through lawmaking or use their control over lawmaking and regulation for personal profit.[31]

More broadly, much of what are now celebrated as instruments of wealth creation for investors used to be called "crimes." During the Clinton presidency, for example, bankers hoping to engage in then-illegal types of derivatives trading paid lobbyists and politicians a lot of money to change words in a federal

statute that transformed, overnight, those doing certain investment banking activities from criminals into philanthropists.[32]

Overt political calculations similarly determine the punishment system's understanding of "terrorism." The federal
government has passed a law to make it a felony to provide
"material support" for "terrorist" groups.[33] This crime includes
providing nonviolent conflict resolution and peaceful advice to
any group a government bureaucrat chooses to put on a list of
"terrorists."[34] And politicians and bureaucrats are constantly
revising who goes on "terrorist" lists and which people are
instead "allies" to whom the U.S. government and private corporations sell weapons.[35] Often, these are the same groups at
different times. To take one example, one of those "terrorist"
groups, the People's Mujahedin of Iran, recently hired dozens
of the most famous retired American politicians to work on its
behalf to remove it from the list of "terrorist" groups, transforming those politicians from felony terrorism offenders to
successful lobbyists.[36] And during America's support for South
African apartheid, the U.S. government not only helped to capture and imprison Nelson Mandela, but it officially categorized
him as a "terrorist" until 2008.[37]

In the same way, the federal government makes it a felony
to disclose "classified" information,[38] and officials secretly
decide what information to deem "classified." There are
between two and three million bureaucrats with the ability to classify (and therefore criminalize) information, and
they did so for nearly fifty million documents in 2017.[39] At
the same time, the federal government does not make it a
crime for bureaucrats to violate Freedom of Information Act
requirements, meaning that officials can fail to document

their activities, refuse to disclose records when they exist, or destroy records without committing a crime.[40] Such violations of the law, even brazen ones, are addressed through *civil* lawsuits.[41] But when a military intelligence officer publicized a video of a mass murder by U.S. troops (including the murder of children arriving at the scene of the massacre to treat the wounded), she became a "criminal" sentenced to thirty-five years in prison because an unknown bureaucrat decided that disclosing the video to the public should be a crime.[42] The soldiers who murdered people on videotape were not prosecuted for their violations of the "rule of law."[43] Similarly, the person who disclosed lies used to justify American involvement in millions of deaths in Vietnam, Cambodia, and Laos was prosecuted in the 1970s for felonies because bureaucrats had decided to make publication of their lies—rather than the lies themselves—a crime.[44]

This political process is also influenced by multibillion-dollar industries with sophisticated marketing and lobbying strategies because many corporations depend on increasing punishment. These interests include pharmaceutical companies lobbying to block marijuana legalization and large meat corporations lobbying to create new felony offenses for videotaping animal abuse at their factories (though, of course, not for the actual animal abuse).[45] They also include private prison corporations and the much larger industry of private contractors in public prisons and jails, who profit from the labor, phone calls, emails, family visits, mail, food, supplies, and medical care of prisoners.[46] The more people in jail or prison and the longer they remain confined to a cage, the more profit the companies make.

Simply put, political power influences what we decide to criminalize. And because political contributions affect voting behavior, groups pay political campaigns and associated entities so that politicians will create laws that benefit those groups. Laws are often passed not because they increase overall well-being, but because politicians need money to stay in power. If a would-be criminal, therefore, has a large amount of money, she can purchase the ability to be viewed as a noncriminal by changing laws. If a group of people wants other people to be called "criminals" and imprisoned, the group can pay for that as well. We could call this behavior "bribery," but instead we have decided to call it "free speech."[47]

To be clear, it is appropriate for a political process to make decisions about what a society should punish and what a society should celebrate. The point here is that our criminal laws are not an objective mechanism for increasing overall well-being by efficiently reducing harmful behavior. Our criminal laws are based on some of the most arbitrary aspects of human existence, like power, racial bias, and economic self-interest—they reflect our demons, past and present.[48]

The Same Processes Determine How Harshly We Punish

Having made certain activity a "crime," society must decide how to punish it. How does the legal system choose how harshly to punish speeding, selling various derivatives of the coca plant, domestic assault, sleeping under a bridge, illegally searching someone, downloading music, committing murder, or tax evasion? Why are penalties for texting or drinking while driving more lenient than for cocaine possession even though impaired driving is more dangerous? And why are the penalties for the same crimes dramatically lower in other countries?

The same forces that determine which conduct is criminal also determine how severely different conduct is punished. To take one example, federal law famously treats crack cocaine offenses more harshly than powder cocaine offenses, even though the two substances are pharmacologically identical. For the first seven years that the disparity existed, not a single white person was prosecuted for a crack cocaine offense in seven of the largest American cities.[49] For decades, even the cautious U.S. Sentencing Commission wanted to remove this disparity because there is no legal or scientific basis for it.[50] And when Congress did reduce the disparity after a unanimous Senate vote in 2010—and millions of years in prison later—no one offered a justification for why it had existed.[51] But for reasons that were never articulated, the government did not remove the disparity; it chose to lower the disparity from 100:1 to 18:1.[52] And for more than eight years after that "Fair Sentencing Act" passed, the government chose not to make even these limited "fair" changes retroactive to help the thousands of human beings already in prison because of a law that everyone agreed had no basis.[53] Close to ten years *after* the celebrated reform under the Obama Administration, the 18:1 punishment disparity is still law, and thousands sentenced to decades in prison under the policy continue to languish.

Besides determining the severity of punishment, these forces influence the *way* people are punished. For many decades, white elites in the South used the punishment system to transfer wealth, confiscate land, and preserve racial hierarchy through convict leasing—that is, criminalizing people so that their bodies could be forced to work for profit.[54] In contemporary prisons throughout the United States, 800,000 people work long hours every day in often dangerous conditions with miniscule wages to produce products for private corporations and government entities so that prisoners can afford to purchase basic necessities sold by other private corporations inside prison walls.[55] In this way, prisoners work to afford phone calls to their families or toilet paper, soap, and nutritious food— needs that the prisons create in order to coerce this labor.[56] This ubiquitous overcharging of prisoners and their families for basic necessities and the monetizing of human contact with one's family are not based on what would help improve health, wellness, and community safety during or after release from prison, but on what maximizes profit.

Our society has created other punishments to promote different political interests. For example, in the early twentieth century, Alabama passed a law that took away a person's ability to vote if the person was caught possessing cocaine. That law was first passed for the purpose of reducing the number of black people voting.[57] In the most recent national election, nearly 6 million Americans could not vote because of the decision to prosecute them in the punishment system, and nearly forty percent of those who could not vote were black.[58] Until recently, Florida alone chose to disenfranchise so many people that 1.5 million people and forty percent of all black males in Florida could not vote in the 2018 election.[59] These Florida laws also had the purpose of limiting the political power of black people.[60] When it became unlawful to deny the right to vote to people based on the color of their skin, a similar result could be accomplished by denying the right to vote if a person committed certain crimes, knowing that "law enforcement" would disproportionately arrest and prosecute people with black skin for those crimes. It is remarkable that many "rule of law" proponents treat these elections as democratic and the laws produced after them as valid even while accepting that large percentages of people are prohibited from casting a ballot because of political decisions made based on their skin color.

In addition to being caged and stripped of the right to vote, people are punished in other ways. One component of contemporary "law enforcement" for drug crimes, for example, is that an entire family can be removed from their home for one person's drug crime, even a grandmother who had no knowledge that her grandson possessed a substance that the government put on a list of substances for which a family could lose a home.[61]

We Have Different Rules of Law, and They Are Inconsistent

How we punish is complicated in another important respect: our laws conflict in ways that make it impossible to apply the "rule of law" without choosing between competing rules. But which laws prevail when rules of law conflict and, thus, which laws come to define the "rule of law" in mainstream consciousness?

One of the bedrock principles of American constitutional law is that when a person has a constitutional right, the government may not deprive a person of that right without sufficient justification.[62] For example, under the First and Second Amendments, I have a right to publish an essay about the dangers of "criminal justice reform" discourse, and to possess a firearm in my home. If the government wants to take away either of these rights, it has to demonstrate that it has good reasons. In the same way, a long line of Supreme Court cases has established that the right to physical bodily liberty is "fundamental" and lies at the "core" of the liberty that the Due Process Clause protects.[63]

The value of bodily liberty has been a central theme of law for centuries. For example, American courts have long required a high constitutional burden of proof in criminal cases: no person can be imprisoned unless the government proves *beyond a reasonable doubt* that she is guilty.[64] This reflects a paramount libertarian concern with agents of the state doing violence to a person's body by confining a person to a cage against her will. But while the legal system thinks of itself as applying extreme rigor to decisions about when a person can be caged, it does not apply any rigor to an antecedent question: is this conduct something for which we should cage a human being?

Consider an example: your friend is stopped by police on the street and searched. The search reveals a small capsule of cocaine powder in her pocket. Your friend is charged with possession of cocaine, which is subject in her state to a penalty of five years in prison. Your other friend, who was also searched, had only a pack of cigarettes in her bag—she was not arrested.

A third friend had a bottle of whiskey in his backpack that the three had just purchased from the nearby alcohol distribution trafficking enterprise—he too was allowed to leave. The cocaine possessor was eventually taken to trial. Because of the foundational importance of human liberty to the constitutional Framers, she was cloaked in innocence and would be caged for five years only if the government proved beyond a reasonable doubt that she knowingly possessed the cocaine powder. But the "reasonable doubt" rule did little for her. It was easy for the government to prove that she knowingly possessed the cocaine found in her own pocket.

However, it would be *very* difficult for the government to prove that putting your friend in a cage for that cocaine possession served a compelling interest, let alone that it served that compelling interest in a *better* way than other alternative responses to cocaine possession—the standard we would apply if the government attempted to forbid the publication of this essay or seize my guns. Indeed, at least with respect to drug laws, it may be an insurmountable burden, given the existing empirical and scientific evidence. One of the remarkable features of the contemporary criminal system is that most punishment bureaucrats are aware of how ineffective caging people who use certain drugs is at addressing any social ill whatsoever, but they continue to enforce that punishment.

To accomplish this result, an entire strand of constitutional law—due process jurisprudence requiring the government to demonstrate a good reason to deprive a person of her bodily liberty—is ignored to enforce drug laws. I have struggled to find a single judicial opinion acknowledging, let alone confronting, this legal problem. The reason for this silence is that the principle of the "rule of law" cannot be applied at the same time to the law requiring a mandatory ten-year prison sentence for a crack cocaine offense and to the law that the government must prove that depriving a person of a fundamental liberty interest such as physical freedom is necessary to serve an identifiable public good.

In contrast, look at how our society has chosen to deal with a variety of other evils. One can be sued for racial discrimination or sexual harassment at work, for instance, but one cannot typically be prosecuted for that conduct, even though it might cause a lot of harm. The political system has chosen to pursue these other important goals without resort to the criminal system. Even assuming that preventing private individuals from choosing to ingest certain non-alcohol and non-tobacco drugs can create a compelling state interest—a proposition that would take its own justification—a variety of other alternatives to human caging exist to reduce drug use: education, employment, companionship, after-school art and theater programs, medical and mental health care, addiction treatment, and stable housing, to name a few. No government in any jurisdiction in the United States has proven that human caging is a way to reduce drug use at all, let alone the least intrusive way. Instead, a mountain of evidence suggests that the punishment approach to drugs has actually *increased* drug use and the harms associated with it, including by diverting funds from evidence-based alternatives.[65]

The pathology through which people who call themselves "law enforcement" officials have come to acquiesce in this punishment is revealing. It would be intolerable to our legal system for a person to spend a moment in a cage for cocaine possession if the person did not possess cocaine. But many "rule of law" proponents care nothing for the question: why is it tolerable for a person to spend a moment in a cage when they *have* possessed cocaine? To answer that question, we would need to ask a further question: is human caging the best way, or even a reasonable way, to minimize the harms that cocaine possession causes?

Thus we have a central paradox of American criminal law: in order to put a person in prison, we have to prove by overwhelming evidence that she merits punishment in a narrow factual sense; but in order to put millions of people in prison, we do not need to show that doing so would do any good. Under the unspoken consensus of the "rule of law," a law authorizing millions of people to be caged for certain conduct will be enforced so long as there is a "rational basis" for it—and the courts define "rational basis" to mean any potential reason, no matter how unpersuasive, and even if it was not the actual reason for the law.[66] This is almost the *exact opposite* of the "beyond a reasonable doubt" approach that we are told the Constitution requires for taking away bodily liberty. In the latter, a person must not be caged so long as there could be a single reason to doubt her factual eligibility for incarceration.

In this way, courts have chosen to enforce certain rules of criminal law over rules of constitutional law that constrain government violence to individual liberty, even though this order of priority defies the most basic "rule of law" in the legal system: that the Constitution trumps other laws. Thus, if a legislature created mandatory ten-year prison punishments for buying products derived from animals or for drinking red wine, it might be difficult for the government to prove that the prison terms were the least restrictive way of promoting a compelling interest in environmental or public health. This scenario is unlikely to happen, but not because the courts would scrutinize whether the law violates a higher rule of constitutional law. It would not happen because such policies would be politically unpopular among groups with power.

Such flouting of foundational rules of law would be unthinkable in noncriminal areas. Consider an example: suppose that a state passes a law establishing that parents lose custody of their children if they endanger their child's health, and that allowing a child to drink sugary sodas is a danger to child health. A federal judge hands her youngest daughter a Coca-Cola drink at a family party. A police officer standing on the street witnesses the incident through the window. Several days later, the judge's house is raided, the child and several cans of soda are removed from the home, and the state petitions to terminate parental rights. If the judge challenged the law that parents could lose their parental rights if they let their children drink soda, the law would be subject to heightened scrutiny because raising one's child is a "fundamental" right under the constitutional "rule of law."[67] Courts would ask whether the law served a compelling government interest (say, for example, child health) and then whether the law's termination of parental rights was the most narrowly tailored way to achieve that health-related goal.[68] The judge would likely win because it would be difficult for the government to prove the necessity of the drastic step of terminating parental rights to promote a Coca-Cola-free life for children.

But what if the law has a companion provision? What if it

also *criminalizes* the distribution of sugary sodas to minors, punishing that behavior with a mandatory sentence of ten years to life in prison? When the federal judge challenges *that* law in court, the courts would, under their current abdication of these principles, refuse to review the criminal law for anything other than a "rational basis." The judge could be sentenced to twelve years of physical confinement. The judge can secure parental rights because the law lacks rigorous justification, but she will lose her bodily liberty and, incidentally, the ability to raise her daughter.

The whole criminal system is pervaded by similar inconsistencies in the "rule of law." To take one ubiquitous example, the Constitution requires that every guilty plea waiving the constitutional right to trial by a jury of one's peers be knowing, intelligent, and voluntary.[69] But no one who works in the criminal system thinks that contemporary plea bargaining produces voluntary agreements. The vast majority of plea bargains are accepted by people who are told that they will be imprisoned for longer if they do not give up their right to a jury trial. Many of these people are in jail and are told that pleading guilty is the only immediate way out of jail.[70] In no other cultural context would the word "voluntary" describe this arrangement. Should my coworker ask a person out on a dinner date but tell the person that, if he does not accept, he will be placed in a cage, no one would view the person's agreement to dine with my coworker as voluntary. That's not how we understand "voluntary" actions. And yet, because we are attempting to arrest and process historically unprecedented numbers of people in the punishment bureaucracy, the system would collapse if people exercised the jury right envisioned by those who wrote the Constitution.[71]

For that reason, the most important "rule of law" in our legal system—the Bill of Rights—is ignored as a matter of practice in millions of cases every year.[72] The U.S. Supreme Court itself has acknowledged that it will not deem threats-based plea bargains involuntary in part *in order to* facilitate the mass caging of human beings.[73] In this respect, the post-arrest criminal system is not "law enforcement," but a bureaucracy designed and permitted to circumvent the "rule of law" when necessary to pursue the aims that political elites have assigned to it.

Similar problems exist throughout the application of the "rule of law" in the punishment bureaucracy. In the case of Ezell Gilbert, the federal courts acknowledged that Mr. Gilbert (like tens of thousands like him) was imprisoned under an illegal sentence that was more than ten years longer than allowed by federal law.[74] He was released after many years in federal prison after a federal appeals court finally granted his second petition for release.[75] But lawyers working for the executive branch, run by President Obama and Attorney General Eric Holder, urged the court to reconsider.[76] A larger group of judges chose to prioritize a legal rule that a prisoner cannot file *two* petitions for release, even if the first one was wrongly denied and even if the person is wrongfully in prison.[77] Despite federal prosecutors and judges admitting that Mr. Gilbert was improperly sentenced, the federal court decided that the legal rule of "finality" was more important than the conflicting legal rule that people should not be in prison illegally.[78] This, it was said, was the result that the "rule of law" required.[79] Despite having been freed from illegal confinement for months, Mr. Gilbert was arrested by U.S. Marshals and sent back to prison to finish his illegal sentence. Take a moment to think about how you might explain that collective social choice to your family over dinner.

The choice by "law enforcement" to prioritize some criminal laws over more fundamental rules of constitutional law that are inconsistent with those criminal laws results in far less actual liberty from imprisonment in the United States than in any other country in the world, even those countries that do not have the procedural protections afforded by the libertarians who wrote the Bill of Rights. If offered a choice between criminal systems, those with brown skin or those living in poverty might rationally choose *any* other country, given that their absolute chances of being imprisoned would be lower.

Modern courts have not reckoned with these issues because the consequences of adhering to the Framers' liberty-advancing principles is the specter that haunts the mass incarceration system built in the last forty years. When the needs of power and bureaucracy conflict with the "rule of law," our punishment system ignores the "rule of law." As Justice Brennan observed, the courts have been afraid that the assembly-line punishment bureaucracy could not withstand "too much justice."[80]

VI

[I]t is forbidden to kill; therefore all murderers are punished, unless they kill in large numbers, and to the sound of trumpets. . . .

—Voltaire[81]

Criminal laws are an important way in which the punishment
bureaucracy accomplishes mass human caging. But the choices
that most define our criminal system today relate to how those
laws are *enforced*.

Nearly everyone commits a crime on a regular basis: "dis-
orderly conduct" by shouting too loud in the street at night,
downloading a song without paying for it, pushing someone
after a heated moment in the schoolyard or the company soft-
ball league, failing to declare cash income at a summer job,
giving a prescription pill to a friend with back pain, using
marijuana to treat a child's seizures, fishing in an undesignated
spot, failing to fully stop at a stop sign, walking a dog without
a leash, hiding money in an offshore bank account, withholding exculpatory evidence in a criminal prosecution, making
misleading statements in a business transaction, stumbling
down the street drunk after a party, hiring a worker who was
born in another country but does not have work authoriza-
tion, stopping and frisking someone without basis, systemi-
cally fabricating mortgage documents, giving a teenager a sip
of wine, ordering drone assassinations, and more. We commit
an incalculable number of legal violations every day. Only a
tiny fraction of those violations, however, are ever targeted for
punishment.

When almost all of us are criminals, the choice of which violations to "enforce" determines what the legal system looks like
in the real world.[82] I have explained how we choose to make
laws authorizing and calibrating punishment for certain conduct. Here, I explore how those laws are *enforced*. Of all the

people who violate laws, how does society decide who will be punished and who will not?

Consider a few snapshots of the decisions that "law enforcement" officials are making: in 2015, more people were handcuffed and caged for marijuana offenses than for all "violent" crimes combined.[83] In many jurisdictions, the single most common criminal prosecution is for driving with a suspended license,[84] and about forty percent of suspended American drivers' licenses were taken away not for any reason related to driving, but because a person was too poor to pay court debts.[85]

I make three points in this part: First, discretionary authority to decide who is punished is vested almost entirely in a group of prosecutors and armed agents. Bureaucrats *decide* which offenses to punish and which to ignore.[86] The people making these choices call themselves "law enforcement."

Second, like society's choices about what conduct is criminalized and how severely that conduct is punished, decisions about who to target (and how and when to target them) are also driven by political, cultural, social, and economic forces. They are also made by particular cohorts of people who bring their life experiences and perspectives to their decisions. For example, American prosecutors are mostly men, almost all white, and share a number of other similarities across religious, class, and educational backgrounds.[87]

Third, the "rule of law" is an important story that the punishment system uses to make its decisions appear to be the natural, inevitable consequences of individual law-breaking rather than distributive choices. Laws are broken. Laws are enforced.

It must be so. One is punished because one breaks the law. "Law enforcement" officials exist not to pursue political, racial, and economic goals through strategic choices, but neutrally to administer mutually agreed-upon rules for everyone's benefit. This conventional story is wrong.

"Law Enforcement" Is About Making Choices

Our apologies good friends
for the fracture of good order
the burning of paper instead of children . . .

—Father Daniel Berrigan[88]

PROSECUTORIAL DISCRETION

Government employees called "prosecutors" decide the people against whom to initiate the state's machinery of physical force. Prosecutors have nearly unlimited authority to decide who to charge with a crime and how harsh a punishment to pursue for it.[89]

Prosecutors make decisions about what crimes to investigate,[90] what crimes to ignore, whether to file charges in any particular case of lawbreaking, whether to seek pretrial detention, whether to seek mandatory minimum prison sentences, whether to permit a plea bargain, and how severe a punishment to seek, including whether to seek the death penalty, life in prison, decades in prison, probation, or diversion from punishment entirely. Because courts have removed themselves from this process and because there is typically no independent oversight of prosecutors, there is effectively no check on the exercise of American prosecutorial power.[91] And in most jurisdictions, there is no mechanism for the public to initiate an independent prosecution.

This power is executed with little fanfare thousands of times every day as prosecutors decide which arrests to convert into prosecutions. In many jurisdictions, large percentages of arrests never end up in prosecution.[92]

Prosecutorial discretion exists all around us. It floats in the ether, largely unnoticed, because the vast majority of its exercise lies in the body of human behavior that prosecutors choose to ignore. Examining virtually any set of prosecutorial actions illustrates that they are political *choices*. Here, I'll look at a few examples that were extensively reported.

It is now known that U.S. government employees committed the crime of torture during what they called the "war on terror."[93] That widespread torture occurred and that it constituted a federal crime is not in dispute. The torture of human beings included, at least as far as we know: physical beatings,[94] anal rape,[95] mutilation of genitals,[96] electric shocks to the body,[97] waterboarding[98] (a crime for which the United States previously prosecuted foreign soldiers[99]), chaining people naked to walls in freezing temperatures until they died,[100] hanging people by their arms until it appeared that their shoulders would break,[101] locking a person in a box with insects,[102] forcing people to remain awake for eleven straight days,[103] and other physical and psychological tactics designed to inflict pain so severe that the inability to bear that pain would lead to people providing information.[104] Many people were killed by government employees during these torture sessions—federal prosecutors knew of at least one hundred such deaths.[105] The details of these crimes and the surrounding criminal conspiracy are set forth in the findings of every public military, civilian, and international investigation conducted, and they are found in the admissions of the torturers themselves.[106] Moreover, no one disputes that further crimes were committed when the CIA destroyed videotapes documenting its employees torturing people.[107]

No person was prosecuted for torture, murder, or for destroying the videos of government employees committing these crimes.[108] Prosecutors chose instead to ignore these violations of federal criminal law.[109] The official prosecutorial reason for the decision not to prosecute these crimes was that we must "look forward, not backward."[110] This is a philosophy of prosecution that every convicted person confined in jails and prisons would love to embrace: every person prosecuted in an American courtroom is charged with committing a crime in the past.

The only person who federal prosecutors used their discretion to prosecute for his role in the torture program was John Kiriakou, a high-level CIA official formerly in charge of the CIA's covert operations.[111] Kiriakou was not prosecuted for torture or for destroying the videos of torture. Instead, Kiriakou's crime was revealing details about the torture to the public, a violation of the rules against disclosure of information that bureaucrats choose to make secret.[112]

Consider an example closer to home: On May 13, 1985, Philadelphia police officers boarded a helicopter and flew over a de-facto segregated black neighborhood.[113] On the orders of the Police Commissioner, when hovering over the home of a group of black liberation activists and their children, the officers dropped a bomb.[114] City officials initially ordered the fire department to "let the fire burn," and police shot at survivors as they ran from the home.[115] Sixty-one houses in the black neighborhood were destroyed by the bombing.[116] Eleven people were killed, including five children between the ages of seven and thirteen who police knew were in the home when they bombed it.[117] Exercising their discretion, local and federal prosecutors chose not to prosecute any of the people who carried out or ordered the bombing.[118] But they did exercise their discretion to prosecute the only adult black liberation activist who survived.[119]

Another high-profile exercise of discretion was the prosecutorial response to the "financial crisis" of 2008 and related subsequent scandals. Employees at banks committed crimes including lying to investors and regulators,[120] fraudulently portraying junk assets as valuable assets,[121] rate-rigging,[122] bribing foreign officials,[123] submitting false documents,[124] mortgage fraud,[125] fraudulent home foreclosures,[126] financing drug cartels,[127] orchestrating and enabling widespread tax evasion,[128] and violating international sanctions.[129]

The massive criminality of financial sector employees caused enormous harm. Leaving aside the millions of home foreclosures[130] and the international effects of the crisis, consider just the lost wealth: in 2000, over 30 million people were living in poverty in the United States,[131] and poverty is estimated to have caused over 100,000 deaths in the year 2000 alone (about 4.5 percent of U.S. deaths).[132] By the end of the financial crisis in 2009, median household wealth in the United States had declined by $27,000,[133] leaving almost 44 million people in poverty[134] and therefore leading to many additional deaths. During the first full year of the crisis, the wealthiest four hundred Americans increased their wealth by $30 billion.[135]

As of 2013, not a single high-ranking banker had been prosecuted by federal prosecutors for actions that led to the 2008 world economic collapse.[136] As one prominent executive famously wrote in an email: "Let's hope we are all wealthy and retired by the time this house of card[s] falters."[137] Again in 2012, the less publicized "Libor scandal" involving many of the same large banks "dwarf[ed] by orders of magnitude any financial scam in the history of markets."[138] That scandal was followed by a new interest-rate swap conspiracy among largely the same banks that former federal regulators called "the height of criminality."[139] Dozens of other bank scandals have each involved the loss of enough money to prevent tens of thousands of deaths.

The highest-ranking federal official overseeing criminal prosecution in the Obama Administration explained that banks, despite having committed federal felony crimes, would generally not be prosecuted because they were too big, and the effects of prosecution could hurt the economy.[140] There are numerous problems with this speculation, including that there is no evidence to support it. The largest U.S. banks are actually *not* profitable without taxpayer money; as *Bloomberg* explained in a seminal editorial, "the profits they report are essentially transfers from taxpayers to their shareholders."[141] And at the same time that large banks escaped prosecution, they retained an estimated $83 billion in yearly taxpayer subsidies—essentially exactly equal to their profits. (They spend hundreds of millions of dollars each election cycle to convince politicians to preserve this taxpayer subsidy.)[142] Thus, entities that are not independently profitable without government welfare, that drain taxpayer money, and that caused massive suffering through flagrant crimes, were protected by federal prosecutors on the unexplained theory that they are essential to social well-being.[143]

In the years that followed, repeated crimes by bankers eventually led to some criminal charges, but prosecutors permitted banks to plead guilty institutionally and to pay fines that represented a small percentage of their annual profits.[144] In these few prosecutions of large banks, *individuals* were typically not prosecuted,[145] even though it was individuals who committed each of the crimes. Individual prosecutions, as opposed to prosecutions of corporate entities, are more likely to achieve the stated goals of punishment given that it is the individual who makes the decision to break a law.[146] Moreover, as a prominent federal judge pointed out,[147] individual prosecutions do not trigger the concern that federal prosecutors used to justify their lack of prosecutions: they do not result in the collapse of the corporation that employed the individual, even if one believes that the collapse of criminal banking corporations would be the result of a prosecution or, beyond that, that such an occurrence would be bad.[148]

To take another prominent example, it came out in June 2013 that James Clapper, the Director of National Intelligence, had lied to Congress—a felony offense[149]—about the scope of federal government surveillance of private electronic communications in March 2013.[150] When his lie was discovered, Clapper sent an apology letter to Congress and offered a series of explanations for his dishonesty.[151] Those explanations ranged from: (1) he intentionally gave "the least untruthful answer possible" to (2) the question was unfair to (3) he did not understand the question.[152] Of course, Clapper could have refused to answer the question in public and answered only in classified communications to the senators.[153] Instead, he chose to give false information, precisely because it would mislead the public about the scope of the NSA's surveillance of ordinary people. Clapper was not prosecuted for this felony.[154] Nor was any NSA official prosecuted for any of the violations of secret FISA court orders in the surveillance programs that related to Clapper's lie.[155] Yet Clapper himself subsequently advocated that prosecutors pursue charges against Edward Snowden, the person who exposed Clapper.[156]

This incident echoes the COINTELPRO scandal, in which the FBI committed felony crimes for years against people who were opposed to racial injustice; poverty; killing millions of human beings in Vietnam, Cambodia, and Laos; and other causes associated with the political left.[157] The FBI's pervasive operation against American leftists and black activists, ordered at the highest levels, included blackmail, burglary, threats, kidnaping, infiltration of groups based on their political beliefs, murder, incitement to criminal activity, illegal wiretapping, intercepting letters and replacing them with changed content, and numerous other tactics (some of the most heinous of which the FBI has not publicly admitted, including the assassination of Fred Hampton and the involvement of an FBI informant in the infamous bombing of children in a Birmingham, Alabama, church).[158] These "law enforcement" officials also targeted black-led organizations on the basis of their race at the behest of J. Edgar Hoover,[159] for whom the organization's headquarters on Pennsylvania Avenue is still named.[160] (Years later, the FBI would provide the explosives that the Philadelphia police dropped from the helicopter.)[161] The FBI even undertook an operation to get Martin Luther King Jr. to commit suicide.[162]

This lawlessness was one of the most significant episodes in modern American history: it was a largely successful effort by elites to derail a growing social movement that sought to help marginalized people and that could have transformed American society. It is now viewed by consensus as one of the darkest periods in the history of modern American "law enforcement." The FBI's crimes even spurred rare congressional reforms establishing new oversight of "law enforcement" agencies.[163]

But the many FBI employees who committed crimes across the country were not outliers or bad apples; they were government bureaucrats following a "national security" program designed and orchestrated at the highest levels. Indeed, when COINTELPRO was uncovered, a team of more than eighty federal "law enforcement" agents was dispatched—not to investigate those responsible for committing the crimes identified in the FBI's files, but instead to search for those who anonymously sent to newspapers and members of Congress the internal documents describing the FBI's crimes.[164] Although numerous people were prosecuted during this period for acts of civil disobedience in protest of government policies now viewed as racist and profoundly harmful, federal prosecutors decided that not a single FBI employee should be prosecuted for their crimes.

Strategic prosecution in order to chill political activism has been, and remains, a through-line in American history. Marcus Mitchell, an engineering student and indigenous activist, is awaiting trial for charges of trespassing and interfering with police after police shot him in the face with a bean bag pellet while he was protesting the Dakota Access oil pipeline.[165] Mitchell was allegedly hidden from his family and interrogated while heavily medicated in a hospital bed, guarded by a for-profit security company. He faces up to two years in jail. In 2016, California police and the FBI decided to work with neo-Nazi groups to surveil and then vigorously pursue charges against civil rights groups and activists, including attempting to prosecute a black anti-fascist protestor who was the victim of a neo-Nazi stabbing attack.[166] Tim DeChristopher went to a federal land auction in 2008 to protest the legality of the sale of federal land in Utah to corporate mining interests.[167] DeChristopher believed that the land auction was not authorized by federal law.[168] Once there, he was offered a bidding number and decided to go into the auction, eventually bidding on a parcel.[169] He was prosecuted for bidding on the land without having the intent to buy it.[170] (DeChristopher later raised enough money to cover his bid,[171] and a federal judge ruled in a civil case that the land sale was indeed unlawful.)[172] During

his trial, at the request of prosecutors, DeChristopher was prohibited from telling the jury about his motives or the illegality
of the land sale, and he was convicted.[173] Prosecutors sought a
lengthy prison sentence, and the judge sentenced him to two
years in federal prison.[174] The police officer who choked Eric
Garner to death was not indicted,[175] but the man who filmed
the murder on his cell phone, Ramsey Orta, was harassed, later
arrested, prosecuted, and sent to prison for ostensibly unrelated crimes.[176]

It is possible that Mitchell trespassed on someone else's
land, that DeChristopher broke a federal law, and that Orta
committed another crime, like those officials in the other
examples discussed here. But who a government goes after and
who it ignores affects what conduct people feel encouraged to
engage in, whether that be political dissent, war crimes, financial fraud, or anything else. The aggregate of these decisions
sends messages to the population about what kind of society
those in charge want to see, what kind of conduct they will not
abide, and what kind of conduct they will tolerate from certain
people.

Consider just a few examples from different contexts:

- Fate Vincent Winslow was sentenced to life in prison
  without the possibility of parole for acting as a go-between
  when he was homeless in the sale of marijuana, worth
  $10 in total, to an undercover police officer.[177] Clarence
  Aaron introduced two of his friends who he knew were
  engaged in selling drugs. Although Aaron had no criminal
  record, he was prosecuted for introducing the drug sellers

to each other.[178] Aaron, a twenty-four-year-old college student, was sentenced to life in prison without parole, meaning that prosecutors used their discretion to ensure that he would die in prison. Stephanie George was also sentenced to die in prison for allowing her boyfriend, the father of her child, to store drugs in her home.[179] George was taken from her child and her family forever. At the request of federal prosecutors, she was given a longer sentence than anyone else involved in the drug conspiracy in which she was prosecuted.[180] There are hundreds of thousands of stories of long prison sentences for similar drug crimes.[181]

- Wage theft by employers costs workers an estimated $50 billion per year.[182] All robberies, burglaries, larcenies, and motor vehicle thefts combined cost $14 billion per year. Prosecutors almost never enforce criminal wage theft laws. Due to policy choices, federal authorities chronically underfund the number of employees assigned to investigate wage theft. As a result, corporations engage in wage theft and view the occasional civil lawsuit forcing compensation for these crimes as a cost of doing business.

- Federal bureaucrats and private corporations working for profit were caught conducting illegal warrantless surveillance of American telecommunications in 2005.[183] At the time, such surveillance was a federal felony punishable by five years in prison.[184] Despite the acknowledged commission of felonies by high-ranking federal government officials and business executives, prosecutors chose not to charge them. And after paying money to lobbyists, telecommunications officials were later given civil immunity from the damages caused by their unprosecuted crimes.[185]

- Children have been physically abused and forced to take psychotropic medication without consent in for-profit immigrant detention jails. Prosecutors have chosen not to file criminal charges.[186] (Federal prosecutors recently chose to pursue charges, sometimes felony charges, against volunteers near the southern border who leave food and water for migrants in commonly lethal parts of the desert.)[187]

- Barack Obama ordered killings when he was President. These killings were often of people whose identities were not known and frequently of medics and children who came to treat the wounded at the scenes of American drone killings.[188] Many of the assassinations went wrong according to their own stated justifications, including the bombings of weddings, funerals, hospitals, journalists, and other civilian targets.[189] American prosecutors decided that Obama should not be charged for these offenses, even after he and other officials were caught lying repeatedly about the murders.[190] Obama likely tells himself a justification about why murdering a sixteen-year-old American child was necessary for the greater good and legally excusable on defense grounds.[191] Should Russia, Iran, Israel, Laos, or Chile[192] determine that assassinations of targets in Chicago and Pittsburgh is necessary to further their interests, or to deter American interference in their elections, those officials would also tell themselves stories about why that preventive violence is necessary to save lives or to "promote democracy."[193]

▪ As alleged in a lawsuit that my organization recently filed, prosecutors in Phoenix have been making false statements in letters to coerce people into paying the District Attorney's office to get it to drop marijuana possession charges in a scheme that has earned the District Attorney's office an average of $1.6 million annually in recent years.[194] This is, paradoxically, both the federal felony of mail fraud and "law enforcement." These prosecutors have not been prosecuted.

▪ California took away 4.2 million drivers' licenses because people could not pay court debts.[195] In the past five years, Tennessee took away more than 250,000 licenses for inability to pay tickets and more than 140,000 licenses for inability to pay other court debts.[196] Because dozens of states have done the same thing, millions more people have lost the ability to do all of the things many of us take for granted in life—go to the grocery store, attend church, commute to work, and visit family—as "driving on a suspended license" has become one of the most commonly charged crimes by prosecutors in many jurisdictions.[197] In such circumstances, that crime serves no function other than to criminalize poverty.

▪ According to an investigation by the District Attorney and the Louisiana State Auditor, judges in New Orleans were extorting money from people, wrongfully jailing people who could not pay, and then illegally using the money to fund their own benefits packages.[198] Despite these investigations and later admissions by judges, prosecutors used their discretion not to prosecute the judges.

- Jail guards in Florida locked a man with mental illness in a shower, turned on scalding hot water, laughed at him, and left him there until he died. Prosecutors chose not to prosecute the guards.[199]

- General David Petraeus was prosecuted for disclosing classified information to a journalist with whom he was having a sexual affair. Although the information Petraeus disclosed included some of what the U.S. government considers to be its most sensitive secrets—more sensitive than the information disclosed by Chelsea Manning,[200] for example—prosecutors permitted him to plead guilty to a misdemeanor and to avoid any time in jail.[201]

- Twelve police officers in Miami Beach shot over one hundred bullets at a car, killing the man inside. The officers also pointed their guns at witnesses, demanding that they stop filming. Police then confiscated and smashed the cell phones of witnesses to the shooting. The officers then lied, claiming that they had not tried to destroy the witnesses' videos of the incident. However, one witness had removed and hidden his phone's memory card in his mouth, and the video given to CNN confirmed the officers' crimes and lies.[202] The officers were not prosecuted.

- Sentencing children to die in prison is illegal in nearly every country in the world, but as of 2012, the United States had over 2,500 people serving sentences to die in prison for crimes committed as children because prosecutors chose to seek life sentences in adult prison.[203]

- Prosecutors have begun charging people for filming animal torture on factory farms and for rescuing animals from them. In one widely reported recent incident, federal bureaucrats raided properties in multiple states searching for the person who rescued two piglets from a factory and ordered doctors to cut off part of a piglet's ear for DNA testing as it screeched in pain.[204]

- Christopher Drew was arrested for selling art on the street in Chicago without a permit, and prosecutors filed charges carrying a fifteen-year prison sentence for recording his own arrest.[205] Throughout my career, I have seen people routinely arrested and charged with crimes for filming police officers committing misconduct or refusing to give police officers their phones after recording police misconduct.

- There is no state, county, or city where a person can afford a two-bedroom home while working forty hours for the federal minimum wage, and it is only possible to afford a one-bedroom home in twenty-two of over three thousand counties while making the federal minimum wage.[206] The majority of criminal cases in Portland, Oregon, are against people who are homeless. The vast majority of those are for nonviolent crimes.[207]

- Prosecutors help for-profit companies collect money on their business contracts by using criminal prosecution when low-income people cannot pay for "rent-to-own" products.[208]

- Since Richard Nixon declared a "war on drugs," there have been twenty million arrests for possession of marijuana offenses,[209] including about 600,000 per year in recent years.[210]

- Each of the three presidents from 1992 to 2016, covering more than two decades of the American incarceration explosion, admitted to committing federal drug crimes when they were younger.[211] Most of society does not (at least for that reason) think of them as "felons" unworthy of basic civil and political rights. Had prosecutors chosen to prosecute them for that conduct, it is possible that we would never have heard their names. It matters who gets investigated, caught, and prosecuted.

- President Clinton's perjury was not prosecuted.[212]

- Prosecutors charged an eleven-year-old child with a felony for pulling a school fire alarm.[213] After many prosecutors adopted "zero tolerance" policies for children committing misconduct in public schools, there was an explosion in the criminalization of child misbehavior.[214] "Law enforcement" employees are typically not involved in misbehavior at private schools, but "law enforcement" employees routinely arrest, jail, prosecute, convict, sentence, imprison, and supervise children after conviction for the same conduct in public schools serving low-income communities.

- Phillip Zimmermann created PGP, the world's first free encryption program that anyone could use to thwart surveillance. It is now ubiquitous and celebrated as a technical computing achievement. He was initially threatened with an indictment because prosecutors treated encryption software to protect individual privacy as a munition and placed it on the same prohibited export control list as guns and missiles.[215]

- Possession of small amounts of marijuana has been decriminalized for years in New York except if possessed "in public view." But police and prosecutors evaded the "public view" exception to create tens of thousands of arrests and prosecutions in New York City by stopping and searching people, ordering them to empty their pockets, and then arresting them because marijuana in their pockets was consequently open to public view.[216]

- Texas officials falsified drug prescriptions that they sought to carry out executions, but they were not prosecuted for this crime.[217]

- Henry Kissinger has never been charged for his war crimes by American prosecutors despite uncontroverted evidence of them.[218]

- Political appointees in the George W. Bush administration intervened to shut down a criminal investigation into environmental felonies being committed by British Petroleum and allowed the company to plead guilty to lesser offenses without the prosecution targeting senior executives.[219]

- Prosecutors have used criminal charges to chill voter turnout from certain groups. In Texas, prosecutors obtained a five-year prison sentence for a woman who cast an uncounted provisional ballot after she purportedly did not know that she could not vote due to her criminal record.[220] Georgia prosecutors attempted to prosecute a black woman city councilmember for showing a confused voter how to operate a voting machine. The woman was acquitted by a jury in twenty minutes.[221]

- From 2004 to 2009, there were over 500,000 violations of the Clean Water Act, resulting in rotting teeth, cancer, kidney failure, and damage to the nervous system. About one in ten Americans was exposed to dangerous chemicals in drinking water. Prosecutors chose to ignore the vast majority of these crimes, admitting when confronted that their enforcement of these laws was "unacceptably low."[222]

The goal in offering these examples is not to provoke an argument about whether what prosecutors decided in any one of them is objectively correct.[223] I mean to give a sense of the kinds of choices that prosecutors make when confronted with alleged illegality and how those choices are tied not to a "rule of law," but rather to particular political preferences.

By choosing to look "backward" and not "forward" in the Winslow or DeChristopher cases, for example, prosecutors sent messages to those interested in possessing marijuana or in acts of civil disobedience in support of environmental causes, in the same way that they sent very different messages to those interested in covering up evidence of torture or lying to Congress about warrantless surveillance. As in South Africa during apartheid or in the United States during the civil rights movement, or in any context where geographic distance or time has given us a different perspective, those who are prosecuted are often those who we later judge to be in better compliance with basic moral values. And in a society characterized by deep, systemic injustices, over time judgments about who is a criminal and who is a hero may be reversed entirely.

INVESTIGATIVE DISCRETION

A personal anecdote: my young client once wondered aloud, "How can I tell you what it's like to leave the house every morning knowing that my body could be searched at any moment? That no one thinks it's wrong? That they call themselves 'law enforcement.'"[224]

Something important happens before a case gets to a prosecutor: bureaucrats decide where to look for crimes. They must decide: should we spend our resources looking for people who possess marijuana? If so, in which neighborhoods should we look for them? Should we stop and search people on the street in the Bronx, or should we use undercover informants to see if students possess marijuana in Columbia University dorms? Or should we instead spend those public resources looking into tens of thousands of tax returns?

There is a massive tax-theft problem in the United States that dwarfs all other types of theft combined.[225] The money recovered from the "law enforcement" of tax crimes could be used to save lives. But every billion dollars spent on informants and surveillance to charge low-level drug cases is a billion dollars not spent on informants and surveillance to investigate tax evaders.[226] Through assignments given to hundreds of thousands of "law enforcement" agents, the government makes decisions about which criminals it will look for. Each police department, for example, decides whether to spend money testing a rape kit or a cocaine sample.[227] Every "law enforcement" agency makes further decisions about which neighborhoods to patrol, which crimes to prioritize, and how many officers to assign to different units.[228] When my organization sued the town of Ferguson, Missouri, for example, the City averaged about "3.6 arrest warrants *per household*" arising out of low-level municipal ordinance violations and tickets,[229] almost exclusively, I uncovered in my investigation, against black people.

Resource-allocation choices determine the response to entire categories of socially harmful behavior. For example, President Ronald Reagan decided to transfer thousands of federal agents from investigating white-collar financial crimes to pursuing the "war on drugs."[230] Similarly, the FBI under Presidents Bill Clinton and George W. Bush oversaw still further declines in its white-collar crime-fighting investigations.[231] The results were stark: federal prosecutors were referred 10,000 white-collar criminal cases by FBI agents in 2000, but that number dropped to 3,500 in 2005,[232] shortly before the worldwide financial system collapsed due to massive fraud.[233] The same is true for the slow depletion of the IRS, which is now unable meaningfully to enforce tax laws against wealthy tax evaders.[234] Indeed, as federal "law enforcement" failed to prevent the $50 billion Bernie Madoff fraud, the FBI alone had at least fifteen thousand informants, many of whom, along with state-level police and private contractors, were monitoring left-leaning political activists across the country.[235]

The government controls a huge "law enforcement" budget. This money could pay for investigating every doctor who writes an improper prescription, chemical testing and surveillance to locate the sources of illegal pollution of local rivers and groundwater, wiretaps to investigate corruption in police departments, and audits to examine prosecutor offices for withholding favorable evidence. "Law enforcement" could infiltrate boarding-school campuses to bust underage drinking and tobacco use or set up sting operations to fight widespread wage theft by employers. The choices that the bureaucracy makes involve direct tradeoffs, for example, from black families to corporate executives or from drug users to sexual abusers.

Tradeoffs exist not only between broad categories of crime (e.g., should we focus our resources on uncovering drug crime or sex crime?), but also within each category. If the government decides that drug possession is a more important priority than is police corruption, water pollution, or rape, it must still decide whether to spend money on police patrols and prisons, or whether to spend money on treatment, medical care, and safe injection sites.[236] If "law enforcement" decides that reducing violent sexual assaults is important, bureaucrats still must decide how they will expend resources looking for criminals; how much they will pay to prosecute and to jail them; or whether they will create programs to reduce gender inequality, help survivors find employment and trauma support, and pay for domestic violence shelters.

Resource choices can be seen not just within police investigation priorities, but also in the money budgeted for other programs, such as housing, drug treatment, mental health care, probation, prisons, and education. For example, under President Clinton, federal public housing expenditures were reduced by $400 million annually, nearly the same amount by which the federal prison budget increased.[237] Today, as police departments turn to "predictive policing" to supposedly prevent *future* crime rather than merely investigating *past* crimes,[238] they are deciding to spend billions of dollars on surveillance instead of investing in lead abatement in poor neigh-borhoods,[239] mental and medical health care, after-school arts programs, or affordable places for people to live.

It is important for people advocating changes to the crimi-nal system to explore why elites are making these investment choices even though, based on all the available evidence, the things bureaucrats are *not* investing in are far more likely to reduce future crime.

Cultural, Political, and Economic Forces Influence Which Laws Are Enforced Against Which People

The Panthers thus became the native Vietcong, the ghetto became the village in which the Vietcong were hid-den, and in the ensuing search-and-destroy operations, everyone in the village became suspect.

—James Baldwin[240]

Police bureaucrats have the discretion to change a person's life at any moment, and they exercise this discretion tens of mil-lions of times every year. A major problem with "criminal jus-tice reform" discourse is that most privileged people have no idea what "law enforcement" looks like in practice. The vast bulk of contemporary policing is discretionary surveillance of and ruthless intervention in the lives of low-income people and people of color.[241]

At any stage, from the street to the courtroom, a govern-ment employee has the power to immunize crime. How many of us have pleaded for a little bit of this discretion when caught breaking a rule? I have a friend who has never received a speeding ticket despite having been stopped by radar-wielding police at least five times. Police officers on city streets have discretion to stop, arrest, or ignore people engaged in a wide variety of conduct and misconduct. Higher-level officials, by deciding geographic placement of officers, drafting department budgets, and setting prosecution priorities, have the ability to ignore lawbreaking in entire neighborhoods or economic sectors. For that reason, the "radical" future of prison and police abolition sought by some on the political left and right effectively already exists for wide swaths of our society: wealthy white people rarely interact with the police, except by choice.

The discretionary exercise of these powers means the opposite for the poor and people of color. What has emerged for them is a metastasized system guided by forces we don't acknowledge as opposed to good policy made transparently to promote shared values.

A major achievement of the punishment bureaucracy is that it has retained mainstream respect even though its "law enforcement" choices crush unprecedented numbers of people with no evidence of any unique social benefit while simultaneously allowing enormous amounts of lawlessness that cause massive harm. Why are these choices still viewed as legitimate?

First, the groups who wield power in our society benefit from the punishment bureaucracy. It privileges their private property, their racial supremacy, their jobs, their voting rights, and their segregated neighborhoods.

Second, the growth of the punishment bureaucracy itself

changes our culture and economy. As the bureaucracy expands, it employs larger and larger numbers of police officers, prosecutors, probation officers, defense attorneys, prison guards, contractors, and equipment manufacturers. People working in the system become dependent on its perpetuation for their livelihoods and even their identities. The path of least resistance is to grow more. Jobs are created, local political power is consolidated, and "law enforcement" activities are normalized and then rendered economically essential—such as roadblocks, prison guards, home raids, drug interdiction teams, neighborhood patrols, armed police in schools, SWAT teams, stop-and-frisk practices, social media monitoring, video surveillance, probation drug testing, and "intelligence" divisions. An ever-expanding set of "criminal justice" products are designed and advertised with billions of dollars from investors and tens of thousands more people involved at every stage of their production and marketing, trade conventions displaying the latest products, and lucrative bureaucrat training schools follow,[242] along with new protocols for using the new products and training methods on those new protocols, and so on.[243] Soon, an entire society is prepared psychologically and institutionally to confront a public health issue like drug addiction with metal shackles, tasers, and cages.

The more police officers and defense lawyers and border agents and weapons makers and training consultants there are, the more people who internalize the norms of the "law enforcement" culture and who come to depend on it. More people's friends and family make their livings in these industries, and private family conversations, public discussions, and media coverage change to tolerate and normalize the jobs performed by all of the normal people we know. This process organically increases support for the "law enforcement" complex, extending its influence, both casually through social norms and directly by expanding its economic power through more profit.

The process of how norms evolve is critical to explaining why it seems reasonable to roll tanks through Ferguson, put handcuffs on twelve million people every year, and monitor the lives of tens of millions of people through electronic surveillance when our society, only a generation ago, would have perceived such government intrusions as an authoritarian revolution. The cultural norms and economic regime that these forces have nurtured have produced a "law enforcement" zeitgeist characterizing the past forty years of American life. So embedded is this spirit that the punishment bureaucracy has become the venue to manage social and public health problems such as poverty, deteriorating education, lack of housing, drug addiction, and mental illness.[244]

Third, it is easier to police and prosecute populations whose pain and inconvenience are not part of the social conscience and who lack economic capital.[245] A decision by police officers to stop, question, and search people is hard to sustain in wealthy neighborhoods. It would *feel* more shocking, strange, and intrusive to those most able to affect policing decisions, and instances of brutality and humiliation would work their way through the web of social connections surrounding the lives of elites. Children of news anchors would be arrested, doctors and their husbands would have their homes raided and their children's faces put to the barrels of assault rifles, and bankers would have their anal cavities searched in their high-rise offices. If that happened, twenty-four-hour news pundits would discuss the violent police behavior with large on-screen fonts, and reporters standing next to news vans would demand explanations.

Fourth, leading punishment bureaucrats exploit these background conditions to obfuscate the functions of the punishment system. Instead of acknowledging that enforcement decisions are made based on cultural norms, money, conscious and subconscious bias, and political connections between officials and the people that they regulate, the punishment bureaucracy masks these deeper forces under slogans like "tough on crime" or "the "rule of law." This propaganda suggests an almost scientific connection between every instance of lawbreaking and an efficient system of enforcement.

The situation is especially ripe for exploitation by punishment bureaucrats in periods when what are marketed as "crime rates" are claimed to be increasing. But the very instinct to respond to perceived increases in (certain types of) crime by more punishment is the response of a ruling class—by those who want to talk about "crime" without changing society.

The zeal for "law enforcement" as punishment means that the legal system does not consider potential causes of misbehavior or ways to reduce it that might have other social benefits— for example, addressing structural inequality,[246] child exposure to lead,[247] gender inequality, or lack of meaningful access to theater, art, music, poetry, and physical wellness activities.[248] The punishment bureaucracy does not ask if these causes of "crime" might be ameliorated without the human cost of prosecution and mass human caging.[249] This lack of care also explains why, in virtually every jurisdiction in which I have worked, I have noticed that the bureaucracy collects virtually no data to rigorously measure its performance.

Consider the drug war—one of the greatest successes of "law enforcement" punishment propaganda. The drug war cost more than a trillion dollars,[250] tens of millions of arrests,[251] hundreds of millions of police stops,[252] tens of millions of years in prison,[253] tens of millions of lost jobs and educations and homes, millions of square acres of spray-poisoned forests,[254] tens of millions of voting rights (including at least one presidential election),[255] tens of millions of children separated from a parent,[256] hundreds of thousands of deaths due to the resulting drug wars and American intervention in Latin America,[257] and massive militarization and surveillance by local police of every American city and town.[258] The vast bulk of these consequences were inflicted on people for personal use of certain substances, an exercise of bodily autonomy that other countries have protected and that this country protects for other harmful substances like alcohol and tobacco. All of this was done in ways that dramatically increased the racial disparities in every stage of the criminal system.[259] For all of these social costs, drug use either did not go down or significantly increased, and teenagers are using dangerous drugs at twice the rate that they did in the 1980s.[260]

Only idiots would pursue strategies that are so counterproductive and destructive for so long—and our legal system's bureaucrats are sophisticated, not idiotic. The "war on drugs" is about something else.

Above all, one thing is true: the punishment bureaucrats

who created the contemporary "criminal justice system" are broadly comfortable with the way that our society looks. They market a crime problem in need of "law enforcement" in order to keep our society looking the way that it does. They do not want to solve the "crime" problem if that means a society that looks much different—say, more equal and with less private profit. Hence they both construct and respond to "crime" with strategies that increase inequality and control, but do little to stop the same problems they purport to care about—and that often make those problems worse, thereby justifying a circular call for more (selective) punishment. And that is why courts do not enforce the rules of law that are intended to make our society more equal when those rules conflict with the goals of the punishment bureaucracy.

The "law enforcement" religion is hostile to the view that a society that is more equal would have less crime, not because that idea is untrue, but because the very *goal* of the criminal legal system is to preserve certain elements of an unequal social order even if that inequality *creates* "crime."[261]

The Myth of the Rule of Law

[T]he alleged protection of our persons from violence is only an accidental result of the existence of a police force whose real business is to force the poor man to see his children starve whilst idle people overfeed pet dogs with the money that might feed and clothe them.

—George Bernard Shaw[262]

To accomplish the "rule of law" trickery, the punishment bureaucracy makes pronouncements about what "crime" is, why people commit crime, and how best to reduce crime by "enforcing the law." The power of this worldview cannot be underestimated: it has won almost every relevant policy debate in the past forty years. It convinced a broad range of people that the solutions to their problems were not changes to the political system or the economic structure or discriminatory social norms, but rather, more police "on the streets" and more poor black people in prison cages.

The "law enforcement" myth is seductive. Many people, including lawyers and judges, want to believe that something like the neutral "rule of law" can exist, and for good reasons. But it is dangerous to do so without understanding that policing and prosecution are used as a tool of politics and power to benefit some and to hurt others.

One of the most insidious notions pervading standard discourse is that people are investigated and punished because they break laws and therefore that, if one breaks the law, one will be investigated and punished. This principle supports a larger idea: our legal system is objective, trying its best to promote well-being, morality, and human flourishing. The myth that an objective "rule of law" determines the outcomes is important to the system's perceived legitimacy and to our acceptance of its authority over us.

A lot of assumptions are imbedded in the everyday assessment of the punishment bureaucracy's legitimacy and effectiveness: Poor people and black people fill jails because they do more bad things than wealthy people and white people. American officials are not arrested for war crimes because they slaughtered people and assassinated democratically elected leaders for good reasons. People are pulled over because they violated a traffic rule or frisked because they were suspicious. Teenagers are searched on their way to school because they live in a "high crime" area and their black and brown bodies are dangerous. A person obtained his wealth legitimately because his ancestors were never prosecuted for acquiring it. Prisoners cannot hug their children or see sunlight because jails are places where we could not safely have family visits or fresh air.

The standard "criminal justice" discourse lulls people into abandoning scrutiny of their assumptions. Government employees who arrest and prosecute people are called "law enforcement" agents; the entire enterprise is referred to in press conferences as an objective entity: "from a law enforcement perspective . . . " or "law enforcement believes that . . . " As we have seen, it would be more accurate to refer to them as "selective enforcement officers" or "white wealth preservation officers" because they usually enforce only *some* laws against *some* people.[263]

Many of the most prominent mass violations of American law were perpetrated or covered up by "law enforcement" officers acting pursuant to official policies, including the Trail of Tears, the ethnic cleansing and forced deportation of more than a million Americans for suspected Mexican heritage,[264] the internment of Japanese Americans, and the arming of right-wing Nicaraguan death squads and the perjury surrounding it.[265] For much of this country's history, black people were lynched—one of the main features of that ritual being that the openness of the public murder communicated that the "law enforcement" apparatus would do nothing to "enforce" criminal laws to protect black bodies and embraced racial terror.[266] To take just one example, not a single white person was prosecuted after the Tulsa massacre, the most deadly terrorist event in an American city until September 11, 2001.[267] Hundreds of years of criminal acts against black people were unpunished such that the "rule of law" was formally converted into a tool to reproduce slavery by another name.[268]

Given this history, one of the central tasks for punishment bureaucrats is to push the myth that the American legal system at some point became *different* and more objective than it has been throughout its entire history.

The way punishment bureaucrats talk is therefore like a newspaper assuring us that it contains "all the news that's fit to print." This marketing technique of feigned completeness and objectivity is a manipulation—its goal to have us ignore editorial decisions about which of the millions of potential news stories to cover. For example, despite its famous motto, the *New York Times* chooses to cover most plane crashes, but does not contain a front-page article every morning about the thousands of children who died of starvation the night before.[269] Filling finite newspaper pages using finite reporting resources and distributing finite resources among "law enforcement" priorities are inescapably political enterprises full of discretion. By presenting as objective decisions that are highly subjective and based on power, both journalists and punishment bureaucrats obscure from debate many of society's political choices.

The work of punishment bureaucrats to convince people to support selective "law enforcement" against certain populations has created a miscalibration of our response to harmful conduct. Seen from the lens of actual social harm, American "law enforcement" priorities are ridiculous. For example, second-hand smoke alone kills 41,000 Americans every year.[270] That is twelve September 11 attacks on innocent people unlucky enough to have come into contact with other people who smoke products produced by corporate traffickers of tobacco. If one includes Americans addicted to tobacco, that drug kills 480,000 Americans[271] and almost 6 million human beings globally every year.[272] Tobacco use is legal, and the marketing and distribution of tobacco is lucrative.[273] Similar examples pervade every aspect of life: the insertion of food additives and cancer-causing agents into products causes enormous harm, but is not typically addressed through the criminal law; the massive financial fraud of *trillions* of dollars of taxpayer money over several decades to secretly inflate the military budget has never been treated as a crime;[274] the contamination of drinking water in major cities is rarely discussed as a criminal issue; the billions of dollars in health costs, deaths, and physical pain caused by sugary sodas are harms not addressed through the punishment system.[275] Mortgage fraud and other financial crimes that result in homelessness and an inability to meet basic needs of life kill, by conservative estimates, tens of thousands of Americans every year, not to mention dramatically reducing the quality of life for millions more.[276] To the contrary, the threat of "terrorism" is almost nonexistent—about the same danger to Americans as shark attacks, and orders of magnitude lower than texting while driving.[277] The vast bulk of "law enforcement" resources are thus spent protecting Americans from relatively miniscule risks. This bureaucracy is therefore pathetic as a means of saving lives, preventing harm, and helping humans flourish.

In societies that our culture portrays as primitive, force was thought to have prevailed in all disputes. Stronger people committed crimes at their pleasure. Cities were sacked, nations conquered, and lords were immune from punishment by the size of their armies. All of this has been replaced with the "rule of law" and institutions to "enforce the law." But, as Camus suggests, there has been something devious in the construction of this bureaucracy. That ingenious element is the illusion of rigorous objectivity, the façade of legitimacy. It's the ability to turn "murderers into judges."[278]

Now that this façade is unraveling amid a new movement challenging the mass imprisonment of black and brown and poor people, many of the bureaucrats who built their careers on the myth of the "rule of law" are trying to rescue the legitimacy of the punishment bureaucracy.

VII

The smart way to keep people passive and obedient is to strictly limit the spectrum of acceptable opinion, but allow very lively debate within that spectrum—even encourage the more critical and dissident views. That gives people the sense that there's free thinking going on, while all the time the presuppositions of the system are being reinforced by the limits put on the range of the debate.

—Noam Chomsky[279]

Powerful systems have a way of shapeshifting. By some measures, we have *more* segregation in schools since 1968 even though courts declared that de jure school segregation is illegal.[280] A push to "reform" federal sentencing laws in the 1980s, ostensibly to reduce judicial bias, *increased* punishment severity across the board.[281] A "bail reform" campaign in the 1960s to eliminate the use of cash bail in federal courts to jail the poor resulted in a system in which the rate of pretrial detention of presumptively innocent people went *up*.[282] Although the Supreme Court has said that pretrial liberty must be the "norm" and pretrial detention the "carefully limited exception,"[283] over seventy-two percent of federal criminal defendants are now confined to jail cells for the entire duration of their prosecution.[284]

And so we find ourselves in a dangerous time. There is broad awareness of the senselessness of the punishment system and a movement of people organizing to dismantle it. But the forces that made the punishment bureaucracy are aligning to shape how it is "reformed." The recognition of the system's unfairness and ineffectiveness has reached such a tipping point that some kind of change must happen in order for the system to preserve its own legitimacy. Accordingly, mass incarceration bureaucrats are looking to become the face of what they call "criminal justice reform." Their success will depend on whether people can tell the difference.

Punishment Bureaucrats and the Rule of Law

On a national level, punishment bureaucrats like Preet Bharara, Eric Holder, Sally Yates, and Kamala Harris are feted as "criminal justice reform" leaders. They and many more punishment bureaucrats have adopted vaguely critical buzzwords about mass incarceration that are trendy in liberal elite circles, and they are calling for "reforms," such as decreasing the use of cash bail in "low level" cases or shorter mandatory minimum prison sentences for some drug crimes. But make no mistake: these former prosecutors devoted a career to mass human caging. For years, each of them prospered professionally by transferring unprecedented numbers of poor people and people of color away from their families and into government confinement. And remember what that means: each of them operated the machinery that abused the bodies and minds of people who lack power in our society without any evidence that the misery they were inflicting was necessary to make our society a better place.

On Twitter, Bharara has billed himself as a "defender of justice and fairness" and a new kind of "sheriff" who has shifted "law enforcement" focus to fighting "big banks, terrorists, hedge funds, and public corruption."[285] But impoverished people of color in New York City saw a different kind of "law enforcement." Bharara began his career as a prosecutor at the height of mass incarceration.[286] Although he had access to essentially any job in the legal profession, he chose to become a drug prosecutor, a job devoted to putting human beings in prison cells for possessing substances on a list of substances that the government has decided that people may not possess.[287] Even later in his career, as he trumpeted a small number of highly marketed Wall Street prosecutions to build his public profile,[288] about eighty percent of the people prosecuted by his office in Manhattan were impoverished.[289] During his time in charge of the office, about *fifty percent* of his cases were prosecutions for drug offenses and of undocumented immigrants accused of crossing a geographic political boundary.[290] In 2016, despite jurisdiction over the New York Police Department (NYPD), he chose not to prosecute a single civil rights case.[291] This is remarkable given that Bharara had jurisdiction to prosecute intentional violation of any person's rights by the NYPD, including any intentionally unlawful stop, search, or arrest. And officers were not prosecuted for perjury, even when they were caught lying in Bharara's cases.[292]

Bharara, like all of us, knew that the people he chose to cage were significantly likely to be physically and sexually assaulted,[293] receive inadequate medical care,[294] and be tortured in solitary confinement.[295] For years, he oversaw all of the things, large and small, that federal prosecution entails in our society: pursuing mandatory minimum sentencing to coerce guilty pleas, working with police with long histories of abuse and constitutional violations, covering up police lying, rejecting science in forensic evidence, placing metal restraints on criminal defendants and immigrants in court so that they could not hug their families, threatening people with longer imprisonment unless they give up their right to a jury trial, imposing pretrial detention in dangerous and grotesque conditions, creating racial disparities, separating children from their parents without evidence that it benefits anyone, and displaying massive disregard for the crimes of elites.

Similarly, Attorney General Holder ran the largest human caging apparatus in the history of western democracies. He was selected for that role in part because of the reputation he built as a tough prosecutor in DC during the 1990s, when he pioneered the now-ubiquitous strategy of police stopping young black men based on pretextual reasons in order to search their bodies.[296] In his later role running the DOJ, among many other things, Holder transferred billions of dollars in cash and military equipment to local police with histories of rampant abuse;[297] managed the largest solitary confinement program in the public record, crushing people for years in isolation; refused to make meaningful changes after the National Academy of Sciences unmasked that federal prosecutors were using junk science for decades to pursue convictions based on testimony that had no scientific basis;[298] supervised an army of prosecutors who sought, virtually every single day, to defend and expand mandatory minimum sentences in federal appellate courts; and presided over a historic expansion of immigrant detention and deportation.[299] More brazenly, he kept thousands of men, mostly black, in prison by fighting against retroactive application of a new law that would reduce the disparity between the punishment of crack and powder cocaine.[300] And he quietly intervened to prevent the release of tens of thousands of black federal prisoners detained illegally for drug offenses in one of the most callous acts that I have witnessed in my legal career.[301]

And Sally Yates, known in the field as a harsh advocate of imprisonment while a federal prosecutor in Georgia,[302] repeatedly undermined the possibility of meaningful changes during her time as Deputy Attorney General. To take just a few of many examples, she argued against application of small reductions in penalties for federal drug sentences to people already confined in prison under harsh sentences,[303] oversaw the DOJ's rejection of Inspector General reports recommending greater compassionate release of terminally ill and elderly prisoners,[304] sat on or rejected the clemency petitions of thousands of federal prisoners,[305] and secretly kept from the White House the contrary opinions of the DOJ Pardon Office in the many cases in which Yates overruled or refused to act on the Pardon Office's recommendation for clemency.[306] Tens of thousands of federal prisoners, mostly poor and disproportionately black—including thousands who were serving sentences that the DOJ itself had declared illegal—never got clemency.[307]

For her part, Harris now calls herself a "progressive prosecutor."[308] When I first encountered Harris, she had spent her prosecutorial career using the cash bail system in California to illegally jail thousands of impoverished people, to extract tens of millions of dollars every year from the poorest families in California for the for-profit bail industry, and to coerce guilty pleas through illegal pretrial detention.[309]

Harris's broader record shows her commitment to the punishment bureaucracy. As a longtime District Attorney, Harris increased felony convictions, largely on the strength of her zealous prosecution of drug offenses.[310] When she was a prosecutor in San Francisco, Harris chose to arrest impoverished black parents whose children were truant.[311] Harris can be seen on video bragging that, against the advice of her political aides, she pushed for punishment of those parents because it was the right thing to do, even if it meant using up her limited political capital.[312] Harris laughed about sending "gang" and "homicide" prosecutors to threaten poor mothers of truant children with prosecution. And she boastfully recalled charging a homeless mother of three with a crime for having truant children.[313] She also pushed legislation to expand such criminal punishment of parents across California.[314] Harris embarked on this crusade despite lacking any evidence that criminal punishment of impoverished parents is the best way to increase school attendance in poor communities of color. In 2010, local prosecutors told the media that Harris "pressured them to take weak cases to trial in an attempt to look tough on crime" before her election.[315] In 2014, she tried to block the early release of people convicted of less serious crimes to reduce deadly prison overcrowding on the ground that "prisons would lose an important labor pool."[316] At the core of Harris's argument was that California needed cheap labor from prisoners, such as to fight dangerous wildfires for $1.45 per day.[317] Perhaps most widely known, she repeatedly fought against exonerations of wrongful convictions and worked to conceal or minimize evidence of false testimony and prosecutorial misconduct.[318]

Across a wide range of areas, each of these former prosecutors is unremarkable as a bureaucrat—their careers reflect a worldview indistinguishable from the consensus that gave rise to mass human caging.

In spite of this, Holder is routinely honored in Washington, DC, society as a "criminal justice reform" leader.[319] After he left the government, he was given a standing ovation at major "criminal justice reform" events that I attended. (He had not renounced his career in human caging or sought accountability for it; instead, he had left the government to get paid large amounts of money to help aggregations of corporate wealth make more money.) Yates was honored by the Southern Center for Human Rights in Atlanta and was given a major award by the National Association of Criminal Defense Lawyers as a "Champion of Justice."[320] (Through her behind-the-scenes assault on the clemency process, Yates may be responsible for the denial of more clemency petitions than any person in American history.)

It says a lot about the "criminal justice reform" culture that someone with the record of Yates or Holder is celebrated as a "reformer." And I predict that Harris and Bharara, despite not having sought accountability for their past actions, will seek higher public office on platforms of "criminal justice reform" with proposals that would do little to remake our punishment bureaucracy. Indeed, when Harris announced her candidacy for President a few days after I had drafted the above para-graphs about her record, the leader of a major national civil rights organization that works on "criminal justice reform" issues praised Harris's prosecutorial record as striking the right "balance" between the "need for public safety and reckoning with civil rights ideals."[321]

My point is not to criticize these four people in particular. They are not unique in their commitment to the punishment bureaucracy. The salient fact about their careers is how ordinary they are—their willingness, along with most of us who have worked in the system, especially lawyers like myself and judges, to go along with unspeakable things, to become desensitized to the pain we cause, and to live our lives without the intellectual and moral rigor that should have prevented so much senseless suffering of powerless people in the name of "law enforcement."

And so these punishment bureaucrats are important because they are *not* outliers. They represent the vast majority of officials that I interact with in dozens of cities and states as I travel the country working on these issues. Mayors, district attorneys, city council members, state legislators, attorneys general, sheriffs, police chiefs, and judges are all adopting some of the language of "reform." To their credit, many with whom I have interacted genuinely believe that reforms need to be made. And like Bharara, Holder, Yates, and Harris, they may have spent their careers as punishment bureaucrats pursuing policies that they genuinely believe in. But almost uniformly, they lack what is necessary for big change: critical analysis of structural problems, genuine self-reflection, and organized political support from groups powerful enough to hold them accountable.[322]

Most reforms being implemented or seriously contemplated suffer from the failure of these bureaucrats to address the nature of the problem. For example, when many "reformer" officials in California finally announced their opposition to cash bail in the summer of 2018, they passed a law ending cash bail. But the law was written in secret by punishment bureaucrats,[323] and the result was a system that could replace cash bail with significantly *expanded* pretrial detention in local jails and that will likely lead to an explosion of for-profit e-carceration[324] through GPS monitoring for people who are released from jail.[325]

In New York, the death of teenager Kalief Browder outraged the public. Kalief committed suicide after he endured three years of pretrial detention on Rikers Island—including eighteen months in solitary confinement and brutal beatings captured on video.[326] Invoking Kalief and standing next to Kalief's brother as he announced "Kalief's Law," Governor Andrew Cuomo used lofty language to announce what punishment bureaucrats portrayed as major "reforms," including raising the age of criminal prosecution in some cases and barring children from being imprisoned with adults. But nearly two years after that announcement, those "reforms" have reinforced the punishment bureaucracy. *More* money is being spent by New York to cage children in *separate* locations, leading to a boom in the construction of child-detention prisons and an *increase* in the number of prison guards; many thousands of children are excluded from the reforms altogether; and new forms of government control over children's bodies are expanding.[327] The public learned that even Kalief Browder would have been excluded from the law that bears his name because the crime for which he was wrongly accused—stealing a backpack from another child—was too serious to qualify for the reforms.[328] In an anecdote that captures "criminal justice reform" culture, Kalief's Law led the State of New York to spend $12 million in 2017 to *reopen* the Harriet Tubman Residential Center—a jail for children named after an abolitionist icon.[329] The facility created eighty-five new jobs and cages disproportionately black children.

A former prosecutor and senior official at a major "criminal justice reform" organization recently wrote an op-ed in the *New York Times* arguing that a way to improve American prisons is to privatize them and to create incentives for the for-profit private prison companies who run them to reduce crime.[330] The article made errors that undermine its conclusions even on their own terms,[331] but most dangerously, the editorial proceeded from a bewildering premise: "Prisons exist to lower crime rates."[332] This factual claim, for which there is no good evidence in American history, is a frequent delusion of punishment bureaucrats. According to them, it is not about race or class or control; it is about good-faith, objective attempts to reduce "crime" for everyone's benefit. Assumptions like this, offered without support or analysis in the public discourse by "rule of law" proponents, are casually asserted as unquestioned wisdom in editorials reaching millions of people. They are a core malignancy that needs to be fought in order to dismantle mass incarceration. No reform, no matter how well intentioned, will be successful if its premise misunderstands why the criminal punishment bureaucracy exists.

Because punishment bureaucrats do not believe that the criminal punishment bureaucracy needs to be dismantled, a movement to dismantle the punishment bureaucracy must learn how to distinguish little tweaks from big changes.

Whatever judgments one makes about punishment bureaucrats as individuals, they serve three main functions in the current conversation. First, they set the outer bounds of acceptable discussion on what should be done to fix the system in order to ensure that more significant changes do not happen. If "reformers" talk about hiring more police officers and spending more money on training them; paying for police body cameras to observe the same officers as they continue to patrol the same poor neighborhoods; creating profitable electronic incarceration instead of jail; using pretrial probation instead of post-trial probation; establishing specialized "drug courts" with "graduated sanctions" instead of immediate punishment; privatizing prisons and immigrant detention jails; and instituting slightly shorter mandatory minimum sentences in cages, then the voices of other people calling for abolition of the police, closing jails and prisons, reparations, new paradigms of restorative justice, and broader economic divestment from punishment are kept outside mainstream discourse. In this way, punishment bureaucrats echo the modern role of the Democratic Party in normalizing American militarism, wealth inequality, neighborhood segregation, incarceration, environmental degradation, and jingoism by defining the boundaries of acceptable dissent from bipartisan policy orthodoxies that lead to these evils.

Second, punishment bureaucrats create confusion. By marketing minor tweaks as huge changes, they make it difficult for the public to figure out who or what promises significant change and who or what does not. If both Kamala Harris and civil rights organizations are calling for "bail reform," ordinary people may think that both groups are proposing the same ideas and that no more change is needed if Harris's version of "reform" passes.

Third, by touting achievements of little significance, they quell popular energy for dramatically changing the punishment system. They burn the areas around the growing fire, ensuring that the fire for reform never threatens the most important punishment infrastructure.

Why are punishment bureaucrats doing this? The origin of these "reforms" is that most elites are happy with the legal system and want it to keep functioning largely as it does. It is not a coincidence that punishment bureaucrats devote their public platforms to promoting America's "rule of law" myth.

Bharara is now the co-chair of a group that calls itself the National Task Force on Rule of Law and Democracy.[333] That group's mission statement portrays American history as democratic and guided by rules and norms that "ensure that officials act for the public good" and that guard against "abuses of power." These rules and norms, Bharara's group claims, historically prevented government from becoming "a chaotic grab for power and self-interest."[334] Armed with this ridiculous picture of America's legal, social, and economic past, the group aims at "*repairing* the rule of law," as if that term had historical content other than to justify *un*democratic exercise of power by elites.[335] Bharara is participating in the long American tradition of developing more and greater obfuscations of a basic truth: the powerful have used the law to dominate the powerless.

Similarly, Yates has been sounding the alarm that the "time-honored" reputation and "legitimacy" of federal "law enforcement" is in danger.[336] She recently explained: "at the Justice Department it is hammered into you that your sole responsibility is to seek justice. It is deeply ingrained in the Department of Justice; that is the ethos."[337] In a characteristic speech to law students entitled "The Rule of Law Under Siege," Yates defended her career working for an organization that accomplished unprecedented mass caging of marginalized people: "When you are part of the Department of Justice . . . [y]our only responsibility is to seek justice. I know that sounds incredibly corny, but that's really what people at DOJ believe. . . . It doesn't get any better than that."[338]

One of Holder's public talking points is that America stands out because it is "a nation of laws" and that, "for the first time in the history of the world, a government was formed based first and foremost on the rule of law" rather than on "the application of force."[339]

In her first words on inauguration as California Attorney General, Harris explained that the elected prosecutor "is one of the most profound innovations in the entire history of the rule of law. . . . [A] crime against any one of us is a crime against all of us. Many times I have looked into the eyes of a crime victim and repeated this promise. It's not you alone versus the defendant. It's the people. The people of the State of California."[340] After fondly recounting her time as a twenty-year line prosecutor in the age of mass human caging, Harris stressed the need to be "tough" on crime and announced that she had secured the help of former police chief Bill Bratton, an architect of "broken windows" policing in which the explicit strategy is to process large numbers of low-level cases, disproportionately targeting poor people of color.[341] She promised the "law enforcement" community: "you will have a forceful advocate for public safety funding at the federal, state and local levels—particularly when it comes to putting more cops on the street."[342]

These punishment bureaucrats thus personify the growing banality of "criminal justice reform": advocates of some of the harshest punishments in the world pushing minor changes in order to preserve faith in the architecture of a bureaucracy used for purposes that they do not acknowledge.

How Can We Tell the Difference?

We must remember that liberty becomes a false ensign—a "solemn complement" of violence—as soon as it becomes only an idea and we begin to defend liberty instead of free [people]. . . . It is the essence of liberty to exist only in the practice of liberty.

—Maurice Merleau Ponty[343]

A lot of attention is turning to local district attorneys. In some ways, the recent interest in "progressive prosecutors" and the growing sums spent on their election campaigns means that more people are acknowledging the myth of the "rule of law." People donating to prosecutorial elections understand that the same "rule of law" will be enforced differently based on the policy choices of the prosecutor.

Perhaps most prominently, there is a wave of "progressive prosecutors" at the local level. Kim Ogg in Houston, Larry Krasner in Philadelphia, Kim Foxx in Chicago, Eric Gonzalez in Brooklyn, Aramis Ayala in Orlando, Kim Gardner in St. Louis, Cyrus Vance in Manhattan, and George Gascón in San Francisco are a few of the dozens of prosecutors embracing a new image as leaders who will "reform" the punishment bureaucracy. While it is wrong to use the same labels to describe each of these actors—Krasner's rhetoric is different from the others, for example, and many would reject Vance's or Gardner's attempts to brand themselves "progressive"—I want to start with some general observations about the entire cohort.[344]

It is remarkable how little these prosecutors have tried to do so far considering that we would need eighty percent reductions in human caging to return to historical U.S. levels and to those of other comparable countries.[345] None of them have reported reducing prosecutions by more than a few percentage points, and most of them have not reported any reductions at all. None of them are calling for smaller prosecutor offices or fewer police. None of them are seeking a massive shift in investigative resources away from investigating the crimes of the poor to investigating the crimes of the rich. None of them have prosecuted a single one of their own employees for withholding evidence or obstruction of justice. None of them have announced a policy of declining to prosecute all drug possession. None of them have stopped prosecuting children as adults. None of them have sought to eliminate fines and fees for the indigent. None of them have opened a systemic civil rights investigation into the brutality, neglect, and crimes against confined people that are rampant in their local jails. None of them have set up a truth and reconciliation commission to confront the past racism and barbarism of their offices and local police. None of them have taken serious steps to transition their approach to a restorative justice model.

All of them do essentially similar things as the offices of their predecessors and the offices of district attorneys around the country: they choose to prosecute a significant majority of low-level misdemeanors and drug crimes, they assume that the response to social problems including violence must be punishment, and they inflict brutal forms of punishment under torturous conditions on a cohort that is disproportionately poor, black, and brown. While a number of them have made initial attempts at less harsh policies in good faith, it is largely business as usual so far.

Krasner, by consensus the most committed to change among this new group, has not made public any data showing that he has reduced the number of people going to prison or the length of sentences relative to other Pennsylvania prosecutors since he took office.[346] In a misdiagnosis of the nature of the problem and of how to make change endure after he leaves office, Krasner worked to *increase* the overall budget for prosecution in Philadelphia.[347]

Although Foxx replaced one of the most notoriously harsh prosecutors in any major American city, the total number of felony prosecutions under Foxx went *up* last year after years of decline, including before she took office.[348] Each year that Foxx has been in office, she has also *increased* the number of cases in which her office chose to prosecute a person for a drug felony.[349] Despite her rhetoric to the contrary, local court watchers have reported to me that Foxx's line prosecutors have taken no action to prevent the use of cash bail in the vast majority of felony cases.

Ogg is sometimes called the least harsh prosecutor in Texas[350]—but her incarceration statistics would be extreme outliers for nearly the entirety of American history. Ogg is a master of the "rule of law" deception. After winning her election on a platform of bail reform because of the supposed injustice of cash bail, Ogg instructed her attorneys to *ignore* the law and to use cash bail to intentionally accomplish pretrial detention of the indigent in cases in which Texas law does not permit transparent pretrial detention.[351] Moreover, Ogg demanded a $20 million budget increase, including for 102 new prosecutors.[352] At the same time, other local officials and lower level prosecutors have told me that they cannot even get her office to stop criminally prosecuting and jailing people for, among other things, driving with a license that was suspended solely because they were too poor to pay court debts. In my experience, over and over again, Ogg appears to want to prosecute more people and to expand her office's bureaucracy. I have watched as she has worked behind the scenes to thwart even modest reforms in Houston like reducing the harms of fines and fees on the indigent and not caging low-level drug possessors in jail cells solely because they cannot pay cash bail amounts requested by her office. As far as I am aware, she has never explained what evidence she possesses that more punishment is the way to solve any of the social problems that she has identified.

Gascón is less harsh than his predecessor, Kamala Harris. But his record of human caging is still alarming by historical and international standards. For years, at the same time that Gascón touted himself as a progressive reformer, attorneys from his office crushed impoverished people and their families every day with relentless use of cash-bail amounts that were five times the national average.[353] Tellingly, after Gascón hyped for months his role in introducing an algorithmic "risk-assessment tool" to the bail process in San Francisco,[354] I asked him and his senior management staff during a meeting to answer the most basic questions about how the tool worked. For example, to explain what the different numerical scores meant in terms of empirical risk prediction. But none of them seemed to have even the rudimentary knowledge about the tool that one could get from reading its instructions, let alone knowledge that public officials implementing the tool should have learned from studying the research and talking to the experts who designed it. This makes sense, because punishment bureaucrats are mostly not interested in using new methods to dramatically reduce pretrial detention—that would remove their ability to coerce guilty pleas through that detention.

And Gascón is not alone: every judge and prosecutor I have interviewed around the country has almost entirely misunderstood or otherwise improperly explained the science, empirical evidence, and function of the risk assessment algorithms that they have touted as their main "reform" of the cash bail system. As a result, Gascón's "progressive" office, like every other jurisdiction I have studied, was misusing the algorithm framework in ways that violated the principles set forth by the researchers who created the tool and that promoted rampant pretrial incarceration of poor people of color. They were also improperly describing the risk-assessment tool to judges in court, including (but not limited to) misstating the purported risk and conflating the algorithm's empirical predictions with their own political choices (but couching the latter in a façade of science without basis). And, again like many other local punishment bureaucracies, because they were not analyzing data and did not have the goal of serious reductions in detention, they neither knew nor cared that they were not using the algorithm properly or changing outcomes significantly. Since then, after we prevailed against Gascón's office in challenging the use of cash bail to detain the poor in San Francisco, Gascón (along with California Attorney General Xavier Beccera) began a campaign to get judges to change the law to expand the ability of the government to detain people without bail,[355] and lawyers at his office even argued in my cases that people should be *presumed guilty* at bail hearings.[356]

I have found Krasner and Gascón to be sincere and smart people. I have talked at length with numerous "progressive prosecutors," and many of them are genuinely attempting to do less harm than other prosecutors. It is prudent to support that harm reduction and to push for more, because "progressive prosecutors" and their rhetoric can play a role in highlighting deeper structural flaws and in energizing a political base to attack them. Importantly, the recent rise of "progressive prosecutors" has already helped to change the overall narrative of punishment in many jurisdictions in which I work by making many more people aware of the injustice and senselessness of much of the punishment system. And I have seen a few of these prosecutors begin some incremental reforms, such as declining some prosecutions, reducing their requests for cash bail, and reducing marijuana possession prosecutions. Perhaps most encouraging, many local organizers are using prosecutor-related issues to engage and mobilize a base who can eventually demand more significant changes.

But we must also guard against the tendency to inflate the importance of existing "progressive prosecutors." We must be clear about who they are; what they are proposing; the differences across the cohort and within each prosecutor office between genuinely transformative changes and minor tweaks; how a newer generation of "progressive prosecutors" can be even more bold than this current cohort; how specifically organizing around prosecutor issues can shift concentrations of local power; and what the theory is for how "progressive prosecutors" can be a stepping stone to much more significant structural change.

After all, as Paul Butler has extensively shown in his writings about a previous generation of what he called "progressive prosecutors" in 2009, these prosecutors are operating under enormous constraints: a powerful local "law enforcement" machine; multibillion-dollar punishment industries; an inherited culture and bureaucracy of line prosecutors and internal office supervisors who believe in mass incarceration; a lack of organized political power among and investment in directly impacted communities; and the broader cultural, racial, and economic forces that fostered our addiction to human caging.[357]

Prosecutors are political actors responding to incentives and, like most of the country, they have been socialized in mass human caging. If left on their own, they will largely preserve mass human caging, if only because none of them have the power to dismantle such a mammoth system even if they wanted to without a social movement articulating it clearly and demanding it. So, although electing different prosecutors and then pushing them to be better can be important in itself and as an organizing tool, anyone interested in significantly dismantling the punishment bureaucracy must have a strategy for creating a reality in which organized political power demands big changes.

VIII

We want land, bread, housing, education, clothing, justice, and peace.

—Black Panther Party, Ten-Point Program[358]

People interested in big change must be clear about what changes they want to see as they build the power in communities to force political actors to accept them. Here, I offer some rules of thumb to differentiate between the "reforms" of punishment bureaucrats and the transformational interventions that would end mass incarceration. The standard "reforms" promoted by punishment bureaucrats typically have several characteristics:

(1) The Silo Mistake

First, at the highest level of generality, they portray the problems of the criminal system as existing in a silo: we can "fix" the criminal system, they say, without confronting deeper problems like white supremacy, lack of access to health care, economic deprivation, educational divestment, neighborhood segregation, gender inequality, banking, lack of access to the arts, unaffordable housing, and environmental destruction.[359] For them, the disproportionate use of the punishment bureaucracy in Boston against black people is not related to the fact that the median net worth of black households in Boston is $8.[360] We must have better policies in this one domain, they concede, but we need not link addressing criminal system failures to remedying broader social inequities.

(2) Misdiagnosing the Problem

Second, they accept the assumptions of the system: we have to deal with social problems through punishment; the existing bureaucracy is trying its best to help people live safe, flourishing lives; "law enforcement" uses the "rule of law" to pursue "criminal justice" and not to further other objectives like protecting profit and racial hierarchy.

(3) Hoarding Control

Third, because punishment bureaucrats accept these assumptions and rely on the bureaucracy's good faith, their proposals retain power and control in the same actors and institutions that created and manage mass human caging.[361] Reformers want to give control, resources, and discretion to prosecutors, judges, police, sheriffs, probation departments, parole boards, private corporations and consultants, and so on. Their reforms are defined by their lack of community self-determination and accountability.[362] They do not shift centers of power and control.

(4) Lack of Reparations, Lack of Justice

Fourth, punishment bureaucrats' reforms are not backward looking. Standard "reforms" pay no attention to repairing the damage done by mass human caging, such as through monetary and property reparations for massive harms caused by the punishment bureaucracy in the past and for the lawlessness against marginalized people and communities that went unprosecuted and uncompensated. Making individual survivors whole is an uncontroversial goal of standard criminal prosecutions, but making whole the many survivors of systemic government atrocities is entirely absent from broader "criminal justice reform" discourse.

(5) Shrinking the Bureaucracy

Fifth, they do not try to shrink the punishment system. They instead tout larger budgets, more police officers, better "predictive" policing and machine learning algorithms, more prosecutors, special "drug" courts with different jail punishment structures, greater use of probation supervision, more parole, fee-based "diversion" programs, and electronic shackles to replace metal ones. In short, they seek expanded control over people's bodies and minds, but they argue that this control should be exercised in different ways.[363]

A good rule of thumb for identifying whether a proposal is meaningful or hollow is asking the question: would this reform result in greater or fewer resources going to the punishment bureaucracy? Virtually every major "reform" pushed by local, state, and federal punishment bureaucrats would result in either the same or more resources flowing into the punishment bureaucracy.

(6) Reinvestment

Sixth, because they shift resources *within* the punishment system (for example, from incarceration to surveillance and supervision) they lack a plan for creating cost savings. Even when there are promises of vague savings due to less incarceration, punishment bureaucrats typically do not propose to reinvest those savings in anti-carceral institutions. They do not attempt to build up institutions that would provide the sustainable infrastructure for dismantling incarceration and shifting toward alternative community-based wellness. The resource savings from reform proposals should be articulated, and every proposal should have a transparent vision for how those savings will be reinvested outside of the punishment bureaucracy.

In contrast with the standard "criminal justice reform" pushed by punishment bureaucrats, people working in communities across the country are situating their work in a deeper politics and are therefore incubating a wide range of transformations. I include here just a small list of the broad range of work being done in communities across the United States:

- Organizers in Cleveland, Detroit, the Bay Area, and elsewhere are cultivating economic models that change distributions of power, such as worker-owned cooperatives that can build the wealth, power, and political engagement of formerly incarcerated people.[364]

- Campaigns to close notorious jails in New York City, St. Louis, and Philadelphia,[365] and campaigns to stop the construction of new jails, such as the JusticeLA campaign to stop the construction of two new jails for $3.5 billion in Los Angeles.[366] All of these organizers understand that the punishment bureaucracy will fill jails and prisons with bodies wherever these facilities exist.

- Policies to reserve profitable marijuana business licenses to people with prior marijuana convictions or people living in communities disproportionately targeted by police for drug arrests.[367]

- Reparations for police torture.[368]

- Community land trusts that attempt to bring affordable housing and neighborhood control to heavily policed neighborhoods.[369]

- Restorative justice that changes norms around how to think about accountability when a person harms another person. Shifting to restorative models in Washington, DC, for example, they have nearly eliminated the use of jails to incarcerate youth in the juvenile system.[370]

- Pilot reinvestment programs to shift savings from decreased parole revocation expenditures to community-based projects led by directly impacted people.[371]

▪ Two-way text messaging, phone-call reminders, childcare in court, and transportation to court are being developed as alternatives to the money bail system, and to the for-profit e-carceration movement that is replacing money bail with GPS monitoring and pretrial supervision.

▪ Hundreds of poetry, theater, and art programs for children and adults who are survivors of human caging have grown organically around the country to involve thousands of people.[372] These programs build community, solidarity, connection, creativity, compassion, and healing, and they help foster empathy and relationships between people impacted by the punishment system and segments of society that have long been indifferent to their stories.

Ideas like these hold enormous promise. But investment in them is dwarfed by the tens of billions of dollars spent on punishing people. Whether we can improve and scale these and other transformative ideas depends on whether we can change the stories that the punishment bureaucracy tells about why it exists and what it does. Only by having an honest conversation about what the punishment bureaucracy is can an informed movement dismantle it. Many human beings have a lot at stake in whether we can.

THE HUMAN LAWYER

I

ROXBURY IS A NEIGHBORHOOD IN BOSTON. IT IS THOUGHT BY some to be one of the "worst" neighborhoods in the city. Roxbury has a very high concentration of black residents. On Warren Street, in the center of the community, lies the Roxbury District Court. Inside the Roxbury District Court sits the bustling local branch office of one of Massachusetts's biggest industries.

One morning, a student attorney was picking up cases at arraignments as part of a third-year legal clinic. She was assigned to represent Maurice.[1] Maurice was being detained in custody, so the young lawyer went upstairs to the lockup to make her introduction. Maurice was short and thin, covered in dirt. As the student introduced herself, a man in another cell drowned out her voice, shouting at officers to flush his toilet. Maurice said "hello" to the student and complained that he, too, couldn't get anyone to flush the toilet in the small cell that he was sharing with two other people.

They began to talk about Maurice's life and about his case.

They weren't as rushed as usual—they still had about twenty minutes before the case would be called. Still, they had to cover all the important details of Maurice's life history: He was homeless. He was cold. He had two children. He had a drug problem. He was a writer. His poetry book had been lost during the arrest. He knew he shouldn't have been in that building, but he wasn't trying to steal anything; he was just looking for shelter. He really wanted the two pieces of jawbreaker candy the officers had taken away but promised to return. He needed her to ask about them right away.

An officer walked down the hallway and slapped the large red button that controlled Maurice's toilet. He then slapped a few others on his way down the hall. The successive sounds of swirling water could be heard all the way down the corridor, each time slightly more distant and distorted.

The officers soon shackled Maurice and took him downstairs for the arraignment. Despite the student lawyer's best efforts, a money bail of $200 was set. After all, Maurice had a habit of getting caught "trespassing." This, for some reason, weighed particularly heavily in the judge's determination that $200 was needed to ensure Maurice's presence at his next court date.

Maurice had no money and nobody he felt comfortable calling for money, so he returned upstairs to the lockup to await transfer to the local jail, where he would spend the next few weeks until his pretrial hearing. Perhaps then he would plead guilty so as not to be jailed several more weeks until a trial was scheduled. His zealous student advocate raced upstairs after him to comfort him. "The food sucks there," he informed her. "And they strip you down and poke around your ass. Plus, they won't let me do any writing," he added. "What'd the judge say about the case from '04?" She looked at her notes and answered, "He said it was for the same charge."

After a few more minutes, she got ready to leave. She had to get back to school for Administrative Law. She promised to visit him the next week at the jail. Then, he surprised her: "Why did I have to sit there behind that glass? I couldn't even hear you." She was startled because Maurice had asked a question that almost nobody else asks each day as they judge, prosecute, and defend inside that courtroom. Why does Roxbury make defendants appear in the courtroom shackled and confined in a glass box? As members of the community fill the courtroom each day, there they are, inside that cage: "us" and "the other."

She thought about every day she had walked into that courtroom and seen the glass cage filled with what seemed to be the same kinds of people charged with the same kinds of crimes. Five or six Roxbury residents were usually stuffed into the box, stepping on and over each other, pressing their faces to its glass walls in a futile effort to hear—much less understand—a snippet of the legal code words being thrown around about their lives.

She thought about that morning after the Red Sox won the World Series, when the arrests had consisted mostly of drunken revelers. Everyone that day had been mesmerized by the sight of the college students inside the glass box. Nobody was quite sure what to say or do; the presence of wealthy white people in that glass box just seemed odd—out of place and somehow silly. The court clerk couldn't hide a smile, the probation officers pointed and joked with each other in the corner, and the lawyers stumbled through their bail arguments, not quite sure what to say. The glass cage suddenly seemed absurd, as if everyone realized they were watching a tragic comedy and their only defense mechanism was laughter.

"Next time just tell the judge I need to stand out there next to you," Maurice told her.

"Well, the judge isn't likely to think the cage is prejudicial, Maurice." She couldn't help but be troubled by her own response. She had answered him almost by reflex, and her legalistic jargon made her feel awkward and embarrassed. But the law student in her also couldn't resist playing out in her head a legal challenge to the use of the glass cage. Her first thought was one of the great, silent fears of public defenders: that the judge would be upset by her request and would not be as lenient on Maurice. But it was more than that. It would involve trying to convince judges that a person shouldn't be in a glass cage and shackles when judges are making decisions about the person's character, guilt, and supposed dangerousness—when judges are deciding whether to revoke probation and send someone like Maurice to jail for a couple years; trying to convince a judge that, psychologically, it is much easier to throw another human in jail if the person already appears inside that box—much easier than if Maurice stood right in front, eye to eye, as a free human being; trying to convince a judge that the judge, as a person, is influenced by seeing a defendant shackled and caged . . .

The student attorney thought about trying to capture in legal writing the tremendous deprivation and insecurity facing the people who find themselves indigent and the sense of hopelessness they feel when they find themselves in a courtroom, pitted against the Commonwealth of Massachusetts in a fight for their liberty—when they cannot afford $200 to avoid stumbling into each court appearance like a caged animal; trying to describe the subtle messages of inferiority that the cage sends to people like Maurice every day; and trying to explain that the cage sends the same message to all of the professionals working in the court and to all of the family members and journalists who fill the courtroom's pews.

And then, with perhaps the four words that best describe the life of a public defender or anyone else caught in the trafficking of inequality, she put her hand on Maurice's shoulder. "But I will try."

II

Michael Riggs was starving and homeless.[2] He had begun using heroin after his young son drowned in the family swimming pool. For many years, he had been living a life of petty crime, depression, and addiction. On October 13, 1995, Michael walked into a grocery store and took a bottle of vitamins without paying for it, perhaps thinking they would help give him strength. In the store's parking lot, he pleaded with employees to let him work at the store, scrubbing their floors to pay off his debt and to help him get food.[3] Instead, he was arrested. The prosecutor decided to file the case as a violation of California's "Three Strikes Law," and Michael was sentenced to twenty-five years to life in prison.[4]

Don't read that paragraph the way the Supreme Court justices and their law clerks read Michael's cruel and unusual punishment petition. Don't read that paragraph as you typically read an article in a newspaper or a law journal. Let down your guard and let each word make you feel something. Think about what Michael Riggs must have felt as he took his first step into his jail cell. Did it have a smell or a flickering light overhead? What did he think as he heard the cell door shut behind him? Did his heart start beating fast? Did he have a brief moment of panic, his hands dampening with sweat? Or was he calm? Was his spirit already broken, resigned to a fraction of the life he could have had? What was the first thing another incarcerated person said to him? Think about the emotions that raced through his body—the moments of uncertainty he felt as he lay in his cell. Maybe he thought about his young son.

We must always remember when those same emotions well up inside each of us. We all have our moments of insecurity and our moments of panic. We all have our moments of loneliness and our moments of pride. Can we see those emotions in others? The debate about rampant incarceration is not just about the billions of dollars that incarceration costs, its stunningly disproportionate impact, and the evidence that it doesn't actually work; it is also about Michael Riggs. It is about a homeless man who was hungry and weak and who stole vitamins from a supermarket. It is about Jorge Andrade, who is serving fifty years to life for stealing nine videos from Kmart, and Gary Ewing, who is serving twenty-five years to life for stealing three golf clubs.[5]

The human lawyer remembers that all abstract policy debates are about real people. We owe it to those people to ensure that their stories are not shortchanged when we make the difficult tradeoffs that governing a society of humans requires. Yet some narratives hold a much more powerful place in our collective psyche than others. There is an empathy displacement that grossly skews our perceptions of social harm.

In individual criminal cases, we employ a heightened standard of proof before imposing a conviction. Liberty is of such great importance that we require evidence "beyond a reasonable doubt" before sending a human being to prison or otherwise depriving a human of her freedom. However, when setting broader policy—for example, in the conception of criminality, the calibration of punishment, and the treatment of accused people—we abandon those heightened standards completely. We resort to strategies that result in massive deprivations of liberty, such as imprisonment or, to borrow from another context, military invasion, with little or no indication that these strategies work, much less evidence that they work *best*. Just as we should be wary of throwing one person in jail if the evidence against her is unsound, so too should we worry about throwing millions in jail if the evidence supporting the connection between massive incarceration and a better society is unproven.[6] The human lawyer reminds her peers that we often fail to internalize negative consequences when these consequences are visited upon certain groups, such as those who look different from us or those who live far away from our tiny bubble of experience. Without great vigilance, these stories and these costs are easily lost, and with this loss disappears any chance of properly evaluating the merits of any given policy.

We forget this when cigarettes kill 443,000 Americans each year[7] and when drunk driving kills nearly the same number of people as all illicit drug use combined (17,000).[8] But we are smokers, and we are drinkers. Smoking has never been criminalized, and drunk driving is barely criminalized in comparison to the severe penalties attached to other drug laws.[9] Because of who is thought to engage in these activities, smoking and drinking hold a different place in our national narrative. Smoking and drinking have been relatively well accepted parts of mainstream and wealthy culture. Because of dominant narratives and incomplete empathy, criminal law has become a woefully imperfect approximation of social harm.

This same narrative displacement, privileging some conception of "us" to "the other," repeats itself over the wide variety of policy areas that make up collective life. It allows great suffering, poverty, and violence all over the world. It is true that many opponents of harsh interrogation techniques or severe criminal punishments or waging wars forget that, while these actions may be quite repulsive, the alternative—omitting to act—may result in an equal or greater number of deaths. But the ease with which we have engaged in these gruesome activities—from imprisoning a significantly higher proportion of our population than any society in the world,[10] to incarcerating black people at almost six times the rate of white people,[11] to waging dozens of wars and supporting countless dictators all over the globe,[12] to spending more on a military than the next forty-five highest spending countries combined[13]—is shocking.

All this because we haven't listened to enough stories and because we haven't experienced enough other ways of life. We treat some lives with a certain nonchalance. The human lawyer is not afraid to make difficult tradeoffs, but she is cavalier with no life. The human lawyer is sensitive to forgotten stories. The human lawyer embraces "costs" and "benefits," but she has a richer understanding of each.

Michael Riggs got out of prison after about ten years due to a claim of ineffective assistance of counsel.[14] But there are many more people like Michael, Gary, and Jorge whose stories never make it into the pages of a law journal.

Human lawyers must weave these stories into the fabric of our culture's narrative.

III

A friend from law school was back at home in New Jersey for winter break, and she got a very expensive speeding ticket. She is a fanatical observer of the speedometer when in her car, and she has a fairly weird obsession with respecting speed limits. On this particular occasion, she was actually driving two or three miles per hour below the labeled limit! There must have been some sort of mistake with the radar gun; perhaps she rubbed the cop the wrong way when she argued with him after being pulled over. In any case, she scheduled a court date for when she would be home from school in January, and she was committed to fighting what she viewed as a minor injustice and a major inconvenience.

When she went into court to make her passionate stand, she was informed that her court date had been changed. She had received no notice. The clerk told her the new date. My friend politely informed the clerk that this wouldn't be possible because she now lived in Boston and could not return for the later date. She asked instead where she could go to contest the ticket right away. The clerk was unsympathetic, and she indicated that if my friend failed to appear on the scheduled date, a warrant would be issued for her arrest. Her other option, according to the clerk, was to admit to the violation and pay several hundred dollars. She had no other recourse.

For just a second, when threatened with an arrest warrant, she felt a powerful feeling of helplessness. She wanted more information. Her eyes darted around the crowded lobby. Who could she talk to about the court's procedures? Who could help her? Who knew what was going on? Was this treatment even legal for speeding tickets? She felt that sensation in her chest— that pang of being treated unfairly. That feeling overwhelmed her as she stood at the courthouse counter.

These moments of emotion are the fires from which the human lawyer is forged. Once she experiences them, she remembers them and holds them close to her heart. *They help her understand other people.*

My friend left the courthouse and went home. She soon felt better. Under that threat, though, my friend ended up just giving in and paying the hefty fine. Luckily she could afford it. Thank goodness the whole thing was relatively minor and would probably never happen to her again.

IV

One morning in the middle of August 2006, forty-three Harvard Law School students gathered in a small classroom in

Hauser Hall, room 102, for the *Harvard Law Review*'s orientation. The thirty men and thirteen women were regaled with stories of their potential impact on legal "scholarship" and their ability to publish student writing.

As long as they gave extra weight to articles from Harvard professors, as long as those articles had a "roadmap" in the beginning, as long as they got permission from respected professors before they published any piece, as long as the articles claimed in their introductions to be entirely novel, and as long as the articles didn't make them think too hard about our culture or their lifestyles, they were completely free to help select the new and exciting wave of legal "scholars."

As long as their own ideas fit within the student writing guidelines and other procedures outlined in their internal manuals—the Greenbook, the Brownbook, the Whitebook, and the Blackbook—and as long as their citations conformed to the Bluebook, they had virtually unlimited control to leave their mark.

V

The first idea for this essay was a choose-your-own-adventure story to be published as a note in the *Harvard Law Review*. It was to be about a law student and the people she met at law school. It would have discussed some of the wonderful things she saw in the law, such as its insistence on requiring reasons and its emphasis on logical rigor in the translation of principles and shared values into outcomes. The note would have also examined the problems she saw in legal education and legal culture, such as restrictions on how reasons are expressed in legal writing, incomplete perceptions of social harm, and systemic flaws that undermine the actual rigor of legal decision-making processes. The note was also to be about the difficult pressures the student faced in her personal life, especially in making decisions like choosing a career. At the end of the adventure, readers would find themselves with a career or with positions on particularly pressing legal problems that were logically consistent with earlier choices they had made about their own stated values.

Another student editor said: "They'll never let you publish that!" I asked why. "Because it's not legal 'scholarship.'" Then the person added, smiling: "Plus, everyone knows that requiring logical consistency with our values would have meant overturning Warren McCleskey's death sentence."[15] In my heart I knew the person was right. People rarely tested (with any rigor) their daily actions or beliefs for logical consistency with their deeply held values. There is comfort and stability in intellectual and moral laziness. My choose-your-own-adventure wasn't going to be published—at least not in that format. The very idea violated the Brownbook, the Greenbook, the Whitebook, and even portions of the Blackbook. The books, like those who depended on them, were all afraid of "too much justice."[16]

VI

After Hurricane Katrina, law students from around the country rushed to New Orleans. Some went because the hurricane was a watershed moment of consciousness—one of those moments when the mind wrestles with striking evidence that the world contains much more of what you abhor than you had thought.

Others went because what Katrina exposed was a little too egregious for comfort, and small amounts of guilt meant that the wounds had to be covered over before life could go on swimmingly. And some went both because they wanted to help and because law schools were offering free trips to warm weather.

But everyone went because, in some sense, they care about other people. Just as an internal computer triangulates the position of millions of tiny ants as they construct a mobile civilization, human colonies, for all their multitude of intricacies, seem to have an internal compass of compassion.

Some of the students who went to New Orleans tell the story of Julian, a public defender who they met. Julian's house had been flooded and destroyed. A fallen tree had almost evenly divided his pickup truck in half, and he was using the bed of the truck as a makeshift office. He didn't have a working phone.

The morning the students met this unforgettable character was a busy one in the local New Orleans courtroom. The students sat in the back of a row of small pews, watching the scene unfold like a group of foreign election observers. In the middle of an arraignment for first-degree murder, the defendant informed the court that he didn't think he was the right "Dwayne Jackson" because he had been picked up for something totally different and because he was in his twenties. Dwayne the murder suspect was in his forties. After a few minutes, the judge apologized to twentysomething Dwayne, but told him that he would have to stay in the city jail for a while since they couldn't transport him back to wherever it was that they had found him. Dwayne was sad because, in the months since the hurricane, he had made some friends and amassed some belongings at a different prison facility, and now he couldn't even go back to that makeshift home.

The judge then started to arraign another murder case. The judge appointed Julian (who by now had taken almost all of the cases since the students arrived) to represent the defendant. The defender calmly raised a few doubts to the judge: "Judge, I don't believe I can take this case. If I do, it'll be my twenty-first pending capital murder case." The judge had no one else there to whom he could assign the case, but had any lawyer in American history ever come close to this total of capital cases? So the judge took a recess in order to complain about the city's punishment system to the visiting law students.

Supreme Court cases about rules of criminal procedure seemed out of touch to the students after they saw Julian. The vague images most of the law students had of the front lines of poverty hardly aligned with the way that law was actually lived and experienced.

After court, the students sought out Julian to tell him how appalled they were at what they had seen in this hurricane-ravaged courtroom. Julian told the students that, even before the hurricane, his office could afford only about half of the lawyers it needed to provide minimal representation to indigent New Orleanians. Now, with only a small fraction of even that already inadequate staff, they were well below even the Supreme Court's definition of effective assistance.[17] Worse still, because of Louisiana's pretrial detention statutes, many of Julian's clients spent weeks in jail before being formally charged with a crime.[18] This period was often longer than the sentence the person would have received had she been found guilty the day she was arrested.

That the hurricane turned those weeks into months perhaps shocked elite law schools enough to send a few of their brightest to the area, but it hardly seemed to rattle this seasoned veteran of the injustice system. The hurricane brought many to the front lines, but it didn't seem at all to change the nature of the battle Julian was fighting there in the trenches. In the fight to improve the lives of marginalized people, the human lawyer has always worked from a broken truck, and every day is hurricane season.

VII

Every year a famous public interest lawyer comes to Harvard Law School to speak to the new class of first-year students. He always speaks in the north classroom in Austin Hall, and he always talks about the wonderful people he has met throughout his life working with disadvantaged communities and throughout his career as a lawyer working against the death penalty. The first-year students sit quietly with tears welling in their eyes and running slowly down their faces. Some cry because they hadn't imagined the poverty and injustice of which he tells and against which his remarkable career has stood as a small fortress of hope. Others cry because of the purity in his eyes and the passion in his words—because it is beautiful to hear about a life devoted to reducing the suffering of others. Every year these students go that night to a drinking event sponsored by student organizations, and they talk over beers and mixed drinks about how it was the best speech they've ever heard.

Every year most Harvard Law School graduates begin their careers at corporate law firms with neither fireworks nor fanfare. Those few hours in Austin Hall are a distant memory of a time when they felt free to think like human lawyers.

VIII

"I'm entitled to my opinion."

"You have no right to judge me."

These two phrases are common in conversation, and they are cousins. These standard verbal shields are surprisingly common phenomena in law school and among law students. We have all heard them from that guy in our first-year Criminal Law class who starts talking about how rape laws are too harsh on men or in response to the class "socialist" telling her classmates that they shouldn't be going to work for corporate law firms.

These shields are dangerous because they are used to neutralize a person who is making us think about our life in an uncomfortable way: "I'm not going to engage with you, friend, because in our culture, it is simply not acceptable to challenge someone else's beliefs or choices." We all do it—we all have this psychological defense mechanism.

Thankfully, this defense mechanism kicks in only when we perceive the challenge to be a relatively close moral call; otherwise, going through our typical days would become difficult. For example, if someone we know robs a homeless person or shoots a child, we generally feel comfortable passing judgment on them. We have no problem saying to them: "What you did was wrong." In fact, as a society, we even require them to give reasons or justifications for their behavior or face punishment.

While perpetuating gender inequality in the law school classroom, or helping America's corporations grow wealthier, or spending hours upon hours watching the National Football League might initially seem less obviously wrong in our minds, our hesitation in judging the decisions of people who engage in these activities is not that they are entitled to behave in any way they wish without regard to the well-being of others. Rather, it is that we don't seem to be as sure empirically that advocating more lenient definitions of rape or working for a corporate law firm or devoting enormous time and energy to watching and discussing corporatized professional sports is leading to serious harm. However, evidence that these activities actually do lead to harms that we care about, if it exists, would have to be taken very seriously. If such evidence exists and is presented, it becomes a sword that we must allow to pierce these verbal shields.

When we say we are each entitled to our opinions and, for example, to our choice of careers, we are simply trading on a background legal rule regarding free speech or freedom from (mostly government) coercion in our everyday decisions. We are not, as some seem to presume, making a moral statement. For in the world of morality, once we have decided our own underlying values, we are not entitled to believe or do anything we wish. Given a set of values, we cannot take positions or engage in activity without regard for the consequences of those positions and actions on the realization of our values, without evaluating the consistency of our positions, or without examining the evidence in support of our beliefs in the same sense that we are not permitted to believe in mathematics that $2 + 2 = 5$. That's just not how morality works.

Moral questions can be extremely difficult. They are intellectually trying; people for many centuries have discussed and debated them without reaching definitive answers. They are also psychologically taxing, because they ask us to evaluate how we are living vis-à-vis others and perhaps even ask us to make some changes to our own lives.

It is precisely when facing such difficult dilemmas that the input of others becomes most valuable. After all, what better way to help us test if we are living well-reasoned lives consistent with whatever our own values might be?

The pervasiveness of anti-intellectual defense mechanisms in law schools is bizarre because legal minds are otherwise trained to support positions with articulable reasons.

The human lawyer leaves these shields at home; she uses her sword.

The human lawyer does not question the *values* of others, but she always supports her beliefs and actions with reasons and asks others to do the same. She understands that there are real effects on people's lives attached to our beliefs and to our actions. She asks herself constantly if she is living her life in accordance with her moral values about how her life should impact other people. The human lawyer also recognizes the daunting practical, emotional, and psychological nature of this task. That is why the human lawyer cries for help: "Please judge me!"

IX

This was one of the most tension-filled trials the court had staged in many years. Both sides had prepared first-rate teams of lawyers, and each day the jury listened carefully to the evidence presented. After all, it was one of the most important decisions in her life.

Many of the arguments and pieces of evidence were the same as last week, when she was deciding between donating her tax refund to a charity or spending it on new headphones. But that trial had been in small claims court, and the decisions are fairly automatic there, based largely on habit and common-law rules previously developed in the higher courts of her mind. Although the Rules of Moral Evidence apply equally there, small claims court is usually too overwhelmed with daily decisions to engage in rigorous litigation over every moral case. Even bigger cases that were fully litigated in the higher courts—such as the one concerning what topic she should choose for her new student law review article or the one concerning whether she should stop spending hours watching professional sports—failed to garner as much media attention as this case.

This case just felt different. Choosing a career was a big deal. There was a series of pretrial motions dates and preliminary hearings in which basic values were discussed and agreed upon.

At least with respect to the issues in this case, there had been surprisingly little disagreement between the parties about what constituted basic moral goods. The sides had no trouble crafting jury instructions detailing the substantive law of her own moral code.

The prosecution was challenging her previously stated desire to work at a corporate law firm. If the jury ruled in its favor, she would have to take a different approach to her career, at least until new evidence surfaced warranting a new trial. The prosecution's position was essentially seeking a significant change in her life, and perhaps in the material lifestyle that she lived. The defense was holding firmly to her way of life and to the way of life practiced by so many of her peers, whose own grand juries had yet to return any moral indictments.

The trial was difficult for the judge. There were a lot of thorny evidentiary questions. For example, the Rules of Moral Evidence clearly prohibited consideration of psychological factors that might *explain* her decisions if those factors were not sufficiently relevant as moral *justifications* under the Rules.

The two sides were hotly contesting several main issues: the extent to which corporate law firms affect pervasive inequality, whether high corporate salaries were excessive personal luxuries in a world of staggering need, and the significance of the opportunity cost involved in working in corporate law when her services were so badly needed elsewhere in the legal system.

The defense began its closing argument. It argued passionately about the need to build wealth so that she could adequately support her family and so that she might later be able to give back to the community. The defense stressed traditional barriers for women in the corporate setting and highlighted the potential expressive message that she could send by working at a corporate law firm.

The prosecution countered with striking evidence about average American and worldwide family incomes and argued that the defense was drastically overestimating the amount of money needed to live a happy life.[19] The prosecution also questioned these asserted rationales and presented evidence that others who had made the defense's arguments were now seen living luxurious lifestyles; going to nice clubs and restaurants; buying expensive cars, televisions, and houses; wearing expensive clothes; taking lavish vacations that harmed the earth's ecological systems; and sending children to costly private schools. The prosecution noted that there were other ways to advance the cause of gender equality that did not contribute to massive economic inequality. The prosecution argued that the desire for an enormous salary was inconsistent with the defense's own positions at the prior motion hearing concerning the moral obligation to help others. Finally, the prosecution presented evidence of the role that corporate law firms pursuing profit played (and continue to play) in some of the most egregious and harmful activities in the history of the United States[20] and evidence that millions of vulnerable people had desperate legal needs that she could attend to instead.

The human lawyer has a courtroom in her head. The human lawyer litigates all her moral decisions.

X

Figure 1: The Supreme Court:[21]

```
MMMMMMMMMMMMMMMMMMMMMMMMMMMM
MMMMMMMMMMMMMMMMMMMMMMMMMMMMMM
MMMMMMMMMMMMMMMMMMMMMMMMMMM
MMMMMMMMMMMMMMWMMMMWMMMWWMM
```

Figure 2: The Supreme Court:

```
WWWWWWWWWWWWWWWWWWWWWWWWWWWW
WWWWWWWWWWWWWWWWWWWWWWWWWWWW
WWWWWWWWWWWWWWWWWWWWWWWWWWW
WWWWWWWWWBWWWWWWWWWBWWWWHWWW
```

Did some of the same flaws that produced these distributions infect the doctrine that the Court crafted at the very same time?

XI

On the third floor of Gannett House, the *Harvard Law Review* has a "Supreme Court Office." Until relatively recently, pictures of the current justices and portraits of the Court in the 1930s filled the walls. Editors inheriting that room as an office have used its space as a temple to worship the justices, old and new. It is one of the many shrines to that institution at Harvard Law School, where larger-than-life portraits of the justices and other legal celebrities follow the students from room to room and building to building.

On their frequent visits to the law school, justices, even more than professors, are treated as emperors. Students huddle in the aisles of large lecture halls just to get a glimpse.

A longtime Harvard professor, known for being uniquely contrarian, famously painted the office red on a personal whim when, as a student, he became Supreme Court Chair of the *Harvard Law Review* in the 1970s. In 2007, a fight ensued after another Supreme Court Chair removed some of the pictures of the justices and marked over the faces of old-time racists like Justice James Clark McReynolds. Some editors were angered: "We have to respect the Supreme Court. It is a great institution."

In the history of that room, these brief moments of color are slowly eroded by the daily tide of law school normalcy—vivid memories turned dull and gray and eventually washed away by wave after wave of thoughtlessness.

Throughout much of its history, the Supreme Court has been openly hostile to or completely out of touch with important social narratives. It has not been sensitive to the stories of people like Maurice and Michael and Dwayne. Idolatry of the Supreme Court and the legal establishment can lead us to sit by while these stories are ignored.

Lawyers, perhaps more than those in other professions, build up their heroes and cheer their rock stars. The human lawyer respects people because of their kindness, the quality of their ideas, and their contributions to alleviating suffering and promoting human flourishing; she never respects someone because other law students do. She challenges idolatry. She is aware that idolatry allows old orthodoxy to go unquestioned and existing flaws in decision-making to go unremedied.

XII

This essay was first written as a student note to be published in the *Harvard Law Review*. The *Harvard Law Review*, as a matter of policy, makes room for every member to publish a note. After the piece was reviewed and edited by a number of student editors and approved by the Notes Committee, the president of the journal, pursuant to his plenary authority, canceled the piece's publication.

XIII

It was nearing 3 p.m., and the professor was moving quickly through another lecture on constitutional law. He had just told a story about a hilarious idiosyncrasy he had discovered in the personality of one of the justices while he was clerking on the Supreme Court. Now he was analyzing the Court's decision in a recent affirmative action case. It was a truly virtuoso performance . . .

A second-year student looked around the room at her friends, their faces staring deeply into the screens of their laptop computers. She sat there quietly, listening to the rhythmic concerto of computer keys that filled the room. What began as her subtle frustration at a potential oversight in his lecture slowly grew into outrage. She didn't want to raise her hand because no one had spoken in the class in over thirty minutes. Maybe she wasn't as smart as him anyway—maybe her idea was stupid. She had often heard other students joke about how useless many of their fellow classmates' comments were. Surely no one cared about her opinion. After all, they were paying money to learn from "expert" legal minds. Maybe she could just ask him after class. She would have to jump out of her seat without putting her stuff into her backpack so she could beat the usual after-class rush down to the podium.

Then she saw Jamie raise his hand. Jamie was one of the few students who consistently spoke in class. Because of his politically libertarian views, Jamie was often in the minority. She often disagreed with him, but she found herself strangely interested and happy whenever Jamie intervened. On affirmative action, Jamie fought back. He engaged the professor, and he spoke to his putative superior with a tone of skepticism that bordered on disrespect. He even interrupted the professor to correct a mischaracterization of his question. It certainly stood out among the general adulation.

Many students seemed annoyed at Jamie, as if he were breaking some unwritten rule. The crescendo of plastic keys, slowly building throughout the lecture, had stopped abruptly in silence. The class waited, their hands perched over the computer keys, for a signal from the puppeteer that would tell them how to regard and record Jamie's arguments.

Jamie worked hard every day so that his views would not be marginalized—reduced to a footnote in the quasi-liberal law school experience. Jamie refused to take the path of least resistance.

The human lawyer, regardless of her political beliefs, sets an example of individuality for her peers. The human lawyer challenges conformity because it prevents us from confronting the issues that our peers are ignoring. It prevents us from feeling the stories that have been systematically hidden with the glosses of legal and popular culture. It also guides our career choices with the same invisible force that holds our hands in the unison of limbo above our keyboards. The human lawyer is aware that pervasive conformity slowly suffocates individual liberty.

XIV

Every night after finishing her reading for the next day at the library, a third-year law student walks home from the law school to her apartment on Massachusetts Avenue. Every night she passes a man who sleeps on a small wooden bench under the street's only broken streetlamp.

A flattened cardboard box always lies at his feet, and a small gym bag full of his possessions always sits on the bench next to him, his arm resting over it as if to protect it. Many nights, the man sits motionless, wrapped in layers of clothing; only his curly beard pokes through the hole between his knit hat and the blanket he has tucked under his neck.

One night, the student was returning late from dinner and drinks, treading through the fresh snow with her rubber boots. She arrived outside her apartment and stopped to look at the ball of cloth and man sleeping upright on his bench. An inch of snow rested precariously on his right shoulder as his head lay tilted to the left. Her heart went out to him. She had gone out of her way to spend a total of less than twenty minutes outdoors the whole day. She knew he would be spending the entire night outside, recoiling with shivers at each gust of wind.

She couldn't imagine what it would be like every night to call that bench home.[22] Not in Boston; not in the winter. How could she pretend to know all that he was going through? At one moment she almost hated herself for pitying him. How could she be worthy to think about him, to share a street with him, to write about him in her journal? The next moment, she hated herself for stupid luxuries she had and for not doing more to help him. In the past, she had placed bread or fruit next to his bag or talked to him if he were awake. Whenever he smiled at her and said, "God bless you," she felt triumphant. He even made her cry one night as she looked back and saw him devouring the bagels she had brought from the law review office's kitchen.

But he was the fourth homeless person she had seen on her walk home. What was she to do? What would it mean to do enough to help him? Where could she draw the line? What about the thousands of people like him who do not have a safe place to live and the millions of others living in poverty or struggling through the other troubles of life?

These are questions that the human lawyer cannot answer. The human lawyer can at most help us think about these things by making sure that the processes we use are as free from coercion and error as possible. She can tell us to be vigilant in ensuring that we always have good reasons when making decisions in our personal lives and when developing our laws. She can tell us to watch out for problems like psychological bias, selfishness, conformity, idolatry, misinformation, logical errors, and defensiveness. She can tell us not to brush aside certain stories—to think about the man on the bench—when we debate broader policy. But each of us must find our own answers to the problems of life that make each day difficult and fascinating.

No doubt we will make mistakes, and we will change our minds, and we will do wonderful things.

XV

On a warm evening in February, I joined a small group of people on the steps of the capitol in Montgomery, Alabama. We stood below the star that proudly commemorates where Jefferson Davis took the oath to become the president of the Confederacy. Behind us was the famous white rotunda, which looked beautiful against the pink sky. In front of us, the sun set over Dexter Avenue, and in the fading light we could just make out the fountain that marked the city's old slave market.

Down the capitol steps stretched a long black tarp on which dozens of names and dates were painted neatly in white. Our group stood at the foot of the steps in an imperfect, quiet circle. As six o'clock neared, we knew Danny Joe Bradley was about to be killed.

I stood still and my eyes darted from the candle in my hands to the faces of my companions to the top of the rotunda. As

I looked at the sky over the rotunda's dome, I began to think about Danny Joe Bradley. Somewhere in Alabama he was being led down a hallway. Was he noticing the tiled walls and the overhead lights? Did he nod his head to the prisoners he passed or meet eyes with the guards that led him from room to room? I wondered what he was thinking. Maybe he was thinking about his family or perhaps of friends he had made on death row. Maybe he was thinking about good and bad things that he had done. Maybe he was worried that it would be painful when the chemicals entered his blood. Maybe he was thinking about something much more mundane. Maybe he was too panicked and nervous to have a coherent train of thought.

Then I realized that I was hungry. I thought about where I might get dinner after I left the vigil. I could cook rice again at home, but I had eaten rice or pasta four days in a row. I thought about stopping to pick up a burrito on the way back to my apartment. But did I really want to go to Moe's? I was pretty mad that even though they had a "hero discount" for military personnel and police officers, the person at the register always refused to give it to public defenders. They were also a fairly large corporation—did I really want to support that business model? I caught myself before I got into yet another internal debate about corporations or factory farming. But then I quickly felt ashamed that my mind had wandered. I felt like I should have been thinking about Danny Joe Bradley. Danny Joe Bradley's mind would never again meander as mine had just then.

I had long been deeply troubled by the death penalty. But in that instant, I suddenly recognized another of its most important conceptual flaws: it denies Danny Joe Bradley that next moment of thought. It ignores that there is always a next moment in which you can decide to do the right thing—to be a better person. It denies that next moment in which you can have hopes and dreams and beliefs and kindness—in which you can actualize your humanity.[23]

Death row inmates in Alabama have founded their own non-profit organization whose board consists entirely of those sentenced to die. It is called Project Hope to Abolish the Death Penalty. That night, we each wore pins with Project Hope's slogan: "Execute Justice, not People."

Project Hope's members produce a print publication every few months in which people living on death row share their thoughts and experiences.[24] The pieces contained within *On Wings of Hope* are, at various times, profound, beautiful, surprising, and funny. The endeavor is, most of all, a testament to what can be done with that next moment.

Danny Joe Bradley never got that next moment. The human lawyer cherishes that next moment, and she understands that, with it, she can always do better.

XVI

Part A of this vignette describes the law's process of reasoning from basic values to doctrinal outcomes. Part B argues that this reasoning process is susceptible to flaws that are often difficult to perceive and suggests general rules of thumb for uncovering when systemic flaws are at work. Part C describes how these flaws also exist in analogous decision-making processes in our personal lives. Part D briefly concludes. (Law journals call what you just read a "roadmap." It is very important to them.)

A

Law promises us what mere chance cannot: intellectual rigor. Outcomes must be consistent with a stated value (or set of values), and a court will invalidate an outcome if it is inconsistent with that value. A court starts from a shared value—whether gleaned from a statute, a constitution, or perhaps something just floating in the ether of our culture, such as: "A person's race should not affect the length of her prison sentence"; or "A person's gender should not affect his salary"; or "Things that tend to interfere with a person's liberty should be minimized"; or "Poverty should not affect the quality of an education or the likelihood of going to jail."

The law then has to explain and justify why a particular outcome is consistent with that principle. This notion of the law as almost a science—indeed, as the science of reasoning—has been a popular conception of legal practice and scholarship throughout much of the field's history.[25] As law schools and legal "scholars" have become increasingly dominated by and intertwined with other disciplines, this technical reasoning and attempted analytical rigor have remained a central authentic characteristic of legal education and law as a distinct discipline. It can be a wonderful characteristic, one that can make a vital contribution to human thought and decision-making.

Consider, for instance, the potential practice of shackling a criminal defendant during pretrial hearings or sentencing. Basic background principles implicated might include the desire to provide fair proceedings and the general rules against restricting bodily liberty and avoiding unnecessary pain. The law would ask if physically restraining a defendant would influence (perhaps unconsciously) the decision-maker, cause pain, inhibit thought or movement, infringe on dignity and humanity, and/or interfere with communication and participation in the defense. It would also ask whether and to what extent shackling responded to any identifiable safety risk by protecting other people present in the courtroom, or if shackling enabled the court to become more efficient and if there were other alternatives that had similar benefits but fewer potential harms. In other words, the law would make a series of empirical assumptions and inquiries about the physical world and human behavior and then make a decision based on reasons and evidence. The assumptions, evidence, and the chain of reasoning from values to outcomes should be explicit so that they can be questioned, reviewed, challenged, and changed if new information or flaws come to light.

B

Often, the law does not actually work like this. Other less obvious things are also happening. Many cases turn on facts and stories that together determine the kind and quality of reasoning eventually employed. Once the mind is made up, legal reasoning is like a game that can be played to perfection, either consciously or unconsciously. Almost any analog or distinctive feature can be seized upon, at least superficially, as a reason to treat a case the same or differently, even if such a move lacks true intellectual rigor.

Judges often reach conclusions first, whether knowingly or unknowingly. That sense of how she might want a case to come out unquestionably infuses her whole decision-making process with a strong psychological undercurrent. A judge may even try to swim straight ahead for a while using the power of her own reasoning, but as we watch her from the shore, she has drifted far away from her desired path.

The central problem is that it is extremely difficult to determine the quality of legal reasoning simply by looking at the process of the reasoning itself. From our judge's perspective, she may have stayed nicely on a straight course, swimming under her own power. No doubt she would be surprised if she looked back and found herself so far adrift from where she entered the water. But judges, like all humans, are filled with subconscious biases and automatic cognitions.[26] They are members of particular social circles, and they read certain sources of information and interact with certain people, all of which contributes to how they think the world works. These attributes, experiences, and relationships shape attitudes, beliefs, and behavior.[27] Unconscious cognitive biases might even lead judges to believe that their rational processes are determining the result when in fact the causal connection was partially or entirely reversed. There also is imperfect information about the world, and judges often have to rely on intuitions about things like human behavior or the potential systemic effects of a given rule. Intuitions can be very dangerous, especially in a culture with so much inequality; after all, if culture shapes our intuitions, flaws in culture will be perpetuated in even the most basic of intuitions.

These cognitive problems are compounded by the fact that many of the most relevant empirical questions leave just enough room for credible belief in multiple mutually inconsistent directions. But we should be skeptical of human cognitive processes and be sensitive to the psychology involved. Empirical beliefs should be independent of wishful thinking, yet lawyers and judges repeatedly come to empirical conclusions that just so happen to support a desired result.[28]

We must search diligently within the ultimate results of legal decisions for patterns, *particularly along dimensions important to our conceptions of social justice.*

Both the physical world and the human mind are too complicated for us to understand with any precision. Perhaps the only way effectively to evaluate any kind of policy, then, is to look at patterns and outcomes. If laws consistently produce outcomes inconsistent with certain fundamental values, we should be extremely skeptical of the social or individual decision-making processes that produced them, even if we cannot precisely identify where the flaws in the reasoning occurred.[29] Identifying these unconscious biases can be difficult. However, if certain groups have consistently fared worse, there may be good reason to believe that something, perhaps something hidden, is consistently creeping into decision-making, especially when cases implicate conflicts between social groups with different levels of power.[30]

C

Similarly, in her own internal debates or in discussions with others about decisions in their personal lives, the human lawyer reasons from basic values to more complicated positions on larger issues.

The brilliance of Socrates's method—still so popular in law schools—is that he recognized that people answer questions differently when they think they know where the line of questioning is going. By failing to disclose the ends, and by building little by little, Socrates minimized this problem. He got honest answers to relatively simple questions. Then he showed how a person's stated beliefs on more complicated issues or a person's behavior in a number of daily situations were inconsistent with the progression of seemingly harmless and unrelated smaller answers they had just given. In the same way, the human lawyer holds the hand of her companion at each stage of the argument; as long as people are taking positions and behaving consistently with their stated values, the human lawyer has done her job. She does not question another person's values.

But in analyzing her own decisions and the decisions of others, the human lawyer understands that students of the law are formidable adversaries. Lawyers are very good at anticipating the logical conclusion of arguments and evidence, and they often construct psychological barriers so that the anticipated arguments and evidence do not have a strong effect on them by the time they are introduced in the chronology of conversation. In this way, because lawyers often do not even actively recognize these barriers, they are similar to the unsuspecting judge drifting away in the strong undercurrent.

After their initial reasons for supporting a certain outcome have been discredited, lawyers are also very adept at changing the reasons for which they support that outcome. In fact, in law school, students are taught to dip quickly into the well of alternate reasons, even if those reasons had little impact on the actual decision or little traction beyond sounding nice at first glance. Instead of leading a lawyer to question why she arrived at that position in the first place, evidence of a faulty decision-making process is usually just the first step in finding some other way to justify maintaining a belief or a way of life with which the lawyer has already become comfortable. Indeed, these skills can be quite useful in the zealous representation of a client or in the professional defense of a legal position. But we cannot afford to be biased advocates in our personal lives.

This would be a fairly innocuous eccentricity in the personality of the lawyer as a species if patterns did not emerge so frequently in the outcomes of their decisions. Much as with the laws discussed in Part B, lawyers (like other people) are not making mistakes that result in a random distribution of errors in their personal lives.

For this reason, the human lawyer reviews the outcomes of personal decisions and looks for trends in her own decision-making. She also seeks to commit her interlocutors to reasons in support of their positions or behavior. After she successfully questions those reasons, she anticipates another battle over a new wave of reasons. With each set of outcomes and each set of new rationalizations, the human lawyer builds evidence about how most people, including herself, make decisions. The human lawyer also remembers each flaw that she finds across many different types of argument and culls the data for patterns.

D

Legal cases and personal decisions implicate a whole range of situations, each with its own subtle differences that make it a part of real life. Law is supposed to unpack these situations, identifying similarities and differences and applying evidence to settle disputed claims. The goal of this endeavor is to develop rules for behavior that create a world consistent with the underlying values we have articulated. The human lawyer never forgets this ultimate mission. The human lawyer vigorously audits our laws and her own personal decisions, and she always wears her outcome glasses to correct for potential myopia.

XVII

Most law review articles begin with a roadmap. Most novels do not. Lawyers are obsessed with the reader getting one meaning from a text. This is perhaps the law's greatest strength and its greatest weakness. For lawyers, arguments progress neatly from one point to another, and assumptions and logical connections can be isolated and evaluated.

Decision-making through rigorous reasoning is surely an underutilized process in other areas of our lives. (We often fail to test each of our personal beliefs and decisions for logical consistency with our values or to make sure that each of our actions is based on deep thought and sound evidence. We often act based on gut feelings or emotions, habit, unreflected assumptions, or cultural norms.) But despite the benefits of rigorous reasoning, a single-minded focus on this reasoning process can be a poor way of introducing and developing new legal paradigms and giving voice to new or different experiences. In the process of isolating and communicating a single meaning, a subset of potential meanings is slowly and systematically suffocated. What starts as a few errant snowflakes becomes an avalanche of forgotten human experiences on the mountain of legal "scholarship" and judicial opinions that define the shared legal universe.

Legal decisions are made and legal commentary is written on the level of shared cultural consciousness. The belief among the faithful seems to be that this shared consciousness can be achieved only through rational argument (or, more precisely, what commonly passes for rational argument in legal discourse). Legal scholarship often appears intentionally to rid itself of emotion and narrative. It is true that a few pages in a judicial opinion or in a law journal is an imperfect medium for communicating the complex workings of the human mind; our thoughts are overwhelmed with panic, insecurity, joy, fear, frustration, sorrow, exhilaration, and other sensations that can only be experienced and can never quite be described.

But these sensations can be *felt*, and legal writing could help us feel them. In particular, stories can help us make these emotional connections—to come to our own understanding about a person or an issue in a way that reasoned argument may not on its own. That is why, in our personal lives, we rely heavily on feelings, relationships, emotional bonds, telling each other stories, and other experiences to inform our sense of how our lives connect to others.

Shared consciousness can and sometimes should be much more than the product of rational argument. We can share in irrationality—in things that we cannot easily derive from or explain with reasons. And we often do; when we meet eyes with one we love or when we look at a picture of an anonymous student standing in front of a tank.

It is this irrationality that narrative helps to capture. It is this irrationality that helps define our humanity. Stories help us create emotional bonds, and they help us sense how others are experiencing the world. The emotions and insights gained from stories are thus vital for developing the kind of holistic understanding of the human experience that is necessary before we can engage in rational argument about the rules that should govern collective human interaction. Legal commentators should thus embrace narrative rather than hide it.

By learning about and experiencing as many different people and ways of life as possible, we learn something that helps us participate in rational argument with a more authentic understanding of *exactly what is at stake.*

Only this way will we become sensitive and humble enough to recognize different, new, or more subtle forms of coercion that are the enemy to all who value liberty. Only through this sharing can we understand and appreciate the possibilities of shared human existence. Thus, prior to making decisions based on reasons through rational argument, the human lawyer embraces the vicissitudes of the human experience and seeks out the narratives and guidance of people directly impacted by her decisions. This is especially important when she does not have direct personal experiences and connections to a particular issue, as is often the case when elite lawyers are involved in issues of social justice. As a result, she has a much richer understanding of the positive and negative effects of legal rules—especially rules that affect others very different from her. She understands, for example, that one would think differently when crafting constitutional legal rules on jail conditions if one had seen and felt and experienced what it is like to be confined to a cage.

We should be more honest about the importance of *both* robust rational argument and emotional connections.

Perhaps while, in our personal lives, we undervalue rationality as a method of decision-making, the legal system undervalues emotion and narrative as a source of a more nuanced understanding of the human beings with which its decisions are designed to interact.

The human lawyer learns a lot from law in her private life and learns a lot from her private life in law.

XVIII

It was the morning of a second-year student's last set of on-campus interviews. She walked to the Charles Hotel, where the corporate law firms had all set up shop. On the way, she was forced into several awkward greetings with people walking busily back and forth—people she hadn't seen since her first-year section meetings. Harvard students traversed Massachusetts Avenue like schools of fish in navy blue and gray business suits.

As she waited in the fancy hotel suite, she suddenly forgot the name of the first firm she was interviewing with at 9:40 a.m. After all, she had already been to seventeen interviews. The panic that precedes inevitable embarrassment abruptly subsided, however, when she noticed the firm's initials molded into the chocolate-covered pretzel that she was about to eat. What a great firm! All the others just gave out generic chocolate-covered pretzels. This one showed style and class, as well as a prescient understanding of the practical problems likely to face a law student in the nervous moments before her interview. Finally a way to tell them apart!

She thought about what she could possibly ask about during her interview. She was, by now, an expert on the wonderful world of pro-bono projects that the firms marketed. She also had a selfish desire not to hear the same speeches again about the firm's extraordinary diversity committee. She felt bored and exhausted—the last couple weeks of interviews had taken their toll, physically and emotionally. Two weeks of rushing around, throwing on her suit and a smile, and then running back to class; in all the commotion, she hadn't had time to think about why she constantly felt anxious. She had a nagging stress—a feeling that something was incomplete. For some reason, she started thinking about it at that moment.

She wondered what life would be like at the firm. Maybe she'd just do it for a little while. It'd probably be really fun in the summer. Most of them promised a lot of group events at nice restaurants and bars. Plus, she had loans, and she would certainly feel more liberated if she could pay them off quickly. Maybe working at a firm wouldn't be so bad because the harm she would be causing would usually be so indirect, and she could still spend some of her time and money on other things. On the other hand, the work seemed kind of boring—would anyone do it if it paid less? Representing great aggregations of wealth also seemed removed from her former work as a teacher. How could she turn away from what she really cared about? Could she really have an impact on the world? She'd be working within the vast corporate system, and any efforts she made, even from such a privileged position, would be like whispering from a mountaintop.

But the firm was so easy. She already had six offers, and four gift boxes of dried fruits, chocolates, and computer accessories covered her kitchen table. The choice seemed rather automatic. It seemed comfortable; removed from anything personal or painful. It seemed like everyone chooses one career or another.

But *her* career choice was important to her. It concerned how she wanted to use her mind every day. It concerned how she wanted to use the energy that animates her body. It would help to define the brief time she has in this world. She could be comfortable financially doing other work; after all, plenty of people, and even many law students, survive without all that money.

But what else could she do? Some of the other options seemed like a waste of her education. And it seemed so hard to get a public interest job—what if she found herself unemployed? After all, she was limited in her choices by the legal market—limited to filling the jobs that were out there. Did she even have a viable alternative? Even if she did, public interest people were sometimes so judgmental and self-righteous. She also hadn't spent that much time doing public interest work; was it too late now? Probably not, but she hadn't yet built the relationships and social capital to compete in that world, and she didn't speak its jargon.

It was so hard because, frankly, not even many public interest jobs seemed to offer real social change. Did civil rights lawyers actually do anything? Were they in touch with and accountable to the communities they purported to represent? Would

defending an indigent person really help the next three or four
who would be arraigned the following day? Maybe none of
these discrete individual choices, even ones as large as the pur-
suits to which she would devote her career, were likely to make
a dent in the vast injustice around her.

Was shouting under water any better than whispering from
a mountaintop?

But maybe these kinds of lawyers were holding the fort, at
least preventing a siege. The poor were getting terrible legal
help in civil and criminal cases in communities everywhere.
She could easily find a job working somewhere representing
people who could not afford a lawyer. Maybe poverty lawyers
were doing their best within the budget constraints of legal
culture and labor markets—amid the constraints of American social conscience. Maybe there was something noble and
authentic in this fight, at least if done right. Maybe one small
choice and one person at a time is all we can ask for. Maybe
it was enough if she could live her life and do her work in a
way that could contribute to a movement that changed who has
power in our society. Maybe she must accept her finitude.

Perhaps all she could do was what she thought was right,
even if the enormity of the task was daunting. Only then could
she understand the kind of synergy needed for real improve-
ment. Through her doing this, and through others doing the
same, there was a slight chance of eventually changing those
broader constraints.

Perhaps her career choice wasn't the kind of decision for
her to make alone. Hopelessness resides in the lonely—in

those who face life's problems without connecting with others. Perhaps it was not even the kind of problem that could be conceptualized on an individual level. Perhaps this was a problem for all human lawyers to tackle together. In the combination of finites, infinity awaits in the distance.

XIX

My friend gave me a picture some time ago that now sits above the desk in my bedroom. In it, a small infant is huddled to the ground, her forehead resting against the dry earth. Her bony arms reach up toward her face, exposing her emaciated rib cage. A small white necklace shines in the sun around her neck. Her legs are coiled, as if she were using them to push slowly forward along the dusty soil. In the background, a few feet away, sits a vulture, waiting to pounce.

My friend told me that this little girl was from the Sudan and that the photo was taken just outside a food station toward which the little girl was attempting to crawl. My friend told me that the photographer did not help the little girl. My friend told me that the photograph won a Pulitzer Prize and that the photographer committed suicide shortly thereafter.[31]

The picture sits on my desk because each day it reminds me what is at stake. It brings life to statistics that I often hear but have trouble feeling.[32] It reminds me that I cannot know what it is like to be a child without food. It reminds me that there are people in desperate need in my neighborhood, in my city, in my state, in my country, and in my world. It reminds me that our individual and collective choices have created that need.

It makes me emotional each day, and it reminds me that I can do more.

XX

Humans are frail, weak, irrational, and insecure. But they are also beautiful, kind, thoughtful, and strong. At their worst, they are automatic flesh robots. At their best, they are dynamic, biological thinking machines. So what is the law student? She is usually floating somewhere between these poles of human possibility.

As a student, she has learned about some of the wonderful things in the law, such as its insistence on requiring reasons and its emphasis on logical and evidentiary rigor in the translation of principles and values into outcomes. She has also learned about some of its flaws, such as restrictions on how reasons are expressed in legal writing and the systemic flaws, biases, and informational deficiencies that undermine the actual rigor of legal decision-making processes.

As a human, she is still developing—still cultivating her intellectual faculties and learning about her own biases, weaknesses, and defense mechanisms. She faces difficult pressures in her personal life, when making decisions like choosing a career. And she is just beginning to come to grips with her own power to affect other people's lives.

The law student is very much an evolving organism. But dangers lurk in the gene pool. Legal reasoning often glides by the intricacies of human life, and the organisms it produces often exhibit a stunted humanity. The totalizing nature of both law school and our culture in general can mask the petty and irrational things that drive us, further preventing us from pursuing with vigilance lives and laws that are consistent with our values.

When we confront these dangers honestly, both in ourselves and in our laws, we can become more human lawyers.

POLICING, MASS IMPRISONMENT, AND THE FAILURE OF AMERICAN LAWYERS

IT DID NOT SURPRISE ME THAT ALMOST EVERY CHILD IN THE DC public high school class raised a hand when I asked if any of them had been stopped and searched by the police. When I told them that being stopped without reasonable suspicion that they were committing a crime is a violation of the U.S. Constitution, one of the students corrected me: "No, you don't understand, these are the Jumpouts,[1] not the police. They're allowed to do that." I'm used to people laughing in disbelief when I do constitutional rights trainings in heavily policed communities. But when I heard those words, my heart sank. In front of me was a child in whose world being stopped and frisked was so regular, such a fact of everyday life, that he had reasonably concluded that it must be lawful. This child was growing up believing that his suspicious body could be probed at will by government employees. One by one, the students described to me the routine that they had developed to turn and face the nearest wall while officers searched through their backpacks and pockets on the way home from school. Like many of the problems in the criminal legal system, there is no genuine dispute that these and more serious illegalities are happening on a massive scale. In the years that I have spent working in American courts and jails, one thing sticks out above all else: the divergence between the law as it is written and the law as it is lived.

The contemporary system of policing and incarceration puts human beings in cages at rates unprecedented in American history and unparalleled in the modern world.[2] It is a considerable bureaucratic achievement to accomplish the transfer of thirteen million bodies each year[3] from their homes and families and schools and communities into government boxes of concrete and metal. It is also a failure of the legal profession.

There is a lot to say about American policing and punishment; they are, of course, tied up in big things that people don't like to talk about in polite company, such as structural racism—which determined virtually every aspect of modern American society, like who owns things, what neighborhoods look like, who we care about, and who seems scary—and capitalism—whose logic proudly depends on the perpetual reproduction of domination and control. But in these few pages, I would like instead to explore carceral America as a failure of legal reasoning and legal practice.

The failure of lawyers is a tragedy in two parts. First, there has been an intellectual failure of the profession to scrutinize the evidentiary and logical foundations of modern policing and mass human caging. Second, the profession has failed in everyday practice to ensure that the contemporary criminal legal system functions consistently with basic rights and values.

Our Intellectual Failure

Lawyers bear some responsibility for the gulf between how we talk about our society and how it is. We have failed to do what lawyers are taught to do: take fundamental shared values and help society translate those principles into results through rigorous argument based on evidence and logic.

I'd like to divide this intellectual failure into two components. First, lawyers have failed properly to catalog, appreciate, and interrogate the negative costs of how we police and how we confine bodies to jail cells. Second, we have failed to scrutinize the purported benefits, both because of an undertheorization of the amount of harm actually caused by what we popularly call "crime" and because of an underdeveloped account of whether caging humans leads to less "crime."

In order for the legal system to unleash police on poor communities and communities of color such that the United States came to imprison black people at a rate six times that of South Africa during the height of apartheid,[4] it was necessary for popular culture and legal culture to develop and nurture serious intellectual pathologies. So deeply have these pathologies captured the legal elite that the wholesale normalization and rationalization of this brutality has become arguably the chief daily bureaucratic function of most of us who work in the system.

We Haven't Confronted the Suffering That We Inflict

Imagine one of the thousands of sentencing hearings every week in which a person is charged with possessing marijuana plants or selling rocks of cocaine or assaulting someone. The prosecutor stands to address the court and produces a wheel. The prosecutor proposes as a punishment that the judge spin the wheel to determine the defendant's fate. The prosecutor declares that, based on the way that her office has constructed the wheel, there is a one in ten chance that the person's punishment is that he will be taken into the next room and raped.[5] Or, to take a slightly different example, consider a judge ordering that a person be whipped in public or stabbed thirty-seven times with a sharp knife in non-life-threatening ways. It is likely that lawyers and judges would come up with persuasive arguments against such punishments. But this is essentially what we do when, in doctrinal silence, we allow people to be sentenced to American jails and prisons.[6]

There are a couple of points to make about this. First, notice the arbitrariness and intellectual vacuousness of the narrow range of standard legal argument. We are stuck inside the box. It should not require a slightly odd sentencing proposal to trigger rigorous examination of the magnitude of the harms that we are causing and to scrutinize whether they are worth it. Second, at some point lawyers allowed the legal system to view caging a person as more acceptable than other physical and psychological punishments and, then, we allowed those cages to degenerate into places in which people will contract life-threatening illness, endure the torture of solitary confinement, be raped and physically assaulted, be deprived of sunlight and fresh air, and experience a variety of other horrors. We then found it unimportant to incorporate those harms into our lawyerly doctrinal thinking.

The legal profession and the doctrines that it produces exhibit a willful blindness to the extent of the physical and psychological punishments that we perpetrate. Putting a human being in a cage is brutal business—one that every lawyer should study in meticulous detail for herself. Lawyers must understand and communicate what it does to a person to strip from the person almost every form of humanity that we take for granted every day: to prevent him for years from eating at a restaurant, going on a date, making love, visiting a museum, traveling to a new place, having walls between his bed and his toilet, hugging his mother, seeing his grandfather before he dies. And the consequences of the policing-to-incarceration pipeline go well beyond the things that come with physical banishment. They include what we do to people in our cages: scandalous medical and mental health care, beatings and stabbings, rampant sexual trauma, extended periods of confinement alone with no one to interact with and no natural light, and coerced labor; obliteration of parental and other friendship and family relationships through unaffordable for-profit prison phone contracts; revocation of the right to vote; unemployment and homelessness for dependent families; deportation; and crushing cycles of debt, despair, and alienation.

We have barely cared about these consequences largely because they aren't happening to wealthy white people. To the contrary, we have smothered, silenced, and erased them. One cannot even engage in a thought experiment about what would happen if other demographic groups were the ones being stopped, probed, strip searched, violently raided, disenfranchised, tased, shot, and caged for years because it is not possible to square such thoughts with how our society works. If criminal laws were enforced on college campuses or investment banks for just a single day at the same rates as in poor communities, there would be twenty-four-hour news vans outside of every local jail and immediate public hearings about the harshness and efficacy of our legal system. Does anyone doubt that our lawyer-made doctrines governing policing interactions, criminal procedure, sentencing, punishment, jail conditions, and every other area of related law would look thoroughly different if they were destroying different people's lives and devastating different people's families? Instead, tens of millions of shackled bodies later, we're starting to have symposia in which people talk about whether everything will be better if we give police more money to buy cameras for their lapels.

It is the intellectual responsibility of lawyers to ensure our fidelity to neutral principles—to ensure that our legal system does not allow practices to develop or to persist because of who they are happening to, and to ensure that the magnitude of grievous harm is witnessed and weighed regardless of the bodies and minds on whom that harm is visited. We have not done that.

We Haven't Bothered to Ask About the Benefits

At the same time that lawyers have failed to ensure a proper accounting of the costs of massive human caging, we have failed to demand a logical and rigorous discussion of its benefits. As I explain in "The Punishment Bureaucracy," under longstanding constitutional precedent, the deprivation of a fundamental right requires the application of strict judicial scrutiny. That is a sensible rule: taking away the most basic human liberty should require compelling reasons and should be done only to the limited extent that it actually achieves those objectives.[7]

Instead of taking this analysis seriously, lawyers have allowed the discourse to be driven by irrational priorities and myths about what kinds of things are likely to cause us harm. The things that we are told to fear in order to justify brutal and repressive policies are hardly ever among the biggest preventable threats to our safety. "Terrorists"—a term whose propagandistic use has rendered it almost entirely devoid of meaning[8]—cause miniscule amounts of harm compared to things like cigarettes,[9] contaminated water,[10] salty food,[11] car accidents,[12] poor access to health care,[13] air pollution,[14] and thousands of other problems that are easily fixable as a policy matter, especially if resources anywhere near the amount expended on what elites call "public safety" or "national security" were devoted to them. Secondhand smoke alone, for example, kills ten times as many nonsmoking people in the United States *every year* as the September 11 attacks,[15] and tobacco as a whole kills fifteen times as many people in this country as secondhand smoke.

Modern policing has been sold using the same myths. For example, we are bombarded with the myths that the most serious types of crime affecting our society are the kinds of crimes that police patrolling the streets supposedly fight, and that entire poor communities are "high-crime areas." The "violent" crime that forms the ostensible justification for modern policing tactics is a small problem compared to other causes of death and trauma, such as inadequate nutrition,[16] water quality, campus sexual assault[17] or any number of other problems that we don't think of as "crime" to be fought, even when they involve illegality. Regardless, the vast majority of modern policing is not even devoted to those "violent" crimes anyway[18]—nor is it devoted to serious institutional white-collar crime or other leading causes of structural violence, such as wage theft, environmental pollution, police brutality, and public corruption.[19]

An intellectually rigorous system would, for example, study in great detail the connection between hundreds of billions of dollars in financial fraud and tax evasion and millions of preventable deaths or homeless families, rather than dramatically reduce every year the resources devoted to fighting crime committed by the wealthy (which our legal system has done for decades).[20] American police forces deliberately gorge on the excess of 750,000 marijuana-related arrests every year[21] in order to profit from quotas, grants, military equipment, and civil forfeiture[22] while allowing hundreds of thousands of rape kits to sit untested for years in police warehouses.[23] Only four percent of all police arrests in the U.S. are for crimes considered "violent" by the FBI, even though those crimes are offered as the justification for enormous public expenditures, wholesale Orwellian surveillance of tens of millions of people, and every violent aspect of modern policing. Yet another myth—one that is behind much of the militarization of modern policing and the development of corresponding legal doctrine to insulate it from accountability—is that policing is a uniquely dangerous job. But contemporary policing is far safer than the work performed by much of the American labor force.[24]

Perhaps the most striking thing, however, about American policing and mass incarceration is that there is no evidence that they work—even on their own terms. Even if the most serious activities harming the greatest number of human lives were the things that we are currently policing and prosecuting in large numbers, we have never bothered to scrutinize whether caging people who do those things is the best way to ensure that fewer of those incidents occur.[25] For example, although a large part of the mass incarceration zeitgeist is ostensibly predicated on fighting "violence" with significant expansion of carceral sentences for "violent crime," there is no serious evidence that caging people who have harmed another person reduces "violent crime," let alone that it is the best way for a community to do so. If I had to pick one pathology at the core of the modern American punishment system, it would be this.[26]

What kind of legal culture allows the massive deprivation of basic liberty and inflicts so much pain without *any* evidence? If we want to put one person into a cage for a single criminal offense, we are required, at least in theory, to present evidence so compelling that there is no reason to doubt the person's guilt. We have to be very close to certain, for example, that the heroin found in the backpack belonged to the accused or that the person who committed the robbery was the defendant before the court. But laws authorizing the imprisonment of millions of people have gotten no such scrutiny—we have not required *any* factual showing that this infliction of pain leads to *any* benefits. Lawyers have never required evidence that caging people with heroin in their backpacks furthers a compelling social purpose.

To take another example that I explore in greater detail in "The Punishment Bureaucracy," if a state legislature passed a law terminating parental rights (which, like bodily liberty, is also considered a "fundamental" constitutional right)[27] of anyone allowing their child to drink Coca-Cola, the law would be struck down under a strict scrutiny analysis. And yet, the same legal system is willing to deprive hundreds of thousands of people of fundamental liberty (and, incidentally, functionally to infringe their parental rights as a consequence collateral to incarceration) for the simple crime of possessing a plant for their own use. To the extent that some types of "crime" are causing a great deal of social harm—and some of them are—lawyers must still require evidence that putting the perpetrators in cages is the best way to create a society in which fewer of those crimes happen. Lawyers must be learned people of evidence and logic ushering society through this difficult terrain, not callous bystanders or, worse, exuberant cheerleaders.

But lawyers have never forced us to ask the basic question: *Are we sure that putting human beings in cages is absolutely necessary to creating a world with fewer people smoking marijuana or physically harming other people?*

All of this makes the failure of lawyers to apply the strictest scrutiny to criminal punishment all the more bizarre. We do not act like a society that treats brutal human caging as a narrowly tailored remedy of last resort. The failure to require reasons and evidence has been a sad chapter in American legal history.

The Legal Profession in Practice

A modern de Tocqueville traveling through America's courts and dedicating herself to reverse engineering a list of the basic principles of American law based on what she finds there would produce a document very different from the Bill of Rights. She might envision, as the boy in my class imagined, a society whose values one could identify by looking at the behavior of public officials in its "palladiums of liberty."[28] But she would be mistaken.

What Do Courts and Jails and People's Experiences Actually Look Like?

Recall the example that I started with in the Punishment Bureaucracy of my first civil rights case: I walked into a local courtroom in Alabama one morning in early 2014 and saw more than sixty people of color led into the courtroom from the jail. All of them had been arrested by local police on warrants for unpaid debt, mostly from old tickets. One by one—single mothers, disabled veterans, the homeless, and other impoverished people—they stood up before the court. The court demanded that they pay their debts and told them that they would be kept in jail unless they could get the money down to the payment window. They begged and pleaded and talked about their poverty. Within seconds, each of their cases was over, and they were returned to the overcrowded city jail to "sit out" their debts at $50 per day. Fifty-eight days for one, ninety-nine days for another, twelve days for a third . . . Local police running the jail informed them that they could get out of jail more quickly by earning $25 toward their debts each day if they performed janitorial labor for the city. I have seen similar assembly line nightmares in virtually every city and every state that I have visited in my brief time as a civil rights lawyer. The rise of modern debtors' prisons is a phenomenon

affecting millions of people all over the country, and it is happening almost entirely outside of the public consciousness. For
example, while the police shooting of an unarmed black teenager
in Ferguson, Missouri, captured mainstream public attention,
especially in the wake of the militarized police assault on journalists and protestors in the weeks that followed, less salient was
the fact that the City of Ferguson had, for several years, averaged
more than 3.6 arrest warrants *per household*,[29] mostly because of
warrants relating to unpaid debt from municipal tickets.[30] In a
single year, Texas alone recently jailed 524,628 people for unpaid
debts and issued more than 2.1 million arrest warrants in cases
involving low-level unpaid fines and fees.[31]

What happens every day in American streets, courts, and
jails bears little resemblance to what is written in our law
books. To get more information about that, I encourage readers to visit their local courts and jails, to learn from people in
heavily policed communities about their daily experiences, and
to read the overwhelming narrative[32] and empirical literature
on the topic.

Consider a few of the many examples:

■ Although the law promises indigent defendants
a zealous attorney, the system almost entirely ignores
that right in practice. Every serious observer recognizes an indigent defense "crisis" in which most of the
millions of American criminal defendants each year
receive barely any individualized representation at all,
let alone a zealous investigation into and presentation
of the questions relevant to their factual guilt and miti-

gation of punishment.[33] On recent trips to Tennessee,
Alabama, and Missouri, for example, I saw hundreds of
defendants in minor misdemeanor cases plead guilty
without a lawyer just so that they could finally get out
of jail after weeks in a cage because they were too poor
to pay for their release pending trial, and I saw judges
routinely inform jailed individuals that they would
refuse to give them a court-appointed lawyer if their
families were able to pay a private for-profit bail corporation to have them released from jail. Local public
defenders reported to me that there was often little that
they could do anyway even if they were appointed to a
person's case, given that they had between one thousand and two thousand cases per year and barely any
investigative resources.

- In a system that guarantees the right to trial unless
the right is waived "knowingly, intelligently, and voluntarily," over ninety percent of all defendants plead
guilty[34] because they are told that they will be given
more serious punishment if they do not plead guilty.

- Although our legal system proclaims that "[i]n our
society liberty is the norm, and detention prior to trial
or without trial is the carefully limited exception,"[35]
several hundred thousand human beings are kept in
American cages *every single day* solely because they are
too poor to make a monetary payment to secure their
pretrial release.[36] I have seen, within the past several
months, a woman confined in jail for two weeks after
being pulled over for failure to stop completely at a stop

sign and for disobeying the order of a police officer
because she could not pay $200, and another woman
who had recently given birth jailed for over a month
because of her inability to pay several hundred dollars
in a case charging her with being a passenger in a car
that contained a burned marijuana cigarette butt in the
ashtray.

▪ After conducting interviews with community
groups, victims, police officers, government officials,
and local lawyers in dozens of cities, as well as performing extensive Internet and case law searching, I have
been unable to find a major metropolitan American
police force without a recent history of systemic constitutional abuses.[37]

▪ For many decades, American courts have allowed
criminal convictions based on policing and forensic
techniques that lack a scientific basis. Even after these
methods were formally exposed as unscientific by the
most prestigious collection of American scientists,[38]
police, prosecutors, and courts continued to use them
every day nonetheless.

▪ Although every member of our culture understands
that armed confrontations with police are pervaded
by coercion and abuse, the legal system presumes such
interactions to be consensual when determining if people voluntarily waive their constitutional rights.

▪ In a society that holds out its police forces and
courts as guardians of justice, an overwhelming driving

force of local policing and municipal court practice in wide swaths of the country is revenue generation.[39]

- In courtrooms across America, people are sent to jail every day on the basis of a single witness's testimony (often a police officer's) with no supporting evidence, even though, as a matter of common sense, it is impossible for a reasonable person not to have a doubt about the observations or motivations of a single human witness.[40] Instead, most lawyers and judges typically view the motion for a directed verdict (the moment when a judge is supposed to independently evaluate the sufficiency of the evidence) as a meaningless formality rather than as a fundamental obligation to ensure that no conviction is entered if a reasonable person would have had a reason to doubt guilt.[41]

- In a society that requires prisoners to be treated humanely, American jails and prisons are cesspools of disease[42] and trauma.[43]

The Distribution of Legal Labor

Contemporary American policing and incarceration creates, every day, an enormous need for civil and criminal legal services for the poor. When people talk vaguely in op-eds, on panels at symposia, and at corporate law banquets about a legal services "crisis" for the poor, they are describing a system in which the basic legal rights of the poor are ignored because there are not enough lawyers offering quality legal services for the poor. For example, even apart from the millions of pending criminal cases for which people are not being provided a well-resourced and zealous defense attorney, every one of the thousands of unlawful stops, searches, home raids, beatings, tasings, shootings, arrests, and denials of medical care in jail that take place every day forms the basis for a freestanding constitutional civil rights suit. A quiet tragedy of the legal system is that these rampant daily violations are almost never litigated by lawyers. No one with a law degree is there to help people tell those stories or to help people repair the damage that this pervasive violence and neglect does to their lives.

Although lawyers have a moral and professional responsibility to address the policing and incarceration crisis, although they possess the training to engage in the intellectual and practical work that needs to be done, and although they possess a virtual monopoly on the ability to use the law to vindicate those rights, the distribution of legal labor is woefully inadequate to deal with this crisis.

We must totally rethink the distribution of legal labor in order to force the system of modern policing adequately to internalize the costs of the human rights violations on which it is predicated. Just as the court system could not physically accomplish the transfer of 2.3 million bodies into cages while also providing in each case a zealous defense and rigorous scrutiny, so too modern policing would cease to function if every constitutional violation were pursued with vigor. The modern criminal legal system thrives on the fact that the Constitution is not self-executing—it needs people devoted to making its promises real. Imagine a world in which lawyers stood ready,

en masse, to use their skills and training and intellects to vindicate these constitutional rights every day. Such a social movement of lawyers would dramatically alter the nature of the legal
system and our society. The system of modern policing, which
depends on callous indifference to basic rights, would crumble
at our simple willingness to hold it to its own formal rules. We
can do it, but only through massive collective action to act on
our professional and moral values.

Lawyers and the schools that produce them must redistrib-
ute their legal labor. Lawyers and law students must organize
collective action to refuse to participate in constitutional violations caused by enormous caseloads and inadequate investigative resources that plague nearly every American indigent
defense system. We must also create better models for legal
careers, using the wealth, knowledge, and connections of law
schools to help develop well-resourced spaces and collective
law practices for graduates to work together as a new vanguard
of lawyers who make a living by vindicating the rights of marginalized people until a system predicated on those violations
can no longer exist.[44]

Legal academics, judges, and lawyers of conscience must
take up this two-pronged challenge: we must bring intellectual
rigor to legal discourse and doctrine that shape the punishment
system, and we must use the energy that animates our bodies
to ensure that the legal system looks in practice as it appears in
our scrolls and on our marble monuments.

AUTHOR'S NOTE

The royalties from this book will be donated to the Essie Justice Group, an organization working to harness the collective power of women with incarcerated loved ones to end mass incarceration.

The views expressed in this book are my own and do not necessarily represent the views of anyone else, including Civil Rights Corps.

NOTES

The Punishment Bureaucracy

1. GEORGE ELIOT, MIDDLEMARCH 194 (Rosemary Ashton ed., Penguin Books 1994) (1872).

2. I am grateful to Salil Dudani for his friendship and for his intellectual contributions to this Essay. I also thank all those who helped me make this piece what it is, including Sarah Stillman, Claire Glenn, James Forman, Jr., Chloe Cockburn, Eric Halperin, K-Sue Park, Deborah Leff, Thomas Harvey, Diane Wachtell, Peter Calloway, Milica Bogetic, and the *Yale Law Journal* editors. I am fortunate to have had the research assistance of David Oyer. Finally, the ideas here owe a great intellectual debt to two of my mentors, Lani Guinier and Derrick Bell.

3. Angela Davis, *Masked Racism: Reflections on the Prison Industrial Complex*, COLOR LINES (Sept. 10, 1998), https://www.colorlines.com/articles/masked-racism-reflections-prison-industrial-complex [https://perma.cc/7GCH-GMKZ].

4. Danielle Kaeble & Mary Cowhig, *Correctional Populations in the United States, 2016*, U.S. DEP'T JUST. (Apr. 2018), https://www.bjs.gov/content/pub/pdf/cpus16.pdf [https://perma.cc/RA2A-VPMC].

5. *See* Peter Wagner & Wendy Sawyer, *Mass Incarceration: The Whole Pie 2018*, PRISON POL'Y INITIATIVE (Mar. 14, 2018), https://www.prisonpolicy.org/reports/pie2018.html [https://perma.cc/7S96-3AAS] (noting that 465,000 pretrial defendants are in the custody of local jails alone).

6. Thomas H. Cohen & Brian A. Reaves, *Pretrial Release of Felony Defendants in State Courts*, U.S. DEP'T JUST. 1 (Nov. 2007), https://www.bjs.gov/content/pub/pdf/prfdsc.pdf [https://perma.cc/UL7X-VXKN] (reporting that of all state-court felony defendants who are detained until the end of their cases, five out of every six are confined because of money bail).

7.   Michelle Ye He Lee, *Does the United States Really Have 5 Percent of the World's Population and One Quarter of the World's Prisoners?*, WASH. POST (Apr. 30, 2015), https://www.washingtonpost.com/news/fact-checker/wp/2015/04/30/does-the-united-states-really-have-five-percent-of-worlds-population-and-one-quarter-of-the-worlds-prisoners [https://perma.cc/Z546-DH5T].

8.   Wagner & Sawyer, *supra* note 5. No one reliably keeps track of how many millions of additional people are on some form of pretrial supervised release or in deferred prosecution programs.

9.   *Report of the Ad Hoc Committee to Review the Criminal Justice Act*, JUD. CONF. xiv (Apr. 2018), https://cjastudy.fd.org/sites/default/files/public-resources/Ad%20Hoc%20Report%20June%202018.pdf [https://perma.cc/98NB-NQRT] ("Fully 90 percent of defendants in federal court cannot afford to hire their own attorney."); John Pfaff, Opinion, *A Mockery of Justice for the Poor*, N.Y. TIMES (Apr. 29, 2016), https://www.nytimes.com/2016/04/30/opinion/a-mockery-of-justice-for-the-poor.html [https://perma.cc/Y5CR-9AHP] ("Approximately 80 percent of all state criminal defendants in the United States qualify for a government-provided lawyer.")

10.   LANI GUINIER & GERALD TORRES, THE MINER'S CANARY: ENLISTING RACE, RESISTING POWER, TRANSFORMING DEMOCRACY 263 (2002).

11.   Marc Mauer & Ryan S. King, *Uneven Justice: State Rates of Incarceration by Race and Ethnicity*, SENT'G PROJECT 11 (July 2007), https://www.sentencingproject.org/wp-content/uploads/2016/01/Uneven-Justice-State-Rates-of-Incarceration-by-Race-and-Ethnicity.pdf [https://perma.cc/9Y9J-E4PT] The disparity appears to have *worsened* since the Sentencing Project's analysis a decade ago. Comparing the D.C. Department of Corrections' data against Census data suggests that the incarceration rate for black people is now twenty-four times worse than it is for white people in Washington, D.C. *Compare Facts and Figures*, D.C. DEP'T CORRECTIONS (Sept. 2018), https://doc.dc.gov/sites/default/files/dc/sites/doc/publication/attachments/DCDepartmentofCorrectionsFactsandFiguresSeptember2018.pdf [https://perma.cc/B92B-VA2P], *with Washington, DC*, CENSUS REPORTER (2017), https://censusreporter.org/profiles/16000US1150000-washington-dc [https://perma.cc/755D-RRYG].

12.   MICHEL FOUCAULT, DISCIPLINE & PUNISH: THE BIRTH OF THE PRISON 234 (Alan Sheridan trans., Vintage Books 2d ed. 1995) (1977).

13.   Toni Morrison, Nobel Lecture (Dec. 7, 1993), http://www.nobelprize.org/prizes/literature/1993/morrison/lecture [https://perma.cc/ZHR4-YWEF].

14. ALBERT CAMUS, THE REBEL 3 (Anthony Bower trans., 1961).

15. *See* Minnesota v. Dickerson, 508 U.S. 366, 372, 378 (1993).

16. *See* Tana Ganeva, *Pot Prisoners: Meet Five Victims of the War on Drugs,* ROLLING STONE (Sept. 13, 2017, 7:32 PM), https://www.rollingstone.com/culture /culture-lists/pot-prisoners-meet-five-victims-of-the-war-on-drugs-200055 /fate-vincent-winslow-200103 [https://perma.cc/J8DH-ZSBW] (telling the story of Fate Winslow, who is serving a sentence of life without parole for selling an undercover police officer two bags of marijuana worth $10 each while he was homeless); Brooke Staggs, *This California Man Will Spend Life in Prison for a Marijuana Conviction Unless Trump or the Supreme Court Helps Him*, MERCURY NEWS (Sept. 10, 2018), https://www.mercurynews.com/2018/09/10/this-man-will-spend-life-in -prison-for-a-marijuana-conviction-unless-donald-trump-or-the-supreme-cour t-helps-him [https://perma.cc/96CQ-TH6Z] (discussing the case of Corvain Cooper).

17. *See* Hutto v. Davis, 454 U.S. 370, 384 (1982) (Brennan, J., dissenting); Laura-Ashley Overdyke, *Life Sentence for a Bag of Marijuana?: Examples of Louisiana's Habitual Offender Law*, KTBS (Apr. 8, 2015), https://www.ktbs.com/news /life-sentence-for-a-bag-of-marijuana-examples-of-louisiana/article_efbef5e8 -85ff-536b-9f6d-b79702e207df.html [https://perma.cc/6FVL-J9ER].

18. *See generally About*, NAT'L INVENTORY COLLATERAL CONSEQUENCES FOR CONVICTIONS (2019), https://niccc.csgjusticecenter.org/about [https:// perma.cc/QAR7-RP4D] (describing the possible collateral consequences for people convicted of crimes).

19. *See* Jack Smith IV, *The End of Prison Visitation*, MIC (Sept. 6, 2016), https://mic.com/articles/142779/the-end-of-prison-visitation [https://perma .cc/4XQP-AETH].

20. Frederick Kaufman, *The Food Bubble: How Wall Street Starved Millions and Got Away with It*, HARPER'S MAG., July 2010, at 27 (describing how highly profitable speculation on wheat futures led to "hundreds of millions" of people starving and enormous profits for American bankers).

21. So too may be dice-wagering, so long as it is done in a large casino facility that has obtained special exemptions through the political process. *See, e.g.*, Jon Delano, *As Communities Opt Out, Process Begins to Award New Pa. Casino Licenses,* CBS PITTSBURGH (Jan. 10, 2018, 2:58 AM), https://pittsburgh.cbslocal.com /2018/01/10/process-begins-award-new-pa-casino-licenses [https://perma.cc /CLL8-PPNM]. Dice-wagering in a private house, in many places, can result in forfeiture of your house. *See, e.g.*, United States v. Real Prop., Titled in the

Names of Godfrey Soon Bong Kang & Darrell Lee, 120 F.3d 947, 948-49 (9th Cir. 1997) (affirming forfeiture of house used for cockfights and dice games). Large corporate wagering houses dominate the skylines of those cities.

22. *Compare* Max Ehrenfreund, *Baltimore Police Once Used a Helicopter to Break Up a Dice Game,* WASH. POST (Aug. 12, 2016), https://www.washingtonpost.com /news/wonk/wp/2016/08/12/baltimore-police-once-used-a-helicopter-to -break-up-a-dice-game [https://perma.cc/Q78F-7CHZ], *with* Dan Roberts, *Wall Street Deregulation Pushed by Clinton Advisers, Documents Reveal,* GUARDIAN (Apr. 19, 2014), https://www.theguardian.com/world/2014/apr/19/wall-street -deregulation-clinton-advisers-obama [https://perma.cc/N7CP-AD5N] (describing lack of opposition to financial deregulation among top policymakers).

23. *Kang,* 120 F.3d at 950.

24. *Compare* Jeremy Waldron, *Why Indigence Is Not a Justification, in* FROM SOCIAL JUSTICE TO CRIMINAL JUSTICE: POVERTY AND THE ADMINISTRATION OF CRIMINAL LAW 98 (William C. Heffernan & John Kleinig eds., 2000) (explaining that recognizing poverty as a defense to theft would threaten the legitimacy of property ownership in a capitalist society), *with* Stephanie Kirchgaessner, *Theft of Sausage and Cheese by Hungry Homeless Man "Not a Crime,"* GUARDIAN (May 3, 2016), https://www.theguardian.com/world /2016/may/03/theft-sausage-cheese-hungry-homeless-man-not-crime-italy [https://perma.cc/3AAR-558K]("Italy's highest court has ruled that the theft of a sausage and piece of cheese by a homeless man in 2011 did not constitute a crime because he was in desperate need of nourishment").

25. *See generally* ANGELA Y. DAVIS, ARE PRISONS OBSOLETE? (2003); MICHEL FOUCAULT, DISCIPLINE AND PUNISH: THE BIRTH OF THE PRISON (Alan Sheridan trans., 1975); BRUCE WESTERN, PUNISHMENT AND INEQUALITY IN AMERICA (2006); RICHARD WILKINSON & KATE PICKETT, THE SPIRIT LEVEL: WHY MORE EQUAL SOCIETIES ALMOST ALWAYS DO BETTER (2009).

26. *See* MICHELLE ALEXANDER, THE NEW JIM CROW: MASS INCARCERATION IN THE AGE OF COLORBLINDNESS (2012); *see also, e.g., Top Adviser to Richard Nixon Admitted "War on Drugs" Was Policy Tool to Go After Anti-War Activists and "Black People,"* DRUG POL'Y ALLIANCE (Mar. 22, 2016), http://www.drugpolicy.org /press-release/2016/03/top-adviser-richard-nixon-admitted-war-drugs-was -policy-tool-go-after-anti [https://perma.cc/J3NL-SYU5].

27. *See* Jeffrey Miron, *Why All Drugs Should Be Legal. (Yes, Even Heroin.),* WEEK (July 28, 2014), https://theweek.com/articles/445005/why-all -drugs-should-legal-yes-even-heroin [https://perma.cc/5NPG-83TU];

cf. Zeeshan Aleem, *14 Years After Decriminalizing All Drugs, Here's What Portugal Looks Like*, MIC (Feb. 11, 2015), https://mic.com/articles/110344/14-years-after-portugal-decriminalized-all-drugs-here-s-what-s-happening [https://perma.cc/DMX9-94XY]; *Ioan Grillo, Mexico's Marijuana Ruling Shakes Up Drug Policy*, TIME *(Nov. 5, 2015)*, http://time.com/4100747/mexicos-marijuana-ruling-shakes-up-drug-policy [https://perma.cc/223V-C4HU] (reporting that marijuana consumption was legalized "to respect personal liberties").

28. *See* Maria Cheng, *Alcohol More Dangerous Than Heroin, Cocaine, Study Finds*, NBC NEWS (Nov. 1, 2010, 2:46 AM ET), http://www.nbcnews.com/id/39938704/ns/health-addictions/t/alcohol-more-dangerous-heroin-cocaine-study-finds [https://perma.cc/8DQV-HTZQ]; Ali H. Mokdad et al., *Actual Causes of Death in the United States, 2000*, 291 JAMA 1238, 1241–42 (2004) (estimating that, in 2000, 17,000 people died from the use or the indirect effects of the use of illicit drugs in the United States, and that 16,653 people were killed in alcohol-related car crashes); *Smoking & Tobacco Use*, CTRS. FOR DISEASE CONTROL & PREVENTION (Feb. 6, 2019), https://www.cdc.gov/tobacco/data_statistics/fact_sheets/fast_facts/index.htm [https://perma.cc/7LWZ-QUJY] ("Smoking is the leading cause of preventable death").

29. *See* Jamie Fellner, *Race, Drugs, and Law Enforcement in the United States*, 20 STAN. L. & POL'Y REV. 257, 263 (2009).

30. *See* Martha Mendoza, Associated Press, *U.S. Drug War Has Met None of Its Goals*, NBC NEWS (May 13, 2010, 4:06 PM), http://www.nbcnews.com/id/37134751/ns/us_news-security/t/us-drug-war-has-met-none-its-goals [https://perma.cc/9H7M-VDD3]; *cf.* Cheng, *supra* note 28.

31. Tamara Keith, *How Congress Quietly Overhauled Its Insider-Trading Law*, NPR (Apr. 15, 2013), https://www.npr.org/sections/itsallpolitics/2013/04/16/177496734/how-congress-quietly-overhauled-its-insider-trading-law [https://perma.cc/A2U2-EVAQ] (explaining that insider trading was legal for Congress until recently); *see also* David Dayen, *Sen. Jeff Merkley Wants to Stop Congress Members from Insider Trading by Banning Them from Owning Stocks*, INTERCEPT (Dec. 17, 2018, 2:03 PM), https://theintercept.com/2018/12/17/jeff-merkley-james-inhofe-ban-stock-trading [https://perma.cc/MHG9-CFCH] (discussing the failure of a new insider trading law to stop profiteering based on insider information by politicians in Congress).

32. They became wealthy even as the newly legal derivatives products contributed to a worldwide financial collapse and massive global suffering. *See* Lynn A. Stout, *Derivatives and the Legal Origins of the 2008 Financial Crisis*,

1 HARV. BUS. L. REV. 1, 29-30 (2011); *see also* Nomi Prins, *Inside the Clintons' Cozy Relationship with the Big Banks*, ALTERNET (May 7, 2015), https://www.alternet. org/news-amp-politics/inside-clintons-cozy-relationship-big-banks [https:// perma.cc/4T4P-5GC9]. The same political dynamics drive much of the tax code. *See generally*, DAVID CAY JOHNSTON, PERFECTLY LEGAL: THE COVERT CAMPAIGN TO RIG OUR TAX SYSTEM TO BENEFIT THE SUPER RICH—AND CHEAT EVERYBODY ELSE (2003).

33.   U.S.C. § 2399B (2018).

34.   David Cole, *The Roberts Court's Free Speech Problem*, N.Y. REV. BOOKS (June 28, 2010), http://www.nybooks.com/blogs/nyrblog/2010/jun/28 /roberts-courts-free-speech-problem [https://perma.cc/MU4P-X3HM].

35.   Jennifer Williams, *Are the Austin Bombings Terrorism? It Depends Who You Ask*, VOX (Mar. 21, 2018, 12:20 PM EDT), https://www.vox.com /2017/10/2/9868048/austin-bombings-terrorism-definition [https://perma.cc /672B-HNZX].

36.   Chris McGreal, *MEK Decision: Multimillion-Dollar Campaign Led to Removal from Terror List*, GUARDIAN (Sept. 21, 2012, 3:20 PM EDT), https:// www.theguardian.com/world/2012/sep/21/iran-mek-group-removed-us -terrorism-list [https://perma.cc/A63K-2L6T]; *see also* United States v. Hayat, 710 F.3d 875, 904 (9th Cir. 2013) (Tashima, J., dissenting) (criticizing "unsettling and untoward consequences of the government's use of [a "material support"] anticipatory prosecution as a weapon in the 'War on Terror'"); Amna Akbar, *How Tarek Mehanna Went to Prison for a Thought Crime*, NATION (Dec. 31, 2013), https://www.thenation.com/article/how-tarek-mehanna-went-prison-thought -crime [https://perma.cc/M8D6-6YHZ]. People would feel differently if Saudi Arabia invaded Minnesota and local residents fought back—it would be seen as patriotic self-defense. Low-income Muslim Americans are prosecuted on charges of "material support of terrorism" for making contributions to political causes in their home countries that the United States deems inappropriate while high-ranking congresspersons and officials aided the "terrorist" group MEK. *Compare* McGreal, *supra*, *with* Akbar, *supra*. Many of the people in the former category had the misfortune of supporting whichever political group the United States happened not to be working with at the time. This can be a difficult thing to predict in advance; after all, active U.S. support for brutal regimes or "terrorist" groups included working with Saddam Hussein to provide chemical weapons to Iraq, General Augustus Pinochet of Chile, Islamic militants in Afghanistan and Syria, and paramilitary death squads and dictators across South America, Africa,

the Middle East, and Asia. *See, e.g.,* Shane Harris & Matthew M. Aid, *Exclusive: CIA Files Prove America Helped Saddam as He Gassed Iran,* FOREIGN POL'Y (Aug. 26, 2013, 2:40 AM), http://www.foreignpolicy.com/articles/2013/08/25/secret _cia_files_prove_america_helped_saddam_as_he_gassed_iran [https://perma. cc/N36F-5V4W]; *see also, e.g., William D. Hartung, Weapons for Anyone: Donald Trump and the Art of the Arms Deal,* TOM DISPATCH *(Apr. 1, 2018, 4:33 PM),* http://www.tomdispatch.com/blog/176405/tomgram%3A_william_hartung %2C_selling_arms_as_if_there_were_no_tomorrow [https://perma.cc/Y88X -YV7N].

37.   David Johnston, *C.I.A. Tie Reported in Mandela Arrest,* N.Y. TIMES (June 10, 1990), https://www.nytimes.com/1990/06/10/world/cia-tie-reported -in-mandela-arrest.html [https://perma.cc/KAF6-FF6R]; Robert Windrem, *U.S. Government Considered Nelson Mandela a Terrorist Until 2008,* NBC NEWS (Nov. 2, 2015, 7:22 PM EST), https://www.nbcnews.com/news/world/us -government-considered-nelson-mandela-terrorist-until-2008-flna2D11708787 [https://perma.cc/E7JN-BREU].

38.   U.S.C. § 798(a) (2018).

39.   Alice Speri, *As FBI Whistleblower Terry Albury Faces Sentencing, His Lawyers Say He Was Motivated by Racism and Abuses at the Bureau,* INTERCEPT (Oct. 18, 2018, 7:00 AM), https://theintercept.com/2018/10/18/terry-albury-sentencing -fbi [https://perma.cc/E3A8-JE5L]; *see also* Heidi Kitrosser, *Classified Information Leaks and Free Speech,* 2008 U. ILL. L. REV. 881, 892–93 & n.68 (2008) (estimating that there were about three million such bureaucrats in 1999, and even more in 2008).

40.   *See* Meredith Fuchs, *Judging Secrets: The Role Courts Should Play in Preventing Unnecessary Secrecy,* 58 ADMIN. L. REV. 131, 148 (2006).

41.   *See, e.g.,* Norman L. Eisen & Noah Bookbinder, Opinion, *Pruitt's Resignation Is Just the Beginning,* N.Y. TIMES (July 6, 2018), https://www.nytimes .com/2018/07/06/opinion/scott-pruitt-resignation-wheeler.html [https:// perma.cc/U7XB-PSHX].

42.   Chris McGreal, *US Private Bradley Manning Charged with Leaking Iraq Killings Video,* GUARDIAN (July 6, 2010, 2:14 EDT), https://www.theguardian. com/world/2010/jul/06/bradley-manning-charged-iraq-killings-video [https://perma.cc/CU3F-2D73]; *Shooters Walk Free, Whistleblower Jailed,* DAS ERSTE (Aug. 11, 2018), https://daserste.ndr.de/panorama/media/panor165.html [https://perma.cc/8L9M-L42X]; Peter Van Buren, *Tomgram: Peter Van Buren,*

in Washington, Fear the Silence, Not the Noise, Tom Dispatch (Feb. 9, 2012, 9:31 AM), http://www.tomdispatch.com/post/175500/tomgram%3A_peter_van _buren%2C_in_washington%2C_fear_the_silence%2C_not_the_noise [https://perma.cc/EB6X-R3XT].

43. *See U.S. "Reviewing" Iraq Killing Video Posted on WikiLeaks*, BBC News (Apr. 8, 2010, 10:20 AM GMT), http://news.bbc.co.uk/2/hi/americas/8608972. stm [https://perma.cc/7MRS-C2J8] (stating that there were "no plans" to reinvestigate the case).

44. Martin Arnold, *Ellsberg Trial: Now the Focus Is on Secrecy*, N.Y. Times (Mar. 5, 1973), https://www.nytimes.com/1973/03/05/archives/ellsberg-trial -now-the-focus-is-on-secrecy.html [https://perma.cc/34KW-JT7Q].

45. *See* Alfonso Serrano, *Inside Big Pharma's Fight to Block Recreational Marijuana*, Guardian (Oct. 22, 2016, 8:00 AM EDT), https://www.theguardian .com/sustainable-business/2016/oct/22/recreational-marijuana-legalization -big-business [https://perma.cc/Z5PF-PJBR]; Leighton Akio Woodhouse et al., *They Rescued Pigs and Turkeys from Factory Farms—and Now Face Decades in Prison*, Intercept (Dec. 23, 2018), https://theintercept.com/2018/12/23/dxe -animal-rights-factory-farms [https://perma.cc/75GD-LZTD] (noting that legislators created an exception to the felony dollar-value threshold for misdemeanor theft to enable felony prosecution of those who rescue factory-farmed animals).

46. Corrections Accountability Project, *The Prison Industrial Complex: Mapping Private Sector Players*, Urban Just. Ctr. (2018), https://static1.squarespace. com/static/58e127cb1b10e31ed45b20f4/t/5ade0281f950b7ab293c86a6/152449 9083424/The+Prison+Industrial+Complex+-+Mapping+Private+Sector +Players+%28April+2018%29.pdf [https://perma.cc/5BU3-S3PY].

47. Citizens United v. FEC, 558 U.S. 310, 365 (2010); *see also, e.g.,* Gary Rivlin, *A Giant Pile of Money*, Intercept (Oct. 20, 2018), https://theintercept.com /2018/10/20/public-pensions-crisis-wall-street-fees [https://perma.cc/G6BU -XU8L] (noting one example in which newly unregulated political donations by hedge funds led to different investment decisions by public pension managers and billions of dollars in public pension losses); *see also, e.g.,* Tom Angell (@tomangell), Twitter (Nov. 26, 2018), https://twitter.com/tomangell/status /1067071136964448257 [https://perma.cc/K524-VDQQ].

48. *See, e.g.,* Douglas A. Blackmon, Slavery by Another Name 53–54 (2008) (explaining that, for the purpose of "reintroducing the forced labor of

blacks" through convict leasing, "[b]eginning in the late 1860s . . . every southern state enacted an array of interlocking laws essentially intended to criminalize black life"); Thomas I. Emerson, *Freedom of Expression in Wartime*, 116 U. Pa. L. Rev. 975, 980–81 (1968) (discussing the "vigorously enforced" espionage acts passed during the First World War).

49.   United States v. Blewett, 719 F.3d 482, 487 (6th Cir. 2013), *rev'd en banc*, 746 F.3d 647 (6th Cir. 2013).

50.   Cocaine and Federal Sentencing Policy, U.S. Sentencing Comm'n iii (Feb. 1995).

51.   *See* Julie Stewart, *Well Done Congress, Now Make Fair Sentencing Act Retroactive*, Huffington Post (Aug. 4, 2010), https://www.huffingtonpost.com/julie -stewart/well-done-congress-now-ma_b_671008.html [https://perma.cc/3LYK -MQMP].

52.   *Id.*

53.   *See* First Step Act of 2018, Pub. L. No. 115-391, § 404, 132 Stat. 5194; United States v. Blewett, 746 F.3d 647, 660 (6th Cir. 2013).

54.   Blackmon, *supra* note 48.

55.   Whitney Benns, *American Slavery, Reinvented*, Atlantic (Sept. 21, 2015), https://www.theatlantic.com/business/archive/2015/09/prison-labor-in- america/406177 [https://perma.cc/QTT7-R78P]; *see also* Luis Gomez, *For $1 an Hour, Inmates Fight California Fires. "Slave Labor" or Self-Improvement?*, San Diego Union Trib. (Oct. 20, 2017), http://www.sandiegouniontribune.com /opinion/the-conversation/sd-how-much-are-california-inmate-firefighters -paid-to-fight-wildfires-20171020-htmlstory.html [https://perma.cc/Y7QZ -KNQB].

56.   Timothy Williams, *The High Cost of Calling the Imprisoned*, N.Y. Times (Mar. 30, 2015), https://www.nytimes.com/2015/03/31/us/steep-costs-of-inmate -phone-calls-are-under-scrutiny.html [https://perma.cc/HQ8J-XDLP].

57.   Mark Joseph Stern, *Alabama's Failure of Moral Turpitude*, Slate (Oct. 6, 2016), http://www.slate.com/articles/news_and_politics/jurisprudence/2016/10 /alabama_s_grossly_unconstitutional_felony_disenfranchisement_scheme.html [https://perma.cc/CCG8-H32L].

58.   Jean Chung, *Felony Disenfranchisement: A Primer*, Sent'g Project 1 (July 17, 2018), https://www.sentencingproject.org/publications/felony -disenfranchisement-a-primer [https://perma.cc/6KS2-7AUL].

59. *See* Steve Bousquet, *Florida's Felon Disenfranchisement System Under Intense National Glare*, TAMPA BAY TIMES (Sept. 11, 2018), https://www .tampabay.com/florida-politics/buzz/2018/09/11/pleading-for-the-right-to -vote-in-florida-one-case-at-a-time [https://perma.cc/J2NK-X72L]. A ballot measure passed in 2018 that was designed to restore the right to vote for most people with felony convictions in Florida. Tim Mak, *Over 1 Million Florida Felons Win Right to Vote with Amendment 4*, NPR (Nov. 7, 2018, 2:46 AM ET), https://www.npr.org/2018/11/07/665031366/over-a-million-florida-ex-felons -win-right-to-vote-with-amendment-4 [https://perma.cc/5BF2-T5LZ].

60. *See* JEFF MANZA & CHRISTOPHER UGGEN, LOCKED OUT: FELON DISENFRANCHISEMENT AND AMERICAN DEMOCRACY 8–10 (2006); Benno C. Schmidt, Jr., *Principle and Prejudice: The Supreme Court and Race in the Progressive Era. Part I: The Heyday of Jim Crow*, 82 COLUM. L. REV. 444, 454 (1982).

61. *See* Dep't of Hous. v. Rucker, 535 U.S. 125, 136 (2002).

62. *See, e.g.*, Washington v. Harper, 494 U.S. 210, 220 (1990).

63. Foucha v. Louisiana, 504 U.S. 71, 80 (1992) (citing Youngberg v. Romeo, 457 U.S. 307, 316 (1982)).

64. *In re* Winship, 397 U.S. 358, 362 (1970). American criminal law recognizes the importance of human liberty in a wide variety of other doctrines— such as the rule of lenity, which requires courts to interpret ambiguity in any criminal law in favor of liberty and against punishment. *See, e.g.*, Leocal v. Ashcroft, 543 U.S. 1, 11 n.8 (2004).

65. *See* Nicholas Kristof, Opinion, *How to Win a War on Drugs*, N.Y. TIMES (Sept. 22, 2017), https://www.nytimes.com/2017/09/22/opinion/sunday /portugal-drug-decriminalization.html [https://perma.cc/C2AZ-8UMJ]; *More Imprisonment Does Not Reduce State Drug Problems*, PEW CHARITABLE TR. 11 (Mar. 2018), https://www.pewtrusts.org/-/media/assets/2018/03/pspp _more_imprisonment_does_not_reduce_state_drug_problems.pdf [https:// perma.cc/DQ4X-S8QK]; Susan Scutti, *Worldwide Drug Use Steady, but Heroin on Rise in U.S., U.N. Report Says*, CNN (June 23, 2016), https://www.cnn.com /2016/06/23/health/un-world-drug-report/index.html [https://perma.cc /6C6U-7TYR]; *see also* Josh Katz, *Drug Deaths in America Are Rising Faster Than Ever*, N.Y. TIMES (June 5, 2017), https://www.nytimes.com/interactive /2017/06/05/upshot/opioid-epidemic-drug-overdose-deaths-are-rising -faster-than-ever.html [https://perma.cc/H2ZM-HCUW].

66. *See, e.g.*, FCC v. Beach Commc'ns, Inc., 508 U.S. 307, 313 (1993).

67. Pierce v. Soc'y of Sisters, 268 U.S. 510, 534–35 (1925). Thus, a law stripping felons of the right to parent would be struck down instantly. But we effect the same result when we put someone in prison for a drug offense.

68. *See* Reno v. Flores, 507 U.S. 292, 301–02 (1993).

69. Brady v. United States, 397 U.S. 742, 748 (1970) ("Waivers of constitutional rights not only must be voluntary but must be knowing, intelligent acts. . . .").

70. *See* Odonnell v. Harris Cty., 251 F. Supp. 3d 1052, 1105 (S.D. Tex. 2017); *see also, e.g.*, Lise Olsen & Anita Hassan, *298 Wrongful Drug Convictions Identified in Ongoing Audit*, HOUST. CHRON. (July 16, 2016), https:// www.houstonchronicle.com/news/houston-texas/houston/article/298 -wrongful-drug-convictions-identified-in-8382474.php [https://perma.cc /9775-K2PL].

71. *See* Lafler v. Cooper, 566 U.S. 156, 186 (2012) (Scalia, J., dissenting) (lamenting the elevation of plea bargaining from a "necessary evil" to a "constitutional entitlement").

72. *See* Robert Schehr, *The Emperor's New Clothes: Intellectual Dishonesty and the Unconstitutionality of Plea Bargaining*, 2 TEX. A&M L. REV. 385, 389 (2015).

73. *Brady*, 397 U.S. at 752–53 (1970) (holding that plea bargains induced by the threat of a higher penalty—in that case, the death penalty—are not involuntary in part because a contrary holding would strain "scarce judicial and prosecutorial resources").

74. Gilbert v. United States, 640 F.3d 1293, 1301 (11th Cir. 2011).

75. *Id.* at 1302.

76. *See id.*

77. *Id.*

78. *See* Alec Karakatsanis, Opinion, *President Obama's Department of Injustice*, N.Y. TIMES (Aug. 18, 2015), https://www.nytimes.com/2015/08/18/opinion/ president-obamas-department-of-injustice.html [https://perma.cc/MAR6 -APT8].

79. *Gilbert*, 640 F.3d at 1327 (Pryor, J., concurring); *see also* Blewitt v. United States, 746 F.3d 647 (6th Cir. 2013) (en banc) (reversing, at the Obama Justice Department's urging, a Sixth Circuit panel's holding that the Fair Sentencing Act's reduction of the 100-to-1 crack-to-powder cocaine sentencing disparity applied retroactively).

80. McCleskey v. Kemp, 481 U.S. 279, 339 (1987) (Brennan, J., dissenting).

81. Voltaire, *Droit [Rights]*, in 4 QUESTIONS SUR L'ENCYCLOPÉDIE [QUESTIONS ON THE ENCYCLOPEDIA] 364, 367 (1771) ("[I]l est défendu de tuer. Tout meurtrier est puni, à moins qu'il n'ait tué en grande compagnie, & au fon des trompettes. . . .") (translated by the author).

82. *Cf.* Radley Balko, *You're Probably a Federal Criminal, Too*, REASON (July 25, 2009), https://reason.com/blog/2009/07/25/youre-probably-a-federal-crimi [https://perma.cc/5BQQ-5UN7]; L. Gordon Crovitz, Opinion, *You Commit Three Felonies a Day*, WALL ST. J. (Sept. 27, 2009), https://www.wsj.com/articles/SB10001424052748704471504574438900830760842 [https://perma.cc/JSU3 -VT9L]; *Luxury to Forget*, WE ARE ALL CRIMINALS (2019), https://www.weareallcriminals.org/category/luxury-to-forget [https://perma.cc/UCD7-SM97].

83. Timothy Williams, *Marijuana Arrests Outnumber Those for Violent Crimes, Study Finds*, N.Y. TIMES (Oct. 12, 2016), https://www.nytimes.com/2016/10/13/us/marijuana-arrests.html [https://perma.cc/CT23-HCW6].

84. *See, e.g.*, Natalie Johnson, *State Senators Propose Reform for Driving with Suspended License Law*, CHRON. (Jan. 12, 2018), http://www.chronline.com/crime/state-senators-propose-reform-for-driving-with-suspended-license-law/article_2996cdf8-f824-11e7-bd9e-ff4084d58384.html [https://perma.cc/6RL6-YG52]; Farida Jhabvala Romero, *Driving with Suspended License Top Crime in Menlo Park, Many Lose Licenses*, PENINSULA PRESS (June 17, 2015), http://peninsulapress.com/2015/06/17/driving-suspended-license-top-crime-in-menlo-park-california [https://perma.cc/56FX-BG89].

85. Joseph Shapiro, *How Driver's License Suspensions Unfairly Target the Poor*, NPR (Jan. 5, 2015, 3:30 AM ET), https://www.npr.org/2015/01/05/37269-1918/how-drivers-license-suspensions-unfairly-target-the-poor [https://perma.cc/VL8Z-HFP5]; *see also* Denise Lavoie, *Drivers Challenge License Suspensions for Unpaid Court Debt*, ASSOCIATED PRESS (July 4, 2018), https://apnews.com/3f83b360a1f141f4a794f4203c7eab2f [https://perma.cc/8UVV-6297] (reporting that there are 4.2 million people with licenses suspended or revoked due to unpaid court debt in Virginia, Tennessee, Michigan, North Carolina, and Texas alone).

86. *See, e.g.*, WILLIAM J. STUNTZ, THE COLLAPSE OF AMERICAN CRIMINAL JUSTICE 3–4 (2011) (observing that prosecutors have wide latitude in deciding whom to target for prosecution).

87. *See, e.g.*, Nicholas Fandos, *A Study Documents the Paucity of Black Elected Prosecutors: Zero in Most States*, N.Y. TIMES (July 7, 2015), https://www.nytimes.com/2015/07/07/us/a-study-documents-the-paucity-of-black-elected-prosecutors-zero-in-most-states.html [https://perma.cc/L9RG-MWSY]; *Justice for All*?*, WHO LEADS, https://wholeads.us/justice [https://perma.cc/KJZ2-SX7R].

88. DANIEL BERRIGAN, THE TRIAL OF THE CATONSVILLE NINE 93 (2004).

89. *See, e.g.*, United States v. Batchelder, 442 U.S. 114, 124–25 (1979).

90. As discussed below, police also have investigative discretion. *See infra* section "Investigative Discretion."

91. *See* David Keenan et al., *The Myth of Prosecutorial Accountability After Connick v. Thompson: Why Existing Professional Responsibility Measures Cannot Protect Against Prosecutorial Misconduct*, 121 YALE L.J.F. 203, 213 (2011).

92. *See* Surell Brady, *Arrests Without Prosecution and the Fourth Amendment*, 59 MD. L. REV. 1, 3, 36–49 (2000).

93. Indeed, as discussed later, some Americans were even convicted in foreign courts of those crimes. *See 3 Americans Convicted of Torture in Afghanistan*, CBC NEWS (Sept. 15, 2004), https://www.cbc.ca/news/world/3-americans-convicted-of-torture-in-afghanistan-1.498047 [https://perma.cc/G5P3-PFNU]; *see also* Lindsay Goldwert, *Iraq: 2 U.S. Soldiers Charged with Murder*, CBS NEWS (July 1, 2007), https://www.cbsnews.com/news/iraq-2-us-soldiers-charged-with-murder [https://perma.cc/B5EF-P62C]; Rebecca Hersher, *Ex-CIA Officer in Rendition Case Is Released After Italy Grants Partial Clemency*, NPR (Mar. 1, 2017), https://www.npr.org/sections/thetwo-way/2017/03/01/517916196/italy-grants-partial-clemency-to-ex-cia-officer-over-extraordinary-rendition [https://perma.cc/CQQ8-KETD].

94. Oliver Laughland, *How the CIA Tortured Its Detainees*, GUARDIAN (May 20, 2015, 11:38 AM EDT), https://www.theguardian.com/us-news/2014/dec/09/cia-torture-methods-waterboarding-sleep-deprivation [https://perma.cc/2QAT-8GVL].

95. Spencer Ackerman et al., *Senate Report on CIA Torture Claims Spy Agency Lied About "Ineffective" Program*, GUARDIAN (Dec. 9, 2014), https://www.theguardian.com/us-news/2014/dec/09/cia-torture-report-released [https://perma.cc/4BD7-L268].

96. Reuters, *CIA Sex Abuse and Torture Went Beyond Senate Report Disclosures, Detainee Says*, GUARDIAN (June 2, 2015), https://www.theguardian.com/us-news/2015/jun/02/cia-sexual-abuse-torture-majid-khan-guantanamo-bay [https://perma.cc/T4C5-NE76].

97. Eric Schmitt & Carolyn Marshall, *In Secret Unit's "Black Room," a Grim Portrait of U.S. Abuse*, N.Y. TIMES (Mar. 19, 2006), https://www.nytimes.com/2006/03/19/world/middleeast/in-secret-units-black-room-a-grim-portrait-of-us-abuse.html [https://perma.cc/AQ6Q-6JU6].

98. *See* Ackerman et al., *supra* note 95.

99. Evan Wallach, *Waterboarding Used to Be a Crime*, WASH. POST (Nov. 4, 2007), http://www.washingtonpost.com/wp-dyn/content/article/2007/11/02/AR-2007110201170.html [https://perma.cc/PQB8-3GL4].

100. *See* Larry Siems, *Inside the CIA's Black Site Torture Room*, GUARDIAN (Oct. 9, 2017), https://www.theguardian.com/us-news/ng-interactive/2017/oct/09/cia-torture-black-site-enhanced-interrogation [https://perma.cc/2XF5-QYUS].

101. Jeremy Scahill, *U.S. Navy Reserve Doctor on Gina Haspel Torture Victim: "One of the Most Severely Traumatized Individuals I Have Ever Seen,"* INTERCEPT (May 17, 2018), https://theintercept.com/2018/05/17/gina-haspel-cia-director-torture [https://perma.cc/H2DM-4LZ5].

102. Michael Scherer, *Bush Torture Memo Approved Use of Insects*, TIME (Apr. 16, 2009), http://content.time.com/time/nation/article/0,8599,1891812,00.html [https://perma.cc/ZZ2V-EGPQ].

103. *CIA Was Authorized to Keep Prisoners Awake for 11 Days*, ALTERNET (May 11, 2009), https://www.alternet.org/story/139953/cia_was_authorized_to_keep_prisoners_awake_for_11_days [https://perma.cc/SPZ9-K7LP].

104. Scahill, *supra* note 101.

105. Glenn Greenwald, *The Suppressed Fact: Deaths by U.S. Torture*, SALON (June 30, 2009), https://www.salon.com/2009/06/30/accountability_7 [https://perma.cc/8ULM-3VZT].

106. *See, e.g.*, GLENN GREENWALD, WITH LIBERTY AND JUSTICE FOR SOME (2011); JANE MAYER, THE DARK SIDE 165–75, 252–55 (2009); SENATE SELECT COMMITTEE ON INTELLIGENCE, COMMITTEE STUDY OF THE CENTRAL INTELLIGENCE AGENCY'S DETENTION AND INTERROGATION PROGRAM 3–4 (2014).

107. *See* Mark Mazzetti, *U.S. Says C.I.A. Destroyed 92 Tapes of Interrogations*, N.Y. TIMES (Mar. 2, 2009), https://www.nytimes.com/2009/03/03/washington/03web-intel.html [https://perma.cc/RQX7-CRQJ].

108.   *See* Brian Ross, *Ex-CIA Operative Says Prison Was Punishment for Whistleblowing on Torture*, ABC NEWS (Dec. 9, 2014), https://abcnews.go.com/International/cia-operative-prison-punishment-whistleblowing-torture/story?id=27474359 [https://perma.cc/UW9H-XXDU]. At least one American was prosecuted and convicted for kidnaping and rendition, but he was prosecuted and convicted by Italy. However, when he was arrested in Panama and Italy requested rendition, the United States intervened and brought him back to the United States to shield him from serving his sentence in Italy. *See* Glenn Greenwald, *This Week in Press Freedoms and Privacy Rights*, GUARDIAN (July 20, 2013), https://www.theguardian.com/commentisfree/2013/jul/20/press-freedoms-manning-risen [https://perma.cc/2XNZ-W2Q8].

109.   Julian Borger, *Senate Report on CIA Torture Could Lead to Prosecution of Americans Abroad*, GUARDIAN (Dec. 10, 2014), https://www.theguardian.com/us-news/2014/dec/10/cia-report-prosecutions-international-law-icc [https://perma.cc/B8KT-MAVX].

110.   *See* Glenn Greenwald, *Obama Justice Department Grants Final Immunity to Bush's CIA Torturers*, GUARDIAN (Aug. 31, 2012), http://www.guardian.co.uk/commentisfree/2012/aug/31/obama-justice-department-immunity-bush-cia-torturer [https://perma.cc/T8L5-P3Z4]; Adam Serwer, *Obama's Legacy of Impunity for Torture*, ATLANTIC (Mar. 14, 2018), https://www.theatlantic.com/politics/archive/2018/03/obamas-legacy-of-impunity-for-torture/555578 [https://perma.cc/F6Q2-STUE]; Sam Stein, *Obama on Spanish Torture Investigation: I Prefer to Look Forward*, HUFFINGTON POST (May 5, 2009), https://www.huffingtonpost.com/2009/04/16/obama-on-spanish-torture_n_187710.html [https://perma.cc/7PR3-EHT3].

111.   Ross, *supra* note 108.

112.   *Id.*; *see also* Kevin Gozstola, *Imprisoned CIA Torture Whistleblower John Kiriakou "Pens Letter from Loretto,"* SHADOW PROOF (May 29, 2013), http://dissenter.firedoglake.com/2013/05/29/imprisoned-cia-torture-whistleblower-john-kiriakou-pens-letter-from-lorett [https://perma.cc/TZ8S-MXA2]; *John Kiriakou, I Went to Prison for Disclosing the CIA's Torture. Gina Haspel Helped Cover It Up*, WASH. POST *(Mar. 16, 2018)*, https://www.washingtonpost.com/outlook/i-went-to-prison-for-disclosing-the-cias-torture-gina-haspel-helped-cover-it-up/2018/03/15/9507884e-27f8-11e8-874b-d517e912f125_story.html [https://perma.cc/MV9J-XUUX]. During the Obama Administration, many news articles on foreign policy contained leaked information that served the goals of politically powerful people, yet they were not prosecuted; on the other

hand, the low-level leakers who disclosed information that exposed misconduct in the administration were prosecuted with vigor. The administration chose to prosecute twice as many leak cases as all previous administrations combined. *See* Conor Friedersdorf, *Behold the Selective Outrage over National Security Leakers*, ATLANTIC (Feb. 13, 2014), http://www.theatlantic.com/politics /archive/2014/02/behold-the-selective-outrage-over-national-security -leaks/283799 [https://perma.cc/TVN3-D5V9].

113.   *See* Gene Demby, *I'm from Philly. 30 Years Later, I'm Still Trying to Make Sense of the MOVE Bombing*, NPR (May 13, 2015), https://www.npr.org/sections /codeswitch/2015/05/13/406243272/im-from-philly-30-years-later-im-still -trying-to-make-sense-of-the-move-bombing [https://perma.cc/XAL8-CNS7].

114.   *Id.*

115.   *Id.*

116.   *Id.*

117.   *Id.*

118.   Alex Q. Arbuckle, *May 13, 1985: The Bombing of MOVE*, MASHABLE (Jan. 10, 2016), https://mashable.com/2016/01/10/1985-move-bombing/#iIbN LWxQmkqG [https://perma.cc/N976-CPNQ].

119.   Connie Langland, *Ramona Africa Still Carrying the MOVE Message*, PHILA. INQUIRER (May 12, 2010), http://www.philly.com/philly/news/special _packages/20100512_Ramona_Africa_still_carrying_the_MOVE_message .html [https://perma.cc/7YZB-UXPT].

120.   *SEC Enforcement Actions: Addressing Misconduct That Led to or Arose from the Financial Crisis*, U.S. SEC. & EXCHANGE COMM'N (Oct. 7, 2016), https:// www.sec.gov/spotlight/enf-actions-fc.shtml [https://perma.cc/4B6K-DD4W].

121.   *Id.*

122.   Reuters, *UBS Libor Rigging May Cost Bank $1.63 Billion Fine*, HUFFINGTON POST (Dec. 15, 2012, 7:33 AM EST), https://www.huffingtonpost.com/201 2/12/15/ubs-libor-rigging_n_2306432.html [https://perma.cc/M67N-8H4D].

123.   Ben Protess & Alexandra Stevenson, *JPMorgan Chase to Pay $264 Million to Settle Foreign Bribery Case*, N.Y. TIMES (Nov. 17, 2016), https://www.nytimes.com/2016/11/18/business/dealbook/jpmorgan-chase -to-pay-264-million-to-settle-foreign-bribery-charges.html [https://perma.cc /2BK9-HSLJ].

124. Catherine Curan, *Wells Fargo Made Up On-Demand Foreclosure Papers Plan: Court Filing Charges*, N.Y. POST (Mar. 12, 2014, 2:06 PM), https://nypost.com/2014/03/12/wells-fargo-made-up-on-demand-foreclosure-papers-plan-court-filing-charges [https://perma.cc/4MB5-9FUB].

125. Binyamin Appelbaum, *How Mortgage Fraud Made the Financial Crisis Worse*, N.Y. TIMES (Feb. 12, 2015), https://www.nytimes.com/2015/02/13/upshot/how-mortgage-fraud-made-the-financial-crisis-worse.html [https://perma.cc/4HTJ-SFEM].

126. David Dayen, The Great Foreclosure Fraud, AM. PROSPECT (May 16, 2016), https://prospect.org/article/great-foreclosure-fraud [https://perma.cc/D4YK-UPCV]; Yves Smith: *Kamala Harris Tells Big Lie: That 2012 Mortgage Settlement Was a Good Deal for Homeowners*, NAKED CAPITALISM, (Jan. 10, 2019), https://www.nakedcapitalism.com/2019/01/kamala-harris-tells-big-lie-2012-mortgage-settlement-good-deal-homeowners.html; Thomas Herndon, *Mortgage Fraud Fueled the Financial Crisis—and Could Again*, INST. FOR NEW ECON. THINKING (Sept. 7, 2018), https://www.ineteconomics.org/perspectives/blog/mortgage-fraud-fueled-the-financial-crisis-and-could-again [https://perma.cc/42RF-W8ZT].

127. Rajeev Syal, *Drug Money Saved Banks in Global Crisis, Claims UN Advisor*, GUARDIAN (Dec. 12, 2009, 7:05 PM EST), https://www.theguardian.com/global/2009/dec/13/drug-money-banks-saved-un-cfief-claims [https://perma.cc/A6CE-A5T2].

128. *See* Ben Protess & Jessica Silver-Greenberg, *Big Swiss Bank Pleads Guilty in Felony Case*, N.Y. TIMES (May 19, 2014, 4:50 PM), https://dealbook.nytimes.com/2014/05/19/credit-suisse-set-to-plead-guilty-in-tax-evasion-case [https://perma.cc/WNY3-Y2UF].

129. Kevin Johnson & Kevin McCoy, *BNP to Pay Almost $9B for Sanctions Violations*, USA TODAY (June 30, 2014, 5:28 PM EST), https://www.usatoday.com/story/money/business/2014/06/30/bnp-paribas-sanctions-announcement/11775681 [https://perma.cc/3CC2-EEH4].

130. FINANCIAL CRISIS INQUIRY COMM'N, THE FINANCIAL CRISIS INQUIRY REPORT xv (2011); *see also* Janet Currie & Erdal Tekin, *Is There a Link Between Foreclosure and Health?* (Nat'l Bureau of Econ. Research, Working Paper No. 729, 1981), https://www.nber.org/papers/w17310.pdf [https://perma.cc/82FM-9LR8] (finding that foreclosures lead to an increase in urgent, preventable hospital admissions).

131. Bureau of Labor Statistics, *A Profile of the Working Poor, 2000*, U.S. DEP'T LAB. (Mar. 2002), https://www.bls.gov/cps/cpswp2000.htm [https://perma.cc/232R-ZGW8].

132. *See How Many U.S. Deaths Are Caused by Poverty, Lack of Education, and Other Social Factors?*, COLUM. MAILMAN SCH. PUB. HEALTH (July 5, 2011), https://www.mailman.columbia.edu/public-health-now/news/how-many-us-deaths-are-caused-poverty-lack-education-and-other-social-factors [https://perma.cc/52SG-W3HK].

133. Leah Hendey et al., *Weathering the Recession: The Financial Crisis and Family Wealth Changes in Low-Income Neighborhoods*, URBAN INST. 6 (March 2012), https://www.urban.org/sites/default/files/publication/25686/412626-weathering-the-recession-the-financial-crisis-and-family-wealth-changes-in-low-income-neighborhoods.pdf [https://perma.cc/J9HE-U84X].

134. *1 in 7 Americans Lived in Poverty in 2009, New Census Data Show*, PBS NEWS HOUR (Sept. 16, 2010, 3:48 PM EST), https://www.pbs.org/newshour/economy/poverty-uninsured-rates-rise-as-recession-continues [https://perma.cc/HK2G-UBKQ].

135. Les Leopold, *The Forbes 400 Shows Why Our Nation Is Falling Apart*, HUFFPOST (Dec. 1, 2009), https://www.huffingtonpost.com/les-leopold/the-forbes-400-shows-why_b_306228.html [https://perma.cc/E9KE-BHYQ]; *see also* Steven Bertoni, *The Rich Are Now Richer Than Before the 2008 Credit Meltdown*, FORBES (Jul. 12, 2011, 1:49 PM), https://www.forbes.com/sites/stevenbertoni/2011/07/12/the-rich-are-now-richer-than-before-the-2008-credit-meltdown/#157a59f74fe9 [https://perma.cc/DS5A-5EZM].

136. *See* Glenn Greenwald, *The Untouchables: How the Obama Administration Protected Wall Street from Prosecutions*, GUARDIAN (Jan. 23, 2013, 7:27 AM EST), https://www.theguardian.com/commentisfree/2013/jan/23/untouchables-wall-street-prosecutions-obama [https://perma.cc/VLT8-UZM2]; Glenn Greenwald, *Wall Street's Immunity*, SALON (May 10, 2012, 2:09 PM UTC), http://www.salon.com/2012/05/10/wall_streets_immunity [https://perma.cc/KT5Q-A6TR]; Gretchen Morgenson & Louise Story, *In Financial Crisis, No Prosecutions of Top Figures*, N.Y. TIMES (Apr. 14, 2011), https://www.nytimes.com/2011/04/14/business/14prosecute.html [https://perma.cc/JYP4-G5B5]; Jed S. Rakoff, *The Financial Crisis: Why Have No High-Level Executives Been Prosecuted?*, N.Y. REV. BOOKS (Jan. 9, 2014), https://www.nybooks.com/articles/2014/01/09/financial-crisis-why-no-executive-prosecutions [https://perma.cc/2SAN-PC6L]; Matt Taibbi, *Why Isn't Wall Street in Jail?*, ROLLING STONE (Feb. 16, 2011, 2:00 PM

EST), http://www.rollingstone.com/politics/news/why-isnt-wall-street-in
-jail-20110216 [https://perma.cc/V8L8-WAPZ].

137.   *See* Matt Taibbi, *The Last Mystery of the Financial Crisis*, ROLLING STONE
(June 19, 2013, 1:00 PM EST), https://www.rollingstone.com/politics/politics
-news/the-last-mystery-of-the-financial-crisis-200751 [https://perma.cc/VBB9
-PU2D].

138.   Matt Taibbi, *Everything Is Rigged: The Biggest Price-Fixing Scandal Ever*, ROLLING STONE (Apr. 25, 2013, 5:00 PM EST), https://www
.rollingstone.com/politics/politics-news/everything-is-rigged-the-biggest
-price-fixing-scandal-ever-82255 [https://perma.cc/5AV7-7EBP] (quoting MIT
professor Andrew Lo).

139.   *Id.* (quoting Michael Greenberger, a former official at the Commodity
Futures Trading Commission).

140.   *See* Ted Kaufman, *Why DOJ Deemed Bank Execs Too Big to Jail*,
FORBES (July 29, 2013, 9:30 AM), https://www.forbes.com/sites/tedkaufman
/2013/07/29/why-doj-deemed-bank-execs-too-big-to-jail/#3eefde093703
[https://perma.cc/QCD2-UTFA].

141.   Editorial Board, *Why Should Taxpayers Give Big Banks $83 Billion a
Year?*, BLOOMBERG (Feb. 20, 2013, 6:30 PM EST), https://www.bloomberg
.com/opinion/articles/2013-02-20/why-should-taxpayers-give-big-banks-83
/-billion-a-year-.

142.   *Id.*

143.   For incisive reporting on the non-prosecution of those responsible for
the financial crisis and how it compares to our government's treatment of the
poor, see MATT TAIBBI, THE DIVIDE: AMERICAN INJUSTICE IN THE AGE OF THE
WEALTH GAP (2014).

144.   *See, e.g.*, Ben Protess & Mark Scott, *Guilty Plea and Big Fine for Bank
in Rate Case*, N.Y. TIMES (Feb. 6, 2013, 8:10 AM), https://dealbook.nytimes
.com/2013/02/06/as-unit-pleads-guilty-r-b-s-pays-612-million-over-rate
-rigging [https://perma.cc/TPQ2-MSK6]; Protess & Silver-Greenberg, *supra*
note 128.

145.   *See* Kaufman, *supra* note 140.

146.   *See* Danielle Kurtzleben, *Too Big to Jail: Why the Government Is Quick to
Fine but Slow to Prosecute Big Corporations*, VOX (July 13, 2015, 10:52 AM EDT),
https://www.vox.com/2014/11/16/7223367/corporate-prosecution-wall-street
[https://perma.cc/53L5-3K33].

147.   Rakoff, *supra* note 136.

148.   *See* Kaufman, *supra* note 140.

149.   *See* 18 U.S.C. § 1001 (2018).

150.   Jeremy Herb, *Intelligence Chief Clapper Apologizes for "Erroneous" State-ment to Congress*, HILL (July 2, 2013), https://thehill.com/policy/defense/308979 -clapper-apologies-for-erroneous-statement-to-congress-on-us-data-collecti on [https://perma.cc/FW5Z-7EVJ].

151.   *Id.*

152.   Dan Roberts & Spencer Ackerman, *Clapper Under Pressure Despite Apology for "Erroneous" Statements to Congress*, GUARDIAN (July 1, 2013, 4:16 PM), https://www.theguardian.com/world/2013/jul/01/james-clapper-apology -congress-erroneous-response [https://perma.cc/6SER-MGGK].

153.   *See* Derek Khanna, *Should the Director of National Intelligence Be Impeached for Lying to Congress About PRISM?*, MEDIUM (Sept. 17, 2013), https://medium. com/politics-and-policy/should-the-director-of-national-intelligence-be-im peached-for-lying-to-congress-about-prism-b09b968c01fd [https://perma.cc /TR59-V8PJ].

154.   Steven Nelson, *James Clapper Avoids Charges for "Clearly Erroneous" Surveillance Testimony*, WASH. EXAMINER (Mar. 10, 2018, 11:10 PM), https:// www.washingtonexaminer.com/james-clapper-avoids-charges-for-clearly -erroneous-surveillance-testimony [https://perma.cc/F8U6-3XR6].

155.   These violations led the Federal Intelligence Surveillance Act (FISA) court reviewing the NSA's actions to accuse federal officials of "an institutional 'lack of candor.'" *See* Tim Johnson, McClatchy, *Secret Court Rebukes NSA for 5-Year Illegal Surveillance of U.S. Citizens*, MIAMI HERALD (May 26, 2017, 5:37 PM), https://www.miamiherald.com/news/nation-world/national/article1529 -48259.html [https://perma.cc/LVF3-WP8T].

156.   *See* Julian Borger & Spencer Ackerman, *Edward Snowden: Republicans Call for NSA Whistleblower to Be Extradited*, GUARDIAN (June 10, 2013, 3:14 AM), https://www.theguardian.com/world/2013/jun/10/the-nsa-files-edward-snowden [https://perma.cc/B6QS-E2YT].

157.   Paul Wolf et al., *COINTELPRO: The Untold American Story*, C.L. DEF. CTR. 3–17 (Sept. 1, 2001), https://cldc.org/wp-content/uploads/2011/12/COIN -TELPRO.pdf [https://perma.cc/3NVV-79JA]; *see generally* NELSON BLACK-STOCK, COINTELPRO: THE FBI'S SECRET WAR ON POLITICAL FREEDOM (1988).

158.   Wolf, *supra* note 157.

159. *Id.*

160. *See FBI Building History*, GEN. SERVS. ADMIN. (Feb. 15, 2018), https://www
.gsa.gov/real-estate/gsa-properties/visiting-public-buildings/j-edgar-hoover
-fbi-building/whats-inside/fbi-building-history [https://perma.cc/E5F3
-3EX2].

161. *See* Arbuckle, *supra* note 118.

162. Beverly Gage, *What an Uncensored Letter to M.L.K. Reveals*, N.Y.
TIMES MAG. (Nov. 15, 2014), https://www.nytimes.com/2014/11/16/magazine
/what-an-uncensored-letter-to-mlk-reveals.html [https://perma.cc/7RCG
-K6HG].

163. BETTY MEDSGER, THE BURGLARY: THE DISCOVERY OF J. EDGAR
HOOVER'S SECRET FBI 489–90 (2014).

164. *Id.* at 294.

165. Will Parrish, *Standing Rock Activist Faces Prison After Officer Shot Him in
the Face*, GUARDIAN (Oct. 4, 2018, 4:00 AM), https://www.theguardian.com/us-
news/2018/oct/04/standing-rock-marcus-mitchell-shooting-charges [https://
perma.cc/8FXA-QC3H].

166. *See* Sam Levin, *California Police Worked with Neo-Nazis to Pursue
"Anti-Racist" Activists, Documents Show*, GUARDIAN (Feb. 9, 2018, 7:00 AM EST),
https://www.theguardian.com/world/2018/feb/09/california-police-white
-supremacists-counter-protest [https://perma.cc/43BX-TCS7]; Sam Levin,
*Revealed: FBI Investigated Civil Rights Group as "Terrorism" Threat and Viewed
KKK as Victims*, GUARDIAN (Feb. 1, 2019, 3:01 AM EST), https://www
.theguardian.com/us-news/2019/feb/01/sacramento-rally-fbi-kkk-domestic
-terrorism-california [https://perma.cc/N2JX-L4DD].

167. *See* United States v. DeChristopher, 695 F.3d 1082, 1087 (10th Cir. 2012).

168. *See id.* at 1095.

169. *Id.* at 1088.

170. *Id.*

171. *See* Travis Holtby, *Bidder 70 Out of Prison*, MOAB SUN NEWS (May 1, 2013,
8:00 AM), http://www.moabsunnews.com/news/article_47888438-b1d3-11e2
-b05b-0019bb30f31a.html [https://perma.cc/BWR6-3655].

172. Impact Energy Res., LLC v. Salazar, 693 F.3d 1239, 1242-44 (10th Cir.
2012).

173. *See DeChristopher*, 695 F.3d at 1088.

186 NOTES

174. Brian Maffly, *Activist Tim DeChristopher to Be Freed After 21 Months in Custody*, SALT LAKE TRIB. (Apr. 17, 2013), https://archive.sltrib.com/article.php?id=56159854&itype=CMSID [https://perma.cc/32DX-7MCZ].

175. *See* Rocco Parascandola et al., *Daniel Pantaleo, the NYPD Officer Who Put Eric Garner in a Fatal Chokehold, Is Loathed, Threatened and an Outcast, but Still Can't Wait to Get Back on the Job*, N.Y. DAILY NEWS (July 11, 2015), http://www.nydailynews.com/new-york/daniel-pantaleo-fatal-choke-ready-back-job-article-1.2289076 [https://perma.cc/NX3D-Y98G].

176. Dale W. Eisinger & Stephen Rex Brown, *Ramsey Orta, Who Filmed Death of Eric Garner, Sentenced to Four Years in Prison for Drugs and Weapons Charges*, N.Y. DAILY NEWS (Oct. 3, 2016), http://www.nydailynews.com/new-york/ramsey-orta-filmed-eric-garner-death-sentenced-4-years-article-1.2815791 [https://perma.cc/U8JL-EXAU].

177. Abby Haglage, *Life in Prison for Selling $20 of Weed*, DAILY BEAST (Feb. 27, 2015), https://www.thedailybeast.com/life-in-prison-for-selling-dollar20-of-weed [https://perma.cc/G7PC-BFUM].

178. Adam Serwer, *Obama Commutes Clarence Aaron's Sentence*, MSNBC (Dec. 19, 2013), http://www.msnbc.com/msnbc/obama-rights-decades-old-injustice [https://perma.cc/D9RU-745S].

179. Erin Fuchs, *How a Florida Beautician and "Bag Holder" in a Drug Conspiracy Got Obama on Her Side After a Life Sentence*, BUS. INSIDER (Aug. 16, 2015), https://www.businessinsider.com/stephanie-george-and-life-after-prison-2015-8 [https://perma.cc/6FB2-MEJ2].

180. John Tierney, *For Lesser Crimes, Rethinking Life Behind Bars*, N.Y. TIMES (Dec. 11, 2012), https://www.nytimes.com/2012/12/12/science/mandatory-prison-sentences-face-growing-skepticism.html [https://perma.cc/52VZ-RYDK].

181. *See, e.g.*, Sari Horwitz, *From a First Arrest to a Life Sentence*, WASH. POST (July 15, 2015), https://www.washingtonpost.com/sf/national/2015/07/15/from-a-first-arrest-to-a-life-sentence [https://perma.cc/N6H3-XLDF]; Alysia Santo, *A Prosecutor's Regret: How I Got Someone Life in Prison for Drugs*, MARSHALL PROJECT (Apr. 7, 2016), https://www.themarshallproject.org/2016/04/07/a-prosecutor-s-regret-how-i-got-someone-life-in-prison-for-drugs[https://perma.cc/VY8N-R3WK]; Annie Sweeney, *Obama Orders Release of Man Jailed for Life for Non-Violent Crime at 17*, CHI. TRIB. (Dec. 19, 2013), http://www.chicagotribune.com/news/ct-xpm-2013-12-19-chi-obama

-orders-release-of-man-jailed-for-life-for-nonviolent-crime-at-17-2013121
9-story.html; John Tierney, *Life Without Parole: Four Inmates' Stories*, N.Y.
TIMES (Dec. 12, 2012), https://www.nytimes.com/2012/12/12/science/life
-without-parole-four-inmates-stories.html [https://perma.cc/G69X-FPE5].

182.   *See* Brady Meixell & Ross Eisenbrey, *An Epidemic of Wage Theft Is Cost-
ing Workers Hundreds of Millions of Dollars a Year*, ECON. POL'Y INST. (Sept. 11,
2014), https://www.epi.org/publication/epidemic-wage-theft-costing-workers
-hundreds [https://perma.cc/88YU-PDN7]; *see also* Terri Gerstein, *Stealing
from Workers Is a Crime. Why Don't Prosecutors See It That Way?*, NATION (May 24,
2018), https://www.thenation.com/article/stealing-from-workers-is-a-crime
-why-dont-prosecutors-see-it-that-way [https://perma.cc/Q9YW-TAQD];
*Report: Wage Theft Is Pervasive in Corporate America; Big Banks, Insurers Are
Among Most-Penalized Firms*, GOOD JOBS FIRST (May 6, 2018), https://www.
goodjobsfirst.org/news/releases/report-wage-theft-pervasive-corporate-
america [https://perma.cc/L2YW-X73Y]; Amy Traub, *The Steal: The Urgent
Need to Combat Wage Theft in Retail*, DEMOS (June 12, 2017), https://www
.demos.org/publication/steal-urgent-need-combat-wage-theft-retail [https://
perma.cc/YK7F-ESYP] (finding just one type of wage theft more prevalent
than all shoplifting combined).

183.   James Risen & Eric Lichtblau, *Bush Lets U.S. Spy on Callers Without Courts*,
N.Y. TIMES (Dec. 16, 2005), https://www.nytimes.com/2005/12/16/politics
/bush-lets-us-spy-on-callers-without-courts.html [https://perma.cc/NY53
-YG5L].

184.   *See* James Bamford, Opinion, *Bush Is Not Above the Law*, N.Y. TIMES
(Jan. 31, 2007), https://www.nytimes.com/2007/01/31/opinion/31bamford.html
[https://perma.cc/ARW5-K2AW].

185.   David Kravets, *Obama to Defend Telco Spy Immunity*, WIRED (Jan.
15, 2009), https://www.wired.com/2009/01/obama-to-fight [https://perma.cc
/8PVA-TSU9].

186.   *See Lost in Detention*, FRONTLINE (Oct. 18, 2011), https://www.pbs
.org/wgbh/frontline/film/lost-in-detention [https://perma.cc/TK7N-CPTF];
Caroline Chen & Jess Ramirez, *Immigrant Shelters Drug Traumatized Teenagers Without Consent*, PROPUBLICA (July 20, 2018), https://www.propublica
.org/article/immigrant-shelters-drug-traumatized-teenagers-without-consent
[https://perma.cc/2TLZ-264M].

187. Editorial Board, *Convicted for Leaving Water for Migrants in the Desert: This Is Trump's Justice*, WASH. POST (Jan. 27, 2019), https://www.washington post.com/opinions/convicted-for-leaving-water-for-migrants-in-the-desert -this-is-trumps-justice/2019/01/27/9d4b3104-2013-11e9-8b59-0a28f2191131 _story.html [https://perma.cc/4HTY-ZYUJ]; Amy Goodman et al., *Arizona Activists Face Jail Time for Providing Life-Saving Aid to Migrants Crossing Sonoran Desert*, DEMOCRACY NOW! (Jan. 15, 2019).

188. *See, e.g.*, Spencer Ackerman, *Obama Claims US Drone Strikes Have Killed up to 116 Civilians*, GUARDIAN (July 1, 2016), https://www.theguardian.com /us-news/2016/jul/01/obama-drones-strikes-civilian-deaths [https://perma.cc /3TTA-KUE2]; Conor Friedersdorf, *The Obama Administration's Drone-Strike Dissembling*, ATLANTIC (Mar. 14, 2016), https://www.theatlantic.com/politics /archive/2016/03/the-obama-administrations-drone-strike-dissembling/473 -541 [https://perma.cc/2K5F-XRQ2].

189. Tom Engelhardt, *The US Has Bombed at Least Eight Wedding Parties Since 2001*, NATION (Dec. 20, 2013), https://www.thenation.com/article /us-has-bombed-least-eight-wedding-parties-2001 [https://perma.cc/H3JB -BTMC]; *see also* Glenn Greenwald, *U.S. Again Bombs Mourners*, SALON (June 4, 2012), http://www.salon.com/2012/06/04/obama_again_bombs_mourners [https://perma.cc/J3FD-PUQQ]; Glenn Greenwald, *U.S. Drones Targeting Rescuers and Mourners*, SALON (Feb. 5, 2012), http://www.salon.com/2012/02/05 /u_s_drones_targeting_rescuers_and_mourners [https://perma.cc/3XZN -E8MM].

190. *See, e.g.*, Friedersdorf, *supra* note 188. After the repeated, false claims that civilians were not being killed, it was revealed that the Obama Administration had internally defined *civilian* to exclude any male of "military age," meaning that any boy or man murdered was automatically reclassified as a combatant. *See* Jo Becker & Scott Shane, *Secret "Kill List" Proves a Test of Obama's Principles and Will*, N.Y. TIMES (May 29, 2012), https://www.nytimes.com/2012 /05/29/world/obamas-leadership-in-war-on-al-qaeda.html [https://perma.cc /RZJ3-N5HK]. Even under this definition, the administration's claims that it did not kill civilians were false by the thousands. *See* Rafiq ur Rehman, Opinion, *Please Tell Me, Mr. President, Why a U.S. Drone Strike Killed My Mother*, GUARDIAN (Oct. 25, 2013), https://www.theguardian.com/commentisfree /2013/oct/25/president-us-assassinated-mother; Jeremy Scahill, *The Assassination Complex*, INTERCEPT (Oct. 15, 2015), https://theintercept.com/drone -papers/the-assassination-complex. In most criminal prosecutions, prosecutors introduce evidence of post-crime lies as evidence of guilt.

191. *See* Nasser Al-Alwaki, Opinion, *The Drone That Killed My Grandson*, N.Y. TIMES (July 17, 2013), https://www.nytimes.com/2013/07/18/opinion /the-drone-that-killed-my-grandson.html [https://perma.cc/39AH-7RRD].

192. For a comprehensive accounting of illegal American interference in foreign democracies, see STEVEN KINZER, OVERTHROW (2007), and WILLIAM BLUM, KILLING HOPE (2003).

193. The child on the south side of Chicago caught in a shootout the previous week has a story that he tells himself about why he should carry a gun for self-defense. *See* Brian Freskos, *How and Why Chicago's At-Risk Youth Carry Guns*, TRACE (Oct. 5, 2018), https://www.thetrace.org /2018/10/chicago-youth-gun-carry-habits-protection [https://perma.cc /S67K-GBPH]. My friends in Alabama who openly carried firearms to protect themselves when we went to lunch together while I lived there felt similarly. Culture, race, economics, and jingoism influence how we think about the validity of self-defense or the degree of criminality in each of these situations.

194. Shaila Dewan, *Caught with Pot? Get-out-of-Jail Program Comes with $950 Catch*, N.Y. TIMES (Aug. 24, 2018), https://www.nytimes.com/2018/08/24 /us/marijuana-diversion-program-maricopa-arizona.html [https://perma.cc /UPL7-R6NW].

195. Alex Bender et al., *Not Just a Ferguson Problem: How Traffic Courts Drive Inequality*, LAW. COMMITTEE FOR C.R. ET AL. 9 (2015), https://www.lccr .com/wp-content/uploads/Not-Just-a-Ferguson-Problem-How-Traffic -Courts-Drive-Inequality-in-California-4.8.15.pdf [https://perma.cc/M55T -MBVZ].

196. Sam Stockard, *Court Orders State to Stop Suspending Licenses of People Too Poor to Pay Debt*, DAILY MEMPHIAN (Oct. 18, 2018, 10:39 AM CT), https:// dailymemphian.com/article/740/Court-orders-state-to-stop-suspending -licenses-of-people-too-poor-to-pay-debt [https://perma.cc/XUD8-XJFA].

197. Justin Wm. Moyer, *More Than 7 Million People May Have Lost Driver's Licenses Because of Traffic Debt*, WASH. POST (May 19, 2018), https://www .washingtonpost.com/local/public-safety/more-than-7-million-people-may-have -lost-drivers-licenses-because-of-traffic-debt/2018/05/19/9767-8c08 -5785-11e8-b666-a5f8c2a9295d_story.html [https://perma.cc/D3ZF-C3X4].

198. Matt Sledge, *New Orleans Judges to Appeal Decisions in Fines and Fees Lawsuits*, NEW ORLEANS ADVOC. (Aug. 21, 2018, 12:59 PM), https://www .theadvocate.com/new_orleans/news/courts/article_fbd197d6-a56b-11e8-befe -abaf6281ca54.html [https://perma.cc/T8G7-Y7UQ].

199. Julie K. Brown, *An M.E. Casts Doubt on Rainey's "Accidental" Death*, MIAMI HERALD (Feb. 4, 2016, 5:54 PM), https://www.miamiherald.com/news/special-reports/florida-prisons/article57413813.html [https://perma.cc/X99C-B9XB] (detailing facts); Laurel Wamsley, *After Inmate with Schizophrenia Dies in Shower, Fla. Prosecutor Finds No Wrongdoing*, NPR (Mar. 19, 2017, 5:11 PM), https://www.npr.org/sections/thetwo-way/2017/03/19/520743255/after-schizophrenic-inmate-dies-in-a-shower-florida-prosecutor-finds-no-wrong-doi [https://perma.cc/AT2A-PEH3] (discussing decision not to prosecute).

200. Alexa O'Brien & David Coombs, *WATCH: Full Extended Interview with Manning's Attorney After 35-Year Sentence*, DEMOCRACY NOW! (Aug. 22, 2013), https://www.democracynow.org/2013/8/22/watch_full_extended_interview_with_mannings_attorney_after_35_year_sentence [https://perma.cc/KHU7-5TKK].

201. *See* Pierre Thomas et al., *Former CIA Head David Petraeus to Plead Guilty*, ABC NEWS (Mar. 23, 2015, 10:33 PM), https://abcnews.go.com/Politics/cia-head-david-petraeus-plead-guilty/story?id=29340487.

202. Rania Khalek, *15 Years in Prison for Taping the Cops? How Eavesdropping Laws Are Taking Away Our Best Defense Against Police Brutality*, ALTERNET (July 28, 2011), https://www.alternet.org/story/151806/15_years_in_prison_for_taping_the_cops_how_eavesdropping_laws_are_taking_away_our_best_defense_against_police_brutality/?page=entire [https://perma.cc/K9CT-H25L].

203. *U.S.: Harsh Conditions for Young Lifers*, HUMAN RTS. WATCH (Jan. 2, 2012, 11:45 PM), http://www.hrw.org/news/2012/01/02/us-harsh-conditions-young-lifers [https://perma.cc/7FY8-XRCB].

204. The piglet's screeches of pain were so terrible that doctors did not subject the second piglet to the same mutilation. Glenn Greenwald, *The FBI's Hunt for Two Missing Piglets Reveals the Federal Cover-up of Barbaric Factory Farms*, INTERCEPT (Oct. 5, 2017, 2:05 PM), https://theintercept.com/2017/10/05/factory-farms-fbi-missing-piglets-animal-rights-glenn-greenwald [https://perma.cc/PDP3-ZH8E] ("[A] six-car armada of FBI agents in bulletproof vests, armed with search warrants, descended upon two small shelters for abandoned farm animals").

205. *Chicago Artist's Protest Backfires as He Faces 15 Years in Jail . . . Because He Recorded His Own Arrest on Video*, DAILY MAIL (Jan. 24, 2011, 4:46 EDT), https://www.dailymail.co.uk/news/article-1349966/Chicago-artist-Chris-Drew-faces-15-years-jail-recorded-arrest.html [https://perma.cc/25H3-PRYP]; Mike Masnick, *Police and Courts Regularly Abusing Wiretapping Laws to Arrest*

People for Filming Cops Misbehaving in Public Places, TECHDIRT (June 4, 2010, 5:45 PM), https://www.techdirt.com/articles/20100603/0859019675.shtml [https://perma.cc/6LE3-QCKJ].

206.   *Out of Reach: The High Cost of Housing*, NAT'L LOW INCOME HOUS. COALI-TION 1 (2018), https://nlihc.org/sites/default/files/oor/OOR_2018.pdf [https://perma.cc/ST97-DCLU].

207.   Rebecca Woolington & Melissa Lewis, *Portland Homeless Accounted for Majority of Police Arrests in 2017, Analysis Finds*, OREGONIAN (June 27, 2018), https://www.oregonlive.com/portland/index.ssf/2018/06/portland_homeless _accounted_fo.html [https://perma.cc/74JW-DYR3] (finding the "vast majority of the arrests" to be for nonviolent crimes and fifty-two percent of all arrests to be of homeless people).

208.   Joshua Vaughn, *Pennsylvania Prosecutors Pursue Charges for People Who Fall Behind on Rent-to-Own Payments*, APPEAL (Sept. 5, 2018), https://theappeal .org/rent-to-own-companies-are-turning-the-criminal-justice-system-into -their-debt-collector [https://perma.cc/U6UH-3NN2].

209.   *Marijuana Arrest Reports*, NORML, https://norml.org/library/arrest -reports [https://perma.cc/Z7FT-H8DL].

210.   Christal Hayes, *Marijuana Arrests Were Up Last Year—and You're Paying Billions for It*, NEWSWEEK (Sept. 26, 2017, 3:22 PM), https://www.newsweek .com/pot-arrests-rising-and-youre-paying-millions-it-671478 [https://perma.cc /6RAM-BTB6]; *see also Marijuana Arrests by the Numbers*, ACLU (last vis-ited Mar. 11, 2019), https://www.aclu.org/gallery/marijuana-arrests-numbers [https://perma.cc/FSK9-BKX8] (finding that "[o]f the 8.2 million marijuana arrests between 2001 and 2010, 88% were for simply having marijuana" and that the marijuana arrests displayed "significant racial bias"); *Nixon Tapes Show Roots of Marijuana Prohibition*, COMMON SENSE FOR DRUG POL'Y 6 (Mar. 2002), http://www.csdp.org/research/shafernixon.pdf [https://perma.cc/4JSA-EKK2] (reporting the annual number of marijuana arrests from 1972 to 2000).

211.   Katharine Q. Seelye, *Barack Obama, Asked About Drug History, Admits He Inhaled*, N.Y. TIMES (Oct. 24, 2006), https://www.nytimes.com/2006/10 /24/world/americas/24iht-dems.3272493.html [https://perma.cc/Y6L8 -8SMK].

212.   Neil A. Lewis, *Special Counsel Puts Lewinsky Case to Rest*, N.Y. TIMES, Mar. 7, 2002, at A18; *cf.* Gwen Ifill, *Clinton Admits Experiment with Marijuana in the 1960's*, N.Y. TIMES, Mar. 30, 1992, at A15.

213. Nancy Flake, *11-Year-Old Arrested, Faces Felony, for Tripping School Fire Alarm*, Hous. Chron. (Feb. 1, 2005, 6:00 PM), https://www.chron.com /neighborhood/article/11-year-old-arrested-faces-felony-for-tripping-9767783 .php [https://perma.cc/WZ9G-ZXJX].

214. *Id.*

215. Juliette Garside, *Philip Zimmermann: King of Encryption Reveals His Fears for Privacy*, Guardian (May 25, 2015, 12:02 PM), https://www.theguardian .com/technology/2015/may/25/philip-zimmermann-king-encryption-reveals -fears-privacy [https://perma.cc/3ECW-NC2G].

216. Benjamin Mueller, *It Wasn't a Crime to Carry Marijuana. Until the Police Found a Loophole.*, N.Y. Times (Aug. 2, 2018), https://www.nytimes.com/2018/08/02/ny /region/marijuana-police-nyc.html [https://perma.cc/7GFL-7KBT].

217. Ross Levitt & Deborah Feyerick, *Death Penalty States Scramble for Lethal Injection Drugs*, CNN (Nov. 16, 2013, 1:44 PM), http://www.cnn.com /2013/11/15/justice/states-lethal-injection-drugs [https://perma/cc/ZG4X -F6MT].

218. *See, e.g.*, Christopher Hitchens, The Trial of Henry Kiss-inger (2001); Zaid Jilani, *REPORT: Henry Kissinger's Long History of Com-plicity in Human Rights Abuses*, Think Progress (Dec. 29, 2010), https:// thinkprogress.org/report-henry-kissingers-long-history-of-complicity-in -human-rights-abuses-ffcb00aafbee [https://perma.cc/7UCY-Z7GJ]; *see gener-ally* Kinzer, *supra* note 192 (describing Kissinger's role in multiple U.S. military interventions based on deception and false claims).

219. Jason Leopold, *How Bush's DOJ Killed a Criminal Probe into BP That Threatened to Net Top Officials*, Truthout (May 19, 2010), https:// truthout.org/articles/how-bushs-doj-killed-a-criminal-probe-into-bp-that -threatened-to-net-top-officials [https://perma.cc/LRZ8-6P4Q].

220. Sandra E. Garcia, *Texas Woman Sentenced to 5 Years in Prison for Voter Fraud Loses Bid for New Trial*, N.Y. Times (June 13, 2018), https://www.nytimes .com/2018/06/13/us/texas-woman-voter-fraud.html [https://perma.cc/PV6C -U5YZ]; *see also* Jack Healy, *Arrested, Jailed and Charged with a Felony. For Voting.*, N.Y. Times (Aug. 2, 2018), https://www.nytimes.com/2018/08/02/us/arrested -voting-north-carolina.html [https://perma.cc/5YQ7-TVFS] (reporting on twelve people on probation or parole who were prosecuted in Alamance County, North Carolina for voting illegally in the 2016 presidential election, nine of whom were black).

221. Carrie Teegardin, *Jury Quickly Says "Not Guilty" in Georgia Elections Case,* ATLANTA J.-CONST. (Mar. 15, 2018), https://www.ajc.com/blog/investigations /jury-quickly-says-not-guilty-georgia-elections-case/uxbnZO4AUxmBQfTm -VGZjXK [https://perma.cc/A64V-7A5R].

222. Charles Duhigg, *Clean Water Laws Are Neglected, at a Cost in Suffering,* N.Y. TIMES (Sept. 123, 2009), https://www.nytimes.com/2009/09/13/us/13water .html [https://perma.cc/P2TW-8F89].

223. Interested readers may also find worthwhile the stories of Tarek Mehanna, Barrett Brown, Thomas Drake, Aaron Swartz, William Binney, Jeremy Hammond, Leonard Peltier, Albert Woodfox, and Lynne Stewart.

224. For illustrations of what the experience of being stopped and frisked can be like, see Gabrielle Bluestone, *This Is What It's Like to Be in a Stop and Frisk,* GAWKER (Oct. 13, 2013, 11:03 AM), http://gawker.com/this-is-what-its -like-to-be-in-a-stop-and-frisk-1444542777 [https://perma.cc/B9LD-4EJJ], *and* Ross Tuttle & Erin Schneider, *Stopped-and-Frisked: "For Being a F**king Mutt" [VIDEO],* NATION (Oct. 8, 2012), https://www.thenation.com/article /stopped-and-frisked-being-fking-mutt-video [https://perma.cc/KD9J-2YVM].

225. *Compare* JANE GRAVELLE, CONG. RESEARCH SERV., R40623, TAX HAVENS: INTERNATIONAL TAX AVOIDANCE AND EVASION 2 (2015), https:// fas.org/sgp/crs/misc/R40623.pdf [https://perma.cc/UN94-HVQH] (estimating annual revenue loss on account of corporate tax evasion due to profit sharing at $100 billion), *with* Meixell & Eisenbrey, *supra* note 182 ("All of the robberies, burglaries, larcenies, and motor vehicle thefts in the nation cost their victims less than $14 billion in 2012, according to the FBI's Uniform Crime Reports"). A problem on a far larger scale is the black hole of international finance that permits tax evasion in complex transactions that are arguably legal in jurisdictions that have changed their laws to permit private individual wealth to be essentially hidden from taxation by other countries. *See* Matthew C. Klein, *How Much Do Tax Havens Cost the Rest of Us?,* BARRON'S (June 19, 2018, 10:58 AM ET), https://www.barrons.com/articles /how-much-do-tax-havens-cost-the-rest-of-us-1529420282 [https://perma.cc /BM2D-N95X].

226. *Cf.* Timothy A. Canova, *Financial Market Failure as a Crisis in the Rule of Law: From Market Fundamentalism to a New Keynesian Regulatory Model,* 3 HARV. L. & POL'Y REV. 369, 385 n.72 (2009) (collecting works by William Black on regulatory capture in financial fraud enforcement).

227. By 2010, major U.S. cities had backlogs of tens of thousands of untested rape kits. *See* Corey Rayburn Yung, *How to Lie with Rape Statistics: America's Hidden Rape Crisis*, 99 IOWA L. REV. 1197, 1246 (2014). Police departments were thus forgoing or slowing rape investigations while they spent money on low-level arrests. Separately, even though we know that rape occurs with frequency on college campuses, the police do not have armies of undercover officers or armies of informants infiltrating college fraternities. And, in my ten years of experience, "law enforcement" essentially ignores uncontroverted evidence of rampant sexual violence against prisoners.

228. For example, police chose to set up a unit of officers to record conversations in religious houses of worship and investigate a community of low-income Muslim residents in their homes. *See* Adam Goldman & Matt Apuzzo, *With Cameras, Informants, NYPD Eyed Mosques*, ASSOCIATED PRESS (Feb. 23, 2012), https://www.ap.org/ap-in-the-news/2012/with-cameras-informants-nypd-eyed-mosques [https://perma.cc/G2AA-TNGN]. The same department presumably did not create a similar team of two hundred agents to infiltrate luxury condos to ferret out evidence of tax evasion and prescription-drug abuse.

229. Class Action Complaint at ¶ 5, Fant v. City of Ferguson, 107 F. Supp. 3d 1016 (E.D. Mo. 2015) (No. 4:15-CV-253) (drawing on data from 2014).

230. *See* JOHN HAGAN, WHO ARE THE CRIMINALS?: THE POLITICS OF CRIME POLICY FROM THE AGE OF ROOSEVELT TO THE AGE OF REAGAN 137–212 (2010).

231. *See* John Hudson, *FBI Drops Law Enforcement as "Primary" Mission*, FOREIGN POL'Y (Jan. 5, 2014, 11:57 PM), http://thecable.foreignpolicy.com/posts/2014/01/05/fbi_drops_law_enforcement_as_primary_mission [https://perma.cc/79PP-FWKA]; Catherine Rampell, Opinion, *How America Stopped Prosecuting White-Collar Crime and Public Corruption, in Charts*, WASH. POST (Aug. 7, 2018), https://www.washingtonpost.com/news/rampage/wp/2018/08/07/how-america-stopped-prosecuting-white-collar-crime-and-public-corruption-in-charts [https://perma.cc/85CN-HAUB] David Sirota, *US Prosecution of White-Collar Crime Hits 20-Year Low: Report*, INT'L BUS. TIMES (Aug. 4, 2015, 7:50 AM), https://www.ibtimes.com/us-prosecution-white-collar-crime-hits-20-year-low-report-2037160 [https://perma.cc/BR6X-7JHL].

232. Hudson, *supra* note 231; *see* Eric Lichtblau et al., *F.B.I. Struggles to Handle Financial Fraud Cases*, N.Y. TIMES (Oct. 18, 2008), https://www.nytimes.com/2008/10/19/washington/19fbi.html [https://perma.cc/YC8U-97SW] ("Prosecutions of frauds against financial institutions dropped 48 percent from 2000 to 2007, insurance fraud cases plummeted 75 percent, and securities fraud

cases dropped 17 percent."); Paul Shukovsky et al., *The Terrorism Trade-Off: Focus on National Security After 9/11 Means that the FBI Has Turned Its Back on Thousands of White-Collar Crimes*, SEATTLE POST-INTELLIGENCER (Apr. 11, 2007), https://www.lathropd.com/projects/terrorism-trade-off/pdfs/terrorism -trade-off-april-11.pdf [https://perma.cc/4KN8-HAK7].

233.   *See supra* notes 120–129.

234.   Paul Kiel & Jesse Eisinger, *How the IRS Was Gutted*, PROPUBLICA (Dec. 11, 2018, 5:00 AM EST), https://www.propublica.org/article/how-the-irs-was -gutted [https://perma.cc/CL3X-8VS8].

235.   *See, e.g.*, Stephan Salisbury, *Tomgram: Stephan Salisbury, Keeping an Eye on Everyone*, TOMDISPATCH (Oct. 3, 2010, 6:03 PM), http://www.tomdispatch.com /archive/175303/stephan_salisbury_keeping_an_eye_on_everyone [https:// perma.cc/VTS5-ULX4].

236.   *See* Katherine Beckett, *The Uses and Abuses of Police Discretion: Toward Harm Reduction Policing*, 10 HARV. L. & POL'Y REV. 77, 89–95 (2016).

237.   Michelle Alexander, *Why Hillary Clinton Doesn't Deserve the Black Vote*, NATION (Feb. 10, 2016), https://www.thenation.com/article/hillary-clin ton-does-not-deserve-black-peoples-votes [https://perma.cc/96QV-E6VC]; *see also* Jeff Stein, *The Clinton Dynasty's Horrific Legacy: How "Tough-on-Crime" Politics Built the World's Largest Prison System*, SALON (Apr. 13, 2015), https://www.salon .com/2015/04/13/the_clinton_dynastys_horrific_legacy_how_tough_on_crime _politics_built_the_worlds_largest_prison [https://perma.cc/5R56-NNMV].

238.   *See* Mara Hvistendahl, *Can 'Predictive Policing' Prevent Crime Before It Happens?*, SCI. (Sept. 28, 2016), http://www.sciencemag.org/news/2016/09 /can-predictive-policing-prevent-crime-it-happens [https://perma.cc/SM5L -D8XK] ("As to whether predictive policing models work as advertised . . . the evidence is scarce, and the few data points are not encouraging.").

239.   Kevin Drum, *Lead: America's Real Criminal Element*, MOTHER JONES (Feb. 11, 2016), http://www.motherjones.com/environment/2013/01/lead-crime -link-gasoline [https://perma.cc/D23V-LRUK].

240.   James Baldwin, *No Name in the Street*, in THE PRICE OF THE TICKET 449, 537 (1985).

241.   *See generally* ISSA KOHLER-HAUSMANN, MISDEMEANORLAND (2018); ALEXANDRA NATAPOFF, PUNISHMENT WITHOUT CRIME (2018); Paul Butler, *The System Is Working the Way It Is Supposed To: The Limits of Criminal Justice Reform*, 104 GEO. L.J. 1419, 1447–75 (2016); NAT'L ASSOC. OF CRIM. DEF. LAWYERS, MINOR CRIMES, MASSIVE WASTE (2009). In New York City, for

example, police recorded stopping and investigating 533,042 people in 2012. NEW YORK CITY BAR ASS'N, REPORT ON THE NYPD'S STOP-AND-FRISK POL-ICY 5 (2013). Eighty-five percent were black and Latino and only six percent of the stops resulted in an arrest. *Id.* at 15; *see also* Vincent Warren, *The Case Against Stop and Frisk*, OPEN SOC'Y FOUND. (Sept. 30, 2016), https://www.open societyfoundations.org/voices/case-against-stop-and-frisk [https://perma.cc /BY55-XZVM]. Black people are significantly more likely than white people to be stopped by police and significantly more likely to be searched after being stopped. Black people are less likely to possess illegal contraband than white people when searched. Jeff Guo, *Police Are Searching Black Drivers More Often but Finding More Illegal Stuff with White Drivers* (Oct. 27, 2015), WASH. POST, https://www.washingtonpost.com/news/wonk/wp/2015/10/27/police-are -searching-black-drivers-more-often-but-finding-more-illegal-stuff-with -white-drivers-2 [https://perma.cc/7PHJ-AUQE]. In Washington, DC, black people are less than half the population but are over 90 percent of those hand-cuffed and jailed for drug offenses, despite using drugs at the same rate as white people. WASHINGTON LAWYERS COMM. FOR CIVIL RIGHTS & URBAN AFFAIRS, RACIAL DISPARITIES IN ARRESTS IN THE DISTRICT OF COLUMBIA, 2009–2011, *at* 2 (2013). When I investigated drug search warrants in Washington, DC, I uncovered that hundreds of them every year were illegal and contained false statements by police. I interviewed dozens of families, who described violent raids executing these illegal searches including strip searches, probing the anuses of innocent people, pointing guns at naked children in the shower, shooting pets, and handcuffing elderly and disabled people. Of these, at least ninety-nine percent were in the homes of black families. John Sullivan, et al., *Probable Cause*, WASH. POST (Mar. 5, 2016), https://www.washingtonpost.com/sf/investigative /2016/03/05/probable-cause [https://perma.cc/DS5C-NDL8].

242.   *See, e.g.*, Shane Bauer, *The Making of the Warrior Cop*, MOTHER JONES (Oct. 23, 2014, 10:00 AM), https://www.motherjones.com/politics/2014/10/swa -warrior-cops-police-militarization-urban-shield [https://perma.cc/L5U4 -D3WB].

243.   Other economic incentives also corrupt this process, including bil-lions of dollars in federal grants for discriminatory and military-style polic-ing, the pursuit of billions of dollars in cash and property through civil forfei-ture, overtime pay policies, performance evaluation metrics, and billions of dollars in weapons transfers from the U.S. military. *See, e.g.*, Eric Blumenson & Eva Nilsen, *Policing for Profit: The Drug War's Hidden Economic Agenda*, 65 U. CHI. L. REV. 35 (1998) (discussing the incentives created by federal grants

and civil forfeiture); Hanqing Chen, *The Best Reporting on Federal Push to Militarize Local Police*, PROPUBLICA (Aug. 19, 2014, 8:30 AM EDT), https://www.propublica.org/article/the-best-reporting-on-the-federal-push-to-militarize-local-police [https://perma.cc/9FQA-EG2A] (explaining a federal program that had provided at least $4.3 billion in military equipment to local police); Mike Maciag, *The Alarming Consequences of Police Working Overtime*, GOVERNING (Oct. 2017), http://www.governing.com/topics/public-justice-safety/gov-police-officers-overworked-cops.html [https://perma.cc/T4AA-YGTU] (describing how police incentives to work overtime have negative consequences, including increased racial bias).

244.   *See generally* LOÏC WACQUANT, PUNISHING THE POOR: THE NEOLIBERAL GOVERNMENT OF SOCIAL INSECURITY (2009) (arguing that the complementary erosion of the social-welfare state and explosion of the penal state has resulted in the criminalization of social insecurity).

245.   *See* Nicholas K. Peart, Opinion, *Why Is the NYPD After Me?*, N.Y. TIMES (Dec. 17, 2011), http://www.nytimes.com/2011/12/18/opinion/sunday/young-black-and-frisked-by-the-nypd.html [https://perma.cc/3TMU-XJJ3].

246.   RICHARD WILKINSON & KATE PICKETT, THE SPIRIT LEVEL: WHY GREATER EQUALITIES MAKES SOCIETIES STRONGER (2011).

247.   *See* Michael Hawthorne, *Studies Link Lead Exposure, Violent Crime*, CHI. TRIB. (June 6, 2015), http://www.chicagotribune.com/news/ct-lead-poisoning-science-met-20150605-story.html [https://perma.cc/7PZU-YXDF].

248.   *See Invest-Divest*, MOVEMENT FOR BLACK LIVES, https://policy.m4bl.org/invest-divest [https://perma.cc/2B9H-PQGF].

249.   William J. Stuntz, *The Pathological Politics of Criminal Law*, 100 MICH. L. REV. 505, 510 (2001).

250.   Associated Press, *AP IMPACT: After 40 Years, $1 Trillion, US War on Drugs Has Failed to Meet Any of Its Goals*, FOX NEWS (May 13, 2010), https://www.foxnews.com/world/ap-impact-after-40-years-1-trillion-us-war-on-drugs-has-failed-to-meet-any-of-its-goals [https://perma.cc/9XPE-4NJE].

251.   *Id.*

252.   See *Findings*, STAN. OPEN POLICING PROJECT (last visited Mar. 11, 2019), https://openpolicing.stanford.edu/findings [https://perma.cc/Z9KR-ZFLB] (finding that more than 20 million motorists are stopped every year, and illustrating graphically that traffic stops in Colorado and Washington reduced by half after the legalization of marijuana in those states).

253.   *See, e.g.*, Mark Motivans, Bureau of Justice Statistics, *Federal Justice Statistics, 2015-16*, U.S. Dep't Just. 10 (Jan. 2019), https://www.bjs.gov/content/pub/pdf/fjs1516.pdf [https://perma.cc/DBU4-K7E2] (reporting in Table 7 that over 100,000 years of prison for drug offenses were imposed in fiscal year 2016 alone, assuming that the median drug sentence approximates the average drug sentence).

254.   *Colombia's Two Anti-Coca Strategies Are at War with Each Other*, Economist (Feb. 20, 2018), https://www.economist.com/the-americas/2018/02/20/colombias-two-anti-coca-strategies-are-at-war-with-each-other [https://perma.cc/QQ8J-Z6VL]; Judith Walcott, *Spraying Crops, Eradicating People*, Cultural Survival Q. Mag. (Dec. 2002), https://www.culturalsurvival.org/publications/cultural-survival-quarterly/spraying-crops-eradicating-people [https://perma.cc/KH4M-AHW2].

255.   *See* Hannah Kozlowska, *What Would Happen if 6 Million Felons Could Vote?*, Quartz (Oct. 6, 2016), https://qz.com/784503/what-would-happen-if-felons-could-vote [https://perma.cc/4VW9-33T4]; *see also* Heather Ann Thompson, *How Prisons Change the Balance of Power in America*, Atlantic (Oct. 7, 2013), http://www.theatlantic.com/national/archive/2013/10/how-prisons-change-the-balance-of-power-in-america/280341 [https://perma.cc/8NMY-MX74].

256.   Brian Elderbroom et. al., *Every Second: The Impact of the Incarceration Crisis on America's Families*, Fwd.US (Dec. 2018), https://everysecond.fwd.us/downloads/EverySecond.fwd.us.pdf [https://perma.cc/D7LZ-39UG] (discussing the effect of incarceration on tens of millions of families).

257.   David Huey, *The US War on Drugs and Its Legacy in Latin America*, Guardian (Feb. 3, 2014), https://www.theguardian.com/global-development-professionals-network/2014/feb/03/us-war-on-drugs-impact-in-latin-american [https://perma.cc/7QMX-G645] (reporting that approximately 100,000 Mexicans have disappeared and 15,000 Colombians have died during the war on drugs).

258.   *See, e.g.*, Chen, *supra* note 243.

259.   Radley Balko, *There's Overwhelming Evidence That the Criminal Justice System Is Racist. Here's the Proof*, Wash. Post (Sept. 18, 2018), https://www.washingtonpost.com/news/opinions/wp/2018/09/18/theres-overwhelming-evidence-that-the-criminal-justice-system-is-racist-heres-the-proof [https://perma.cc/EU44-SM8Q].

260.   Associated Press, *supra* note 250.

261. *See* ALEXANDER, *supra* note 26, 173–208; THE DERRICK BELL READER 27-54 (Richard Delgado & Jean Stefancic eds., 2005).

262. GEORGE BERNARD SHAW, THE COLLECTED ARTICLES, LECTURES, ESSAYS & LETTERS OF GEORGE BERNARD SHAW (2017).

263. *See* HAGAN, *supra* note 230.

264. Diane Bernard, *The Time a President Deported 1 Million Mexican Americans for Supposedly Stealing U.S. Jobs*, WASH. POST (Aug. 13, 2018), https://www.washingtonpost.com/news/retropolis/wp/2018/08/13/the-time-a-president-deported-1-million-mexican-americans-for-stealing-u-s-jobs [https://perma.cc/P464-ASPG].

265. Noam Chomsky, Opinion, *From Central America to Iraq*, KHALEEJ TIMES (Aug. 6, 2004), https://www.khaleejtimes.com/article/20040806/ARTICLE/308069989/1098 [https://perma.cc/KL3K-JGVV]; *see also* Tuttle & Schneider, *supra* note 224.

266. *See* David Garland, *Penal Excess and Surplus Meaning: Public Torture Lynchings in Twentieth-Century America*, 39 LAW & SOC'Y REV. 793, 797–99 (2005).

267. OKLA. COMM'N TO STUDY THE TULSA RACE RIOT OF 1921, TULSA RACE RIOT 11–15 (2001).

268. *See* BLACKMON, *supra* note 48, at 99–100.

269. *Cf.* Robert E. Black et al., *Maternal and Child Undernutrition and Overweight in Low-Income and Middle-Income Countries*, 382 LANCET 427 (2013).

270. *Tobacco-Related Facts*, CTRS. FOR DISEASE CONTROL & PREVENTION (May 15, 2017), https://www.cdc.gov/tobacco/data_statistics/fact_sheets/health_effects/tobacco_related_mortality/index.htm [https://perma.cc/JRD5-FUMV].

271. *Id.*

272. *Smoking and Tobacco Use: Fast Facts*, CTRS. FOR DISEASE CONTROL & PREVENTION (Feb. 20, 2018), https://www.cdc.gov/tobacco/data_statistics/fact_sheets/fast_facts/index.htm [https://perma.cc/9XEZ-F9CF].

273. *Cf.* Anna Gilmore, *Big Tobacco Targets the Young in Poor Countries— with Deadly Consequences*, GUARDIAN (Dec. 1, 2015), https://www.theguardian.com/global-development/2015/dec/01/big-tobacco-industry-targets-young-people-poor-countries-smoking [https://perma.cc/8WC4-953D].

274. Dave Lindorff, *The Pentagon's Massive Accounting Fraud Exposed*, NATION (Nov. 27, 2018), https://www.thenation.com/article/pentagon-audit-budget -fraud [https://perma.cc/FPW3-N4Z4].

275. *See* Gretchen Frazee, *How Taxing Sugary Drinks Affects a Community's Health and Economy*, PBS NEWSHOUR (Oct. 4, 2018, 5:57 PM), https:// www.pbs.org/newshour/economy/making-sense/how-taxing-sugary-drinks -affects-a-communitys-health-and-economy [https://perma.cc/DR8F-EEGL].

276. *See supra* notes 131–134 and accompanying text.

277. *See* Andrew Shaver, *You're More Likely to Be Fatally Crushed by Furniture than Killed by a Terrorist*, WASH. POST (Nov. 23, 2015), https://www.washington post.com/news/monkey-cage/wp/2015/11/23/youre-more-likely-to-be-fatally -crushed-by-furniture-than-killed-by-a-terrorist [https://perma.cc/DX5N-NWSW].

278. ALBERT CAMUS, THE REBEL: AN ESSAY ON MAN IN REVOLT 3 (1951).

279. NOAM CHOMSKY, THE COMMON GOOD 43 (1998).

280. *See* Beverly Daniel Tatum, Opinion, *Segregation Worse in Schools 60 Years After* Brown v. Board of Education, SEATTLE TIMES (Sept. 14, 2017, 3:06 PM), https://www.seattletimes.com/opinion/segregation-worse-in -schools-60-years-after-brown-v-board-of-education [https://perma.cc/Y8U6 -YRXS]; *see also, e.g.,* Gary Orfield et al., Brown *at 60: Great Progress, a Long Retreat, and an Uncertain Future*, C.R. PROJECT (2014), https://civilrightsproject. ucla.edu/research/k-12-education/integration-and-diversity/brown-at-60 -great-progress-a-long-retreat-and-an-uncertain-future/Brown-at-60-051814. pdf [https://perma.cc/YQQ9-DUVN]; Fred Harris & Alan Curtis, Opinion, *The Unmet Promise of Equality*, N.Y. TIMES (Feb. 28, 2018), https://www.nytimes .com/interactive/2018/02/28/opinion/the-unmet-promise-of-equality.html [https://perma.cc/LAC5-7CM4].

281. Note, *Bail Reform and Risk Assessment: The Cautionary Tale of Federal Sentencing*, 131 HARV. L. REV. 1125, 1134–36 (2018).

282. Shima Baradaran, *Restoring the Presumption of Innocence*, 72 OHIO ST. L.J. 723, 741 (2011). The overall rate of pretrial detention prior to the reforms was 24 percent, which means that pretrial detention has exploded by a factor of three. *See* United States Department of Justice, Bureau of Justice Statistics, Pretrial Release and Detention: The Bail Reform Act of 1984 (1988), available at https://www.bjs.gov/content/pub/pdf/prd-bra84.pdf (last visited June 16, 2019).

283. United States v. Salerno, 481 U.S. 739, 755 (1987).

284. *See Table H-14—Federal Pretrial Services Judicial Business (September 30, 2017)*, U.S. COURTS (Sept. 30, 2017), http://www.uscourts.gov/statistics/table/h-14/judicial-business/2017/09/30 [https://perma.cc/3YRT-HMKK].

285. Preet Bharara (@PreetBharara), TWITTER (Oct. 9, 2018, 2:38 PM), https://twitter.com/PreetBharara/status/1049776018943143936 [https://perma.cc/CZ5C-KVJ2].

286. *See* Benjamin Weiser, *For Manhattan's Next U.S. Attorney, Politics and Prosecution Don't Mix*, N.Y. TIMES (Aug. 9, 2009), https://www.nytimes.com/2009/08/10/nyregion/10bharara.html [https://perma.cc/2UWC-BU9R].

287. *See id.; see also, e.g.,* Nicole Hong, *U.S. Attorney Preet Bharara Sets His Sights on Drug Dealers in Opioid Overdoses*, WALL ST. J. (Nov. 20, 2016, 8:30 AM), https://www.wsj.com/articles/u-s-attorney-preet-bharara-sets-his-sights-on-drug-dealers-in-opioid-overdoses-1479643209 [https://perma.cc/4HAN-JW6D] (outlining Bharara's initiative to charge dealers for their buyers' deaths); David Patton, Opinion, *An Honest Assessment of Preet Bharara's Record: Harsh Prosecutions Put More African-Americans and Hispanics Behind Bars*, N.Y. DAILY NEWS (Mar. 15, 2017) http://www.nydailynews.com/opinion/honest-assessment-preet-bharara-record-article-1.2999367 [https://perma.cc/9HTQ-LRKS] (providing statistics on Bharara's tenure); Press Release, *Manhattan U.S. Attorney Charges 34 Members of Bronx Drug Trafficking Crews with Distributing Crack Cocaine*, DRUG ENFORCEMENT AGENCY (Dec. 15, 2011), https://www.dea.gov/press-releases/2011/12/15/manhattan-us-attorney-charges-34-members-bronx-drug-trafficking-crews [https://perma.cc/Q5BU-H2VU] (quoting Bharara as stating that "[d]rug dealers infect neighborhoods with their presence and poison a community's lifeblood" and that "[t]ogether with our law enforcement partners, our commitment to cleaning up the streets of New York for its citizens is a top priority").

288. Keith J. Kelly & Kaja Whitehouse, *Preet Bharara Scores $1M Book Deal for Debut*, N.Y. POST (June 22, 2017, 12:27 PM), https://nypost.com/2017/06/22/preet-bhararas-debut-book-will-be-about-the-search-for-justice [https://perma.cc/2DLL-ETP5].

289. Patton, *supra* note 287.

290. *Statistical Information Packet: Fiscal Year 2015: Southern District of New York*, U.S. SENT'G COMMISSION (2015), https://www.ussc.gov/sites/default/files/pdf/research-and-publications/federal-sentencing-statistics/state-district-circuit/2015/nys15.pdf [https://perma.cc/9WAG-CJ4C].

291. *Statistical Information Packet: Fiscal Year 2016: Southern District of New York*, U.S. SENT'G COMMISSION (2016), https://www.ussc.gov/sites/default/files/pdf/research-and-publications/federal-sentencing-statistics/state-district-circuit/2016/nys16.pdf [https://perma.cc/WE8J-K8ZG].

292. *See, e.g.*, David E. Patton, *Policing the Poor and the Two Faces of the Justice Department*, 44 FORDHAM URB. L.J. 1431 (2017).

293. Allen J. Beck et al., *Sexual Victimization in Prisons and Jails Reported by Inmates, 2011-12*, U.S. DEP'T JUST. (2013), https://www.bjs.gov/content/pub/pdf/svpjri1112.pdf [https://perma.cc/9RQ8-SBBZ].

294. *See generally Medical Treatment in Prison: A Curated Collection of Links*, MARSHALL PROJECT (Mar. 10, 2019, 6:15 PM), https://www.themarshallproject.org/records/868-medical-treatment-in-prison [https://perma.cc/6TFN-VFXD]; *see also, e.g.*, Brown v. Plata, 563 U.S. 493, 501 (2011) ("For years the medical and mental health care provided by California's prisons has fallen short of minimum constitutional requirements and has failed to meet prisoners' basic health needs. Needless suffering and death have been the well-documented result."); NATIONAL RESEARCH COUNCIL, THE GROWTH OF INCARCERATION IN THE UNITED STATES 222-226 (2014), https://www.nap.edu/read/18613/chapter/9#222 [https://perma.cc/M42L-T9DG]; Amanda Aronczyk & Katie Rose Quandt, *Angola Prison Lawsuit Poses Question: What Kind of Medical Care Do Inmates Deserve?*, NPR (Mar. 10, 2018, 7:46 AM ET), https://www.npr.org/sections/health-shots/2018/03/10/591624904/angola-prison-lawsuit-poses-question-what-kind-of-medical-care-do-inmates-deserv [https://perma.cc/C263-SFCE]; Mike Cason, AL.COM (Feb. 11, 2019), *Judge Finds Alabama Prisons "Deliberately Indifferent" to Isolated Inmates*, https://www.al.com/news/2019/02/judge-finds-alabama-prisons-deliberately-indifferent-to-isolated-inmates.html [https://perma.cc/MA2J-R257]; Greg Dober, *Corizon Needs a Checkup: Problems with Privatized Correctional Healthcare*, PRISON LEGAL NEWS (Mar. 15, 2014), https://www.prisonlegalnews.org/news/2014/mar/15/corizon-needs-a-checkup-problems-with-privatized-correctional-healthcare [https://perma.cc/SA4J-B24G]; Bob Egelko, *Report Rips California Prison Psychiatric Care, Cites Case of Inmate Who Ate Her Eyeball*, SFGATE (Nov. 2, 2018, 4:34 PM PDT), https://www.sfgate.com/bayarea/article/Report-rips-California-prison-psychiatric-care-13356438.php [https://perma.cc/39K7-KARQ]; Jennifer Gonnerman, *Do Jails Kill People?*, NEW YORKER (Feb. 20, 2019), https://www.newyorker.com/books/under-review/do-jails-kill-people [https://perma.cc/CE8R-5SRP] (discussing HOMER VENTERS, LIFE AND DEATH IN RIKERS ISLAND (2019); Jimmy Jenkins, *On the Inside:*

The Chaos of Arizona Prison Health Care, PRISON LEGAL NEWS (Nov. 6, 2018), https://www.prisonlegalnews.org/news/2018/nov/6/inside-chaos-arizona -prison-health-care [https://perma.cc/7GFW-5EN7].

295. Atul Gawande, *Hellhole*, NEW YORKER (Mar. 30, 2009), https://www .newyorker.com/magazine/2009/03/30/hellhole [https://perma.cc/2GYA-6QWV].

296. *See* JAMES FORMAN JR., LOCKING UP OUR OWN 194–204 (2017).

297. *See supra* note 241 and accompanying text; *infra* note 362 and accompanying text.

298. Rachel E. Barkow & Mark Osler, *Designed to Fail: The President's Deference to the Department of Justice in Advancing Criminal Justice Reform*, 59 WM. & MARY L. REV. 387, 449 (2017); *see also* Spencer S. Hsu, *Convicted Defendants Left Uninformed of Forensic Flaws Found by Justice Department*, WASH. POST (Apr. 16, 2012), http://www.washingtonpost.com/local/crime/convicted-defendants-left-uninformed-of-forensic-flaws-found-by-justice-dept/2012/04/16/gIQAW -TcgMT_story.html [https://perma.cc/KRT2-PRFS]; Spencer S. Hsu, *Forensic Techniques Are Subject to Human Bias, Lack Standards, Panel Found*, WASH. POST (Apr. 17, 2012), http://www.washingtonpost.com/local/crime/forensic-tech -niques-are-subject-to-human-bias-lack-standards-panel-found/2012 /04/17/gIQADCoMPT_story.html [https://perma.cc/B6BA-BDX3] ("[N]ew DNA testing appeared to clear convicted defendants in 16 percent of Virginia criminal convictions between 1973 and 1988 in which evidence was available for retesting. A 2009 study of post-conviction DNA exonerations—now up to 289 nationwide—found invalid testimony in more than half the cases.").

299. *See, e.g.*, Serena Marshall, *Obama Has Deported More People Than Any Other President*, ABC NEWS (Aug. 29, 2016, 2:05 PM ET), https://abcnews. go.com/Politics/obamas-deportation-policy-numbers/story?id=41715661 [https://perma.cc/64RP-BZV2]. The number of border patrol agents feeding this bureaucracy increased from 4,139 in 1992 to more than 20,000 in 2015. Daniel Denvir, Opinion, *Obama Created a Deportation Machine. Soon It Will Be Trump's*, GUARDIAN (Nov. 21, 2016, 7:30 AM ET), https://www.theguardian .com/commentisfree/2016/nov/21/obama-deportation-mcahine-damage -trump [https://perma.cc/Q9BN-K9SZ].

300. *See* United States v. Blewett, 746 F.3d 647 (6th Cir. 2013).

301. *See* Karakatsanis, *supra* note 78.

302. *See, e.g.*, Josh Gerstein, *Sally Yates Confirmed as No. 2 at Justice Department*, POLITICO (May 13, 2015, 2:35 PM ET), https://www.politico. com/blogs/under-the-radar/2015/05/sally-yates-confirmed-as-no-2-at

-justice-department-207069 [https://perma.cc/87SS-EHB8] (reporting that Senator Jeff Sessions had "no quibble with [Yates's] track record"). To take one of many examples from her career, Yates's office argued that a judge should disregard a jury's determination about how much cocaine was possessed by the defendants, arguing that the judge should sentence one defendant with no criminal record to ten years in prison and another man to twenty years in prison. Yates then chose to defend the mandatory minimum sentences on appeal. Yates eventually lost because the Supreme Court determined that judges cannot sentence people to mandatory minimum prison terms based on facts that were not found by a jury beyond a reasonable doubt. United States v. Jordan, 531 F. App'x 995, 996 (11th Cir. 2013) (vacating the sentences and remanding to the district court following review by the Supreme Court).

303. *See Public Hearing on Retroactivity of 2014 Drug Amendment,* U.S. SENT'G COMMISSION 110-11 (June 10, 2014), https://www.ussc.gov/sites/default/files/transcript_1.pdf [https://perma.cc/D92V-DX9T].

304. Barkow, *supra* note 298, at 441-49.

305. *See* Resignation Letter from Deborah Leff, Pardon Attorney, U.S. Dep't of Justice, to Sally Quillian Yates, Deputy Attorney General, U.S. Dep't of Justice (Jan. 15, 2016), https://www.documentcloud.org/documents/2777898-Deborah-Leff-resignation-letter.html [https://perma.cc/Q78S-6HDB] (citing as reasons for her resignation, Pardon Attorney Deborah Leff noted that she was "instructed to set aside thousands of [clemency] petitions," that Sally Yates reversed her staff's recommendations for clemency in an "increasing number of cases," and that she was denied access to the White House, preventing President Obama from learning of her disagreements with Ms. Yates); *see also* Mark Osler, Opinion, *Obama's Clemency Problem,* N.Y. TIMES (Apr. 1, 2016), https://www.nytimes.com/2016/04/01/opinion/obamas-clemency-problem.html [https://perma.cc/8FJH-QD7M] (discussing the Administration's inadequate approach to clemency generally).

306. *Id.*

307. *See* Office of the Pardon Att'y, *Commutations Denied by Barack Obama,* U.S. DEP'T JUST. (Jan. 23, 2017), https://www.justice.gov/pardon/obama-denials/commutations-denied-president-barack-obama [https://perma.cc/L96N-CRXW].

308. C.J. Ciaramella, *Kamala Harris' New Book Tries to Massage Her Record as a Prosecutor, but the Facts Aren't Pretty,* REASON: HIT & RUN BLOG (Jan. 9, 2019, 2:56 PM), https://reason.com/blog/2019/01/09/kamala-harris-new-book-tries-to-massage? [https://perma.cc/HEK5-BJGM].

309. *See* Branko Marcetic, *The Two Faces of Kamala Harris*, JACOBIN (Aug. 10, 2017), https://www.jacobinmag.com/2017/08/kamala-harris-trump-obama -california-attorney-general [https://perma.cc/D9SW-XFZF]; Marisa Lagos, *Report: Bail Hits People of Color Hard, Strips $15 Million a Year From S.F. Residents*, KQED NEWS (June 28, 2017), https://www.kqed.org/news/11535497/report-bail -hits-people-of-color-hard-strips-15-million-a-year-from-s-f-residents.

310. Hannah Giorgis, *Kamala Harris's Political Memoir Is an Uneasy Fit for the Digital Era*, ATLANTIC (Jan. 11, 2019), https://www.theatlantic.com/entertain-ment/archive/2019/01/kamala-harris-truths-we-hold-review/579430 [https://perma.cc/SGA7-77TR].

311. Marcetic, *supra* note 309.

312. Walker Bragman (@WalkerBragman), TWITTER (Jan. 28, 2019, 2:24 AM), https://twitter.com/walkerbragman/status/1089831581030797312?la ng=en[https://perma.cc/2BE3-QJLL].

313. Walker Bragman (@WalkerBragman), TWITTER (Jan. 28, 2019, 11:51 AM), https://twitter.com/WalkerBragman/status/1089974205284798464 [https://perma.cc/BZL5-UKDN].

314. Marcetic, *supra* note 309.

315. Kate Zernike, *"Progressive Prosecutor": Can Kamala Harris Square the Circle?*, N. Y. TIMES (Feb. 11, 2019), https://www.nytimes.com/2019/02/11/us /kamala-harris-progressive-prosecutor.html [https://perma.cc/WG5A-8Q8W].

316. Paige St. John, *Federal Judges Order California to Expand Prison Releases*, LA. TIMES (Nov. 14, 2014), https://www.latimes.com/local/political /la-me-ff-federal-judges-order-state-to-release-more-prisoners-2014 1114-story.html [https://perma.cc/WM7J-JPGB].

317. David C. Fathi, Opinion, *It's Time to Give Prisoners a Big Raise*, WASH. POST (Sept. 3, 2018), https://www.washingtonpost.com/opinions/its-time -to-give-prisoners-a-big-raise/2018/09/03/6be40364-ad5b-11e8 -8a0c-70b618c98d3c_story.html [https://perma.cc/QER9-CUCC].

318. Lara Bazelon, Opinion, *Kamala Harris Was Not a "Progressive Prosecu-tor,"* N.Y. TIMES (Jan. 17, 2019), https://www.nytimes.com/2019/01/17/opinion /kamala-harris-criminal-justice.html [https://perma.cc/A72X-C8F6] (detailing Harris's record on wrongful convictions and prosecutorial misconduct).

319. *See, e.g.*, Angela J. Davis, *Eric Holder Transformed the Attorney General into an Advocate for the Poor*, NEW REPUBLIC (Sept. 26, 2014), https://newrepublic .com/article/119616/eric-holders-criminial-justice-legacy [https://perma l.cc/99ZM-HLXF] ("[T]his former prosecutor became a champion of liberty").

320. *NACDL Presents Champion of Justice Restoration of Rights Award to Georgia Gov. Nathan Deal and Former U.S. Deputy Attorney Sally Q. Yates,* NAT'L ASS'N CRIM. DEF. LAW. (Aug. 28, 2018), https://www.nacdl.org /Deal-Yates-Rights-Restoration-Award [https://perma.cc/3CT2-6TMZ].

321. *See* Astead W. Herndon, *Kamala Harris Declares Candidacy, Evoking King and Joining Diverse Field,* N.Y. TIMES (Jan. 21, 2019), https://www.nytimes .com/2019/01/21/us/politics/kamala-harris-2020-president.html [https:// perma.cc/53W8-BCSA] (quoting Kristen Clark, President and Executive Director of the Lawyers' Committee for Civil Rights Under Law).

322. I have seen this in dozens of cities and counties in which I work. Sheriff Tom Dart in Chicago, for example, announced himself as a leader on bail reform, but I saw him work behind the scenes to undermine that reform; then to promote increased use of pretrial detention; and then to advocate for expansion of e-carceration. At one point, the sheriff simply refused to enforce court orders releasing pretrial detainees from his jail cells in flagrant violation of the "rule of law." *See* Rick Tulsky, *Lawsuit Contends Dart Illegally Holding Inmates Despite Judges' Bond Decisions,* INJUSTICE WATCH (Feb. 28, 2018), https://www.injusticewatch.org/news/2018/developing-cook -county-jail-inmate-contends-dart-illegally-holding-inmates [https://perma .cc/F2ME-4L8Y]. After pretrial reforms by the Chief Judge in response to a lawsuit in which I was involved led to a 44 percent decrease in the number of people physically confined in the Cook County jail, the sheriff's department bureaucracy expanded electronic custody to include thousands of people being monitored every day, and despite the dramatic decrease in jail population, the Sheriff's bureaucracy actually *increased* its budget by 28 percent to reach $588 million in 2018. *Money for Communities, Not Cages,* CHI. COMMUNITY BOND FUND 4 (Oct. 2018), https://chicagobond.org/wp-content/uploads /2018/10/money-for-communities-not-cages-why-cook-county-should-reduce -the-sheriffs-bloated-jail-budget.pdf [https://perma.cc/4BUZ-J4RW].

323. *See* Dan Walters, *Bail Reform Bill Stretches the 72-Hour Notice Law,* CALMATTERS (Aug. 27, 2018), https://calmatters.org/articles/commentary/bail -reform-bill-stretches-the-72-hour-notice-law [https://perma.cc/FUT8-28LQ].

324. *See* Michelle Alexander, *The Newest Jim Crow,* N.Y. TIMES (Nov. 8, 2018), https://www.nytimes.com/2018/11/08/opinion/sunday/criminal-justice -reforms-race-technology.html [https://perma.cc/6T77-U2Q9].

325. I represent a habeas petitioner in the California Supreme Court in a pending case arguing that this expansion of pretrial detention would violate the California Constitution. *See In re* Humphrey, 228 Cal. Rptr. 3d 513 (Cal. Ct. App. 2018), *rev. granted,* 417 P.3d 769 (Cal. 2018).

326.   *See* Jennifer Gonnerman, *Before the Law*, NEW YORKER (Oct. 6, 2014), https://www.newyorker.com/magazine/2014/10/06/before-the-law [https://perma.cc/TVU3-7SUN]; Jennifer Gonnerman, *Kalief Browder, 1993–2015*, NEW YORKER (June 7, 2015), https://www.newyorker.com/news/news-desk/kalief-browder-1993-2015 [https://perma.cc/FRX9-VYPP].

327.   *See* Zhandarka Kurti & William Martin, *Cuomo's "Carceral Humanism,"* JACOBIN (Nov. 2018), https://www.jacobinmag.com/2018/11/andrew-cuomo-juvenile-justice-carceral-humanism-kalief-browder [https://perma.cc/7PCY-P9D3].

328.   Akeem Browder, Kalief's brother, refused to endorse Cuomo in the 2018 primary. *Id.*

329.   *See* Samantha House, *After $12 Million Update, Former Cayuga County Center Will Again House Youth Offenders*, SYRACUSE.COM (Sept. 22, 2017, 3:33 PM), https://www.syracuse.com/crime/index.ssf/2017/09/state_plans_to_create_12_million_center_for_youth_offenders_in_cayuga_county.html [https://perma.cc/J4G5-V3T3].

330.   *See* Lauren-Brooke Eisen, *Down Under, More Humane Private Prisons*, N.Y. TIMES (Nov. 14, 2018), https://www.nytimes.com/2018/11/14/opinion/private-prisons-australia-new-zealand.html [https://perma.cc/649A-JZ33].

331.   The piece makes logical errors, has no analysis of or engagement with scholarship concerning the larger implications of increasing the economic and political power of private prison corporations, provides no empirical evidence to support its central claims, and ignores contrary evidence of the systemic mistreatment of detainees by private prisons in Australia and the United States. *See, e.g.*, Nick Olle et al., *At Work Inside Our Detention Centres: A Guard's Story*, GLOBAL MAIL (last visited Mar. 11, 2019), http://tgm-serco.patarmstrong.net.au [https://perma.cc/6TWG-MKUR]; Mark Willacy & Alexandra Blucher, *Inside Australia's 'Powder Keg' Private Prison*, ABC (June 19, 2018, 9:45 PM), https://www.abc.net.au/news/2018-06-20/inside-arthur-gorrie-correctional-centre/9837260 [https://perma.cc/3V73-TQJD]. Most brazenly, for example, although praising privatization of prisons in Australia was the supposed occasion for writing the op-ed, the author notes at the end of the op-ed that *there is no data available yet to evaluate private prisons in Australia.*

332.   *Id.*

333.   *See* Colleen O'Dea, *Former NJ Gov. Whitman to Chair National Task Force to Fix U.S. Democracy*, NJ SPOTLIGHT (Feb. 1, 2018), https://www

.njspotlight.com/stories/18/01/31/former-nj-gov-whitman-to-chair-national
-task-force-to-fix-u-s-democracy [https://perma.cc/85YE-AF8G].

334. *See* Preet Bharara et al., *Proposals for Reform: National Task Force on Rule of Law & Democracy*, BRENNAN CTR. FOR JUST. (Oct. 2, 2018), https://www.brennancenter.org/publication/proposals-reform-national-task-force-rule-law-democracy [https://perma.cc/F6X7-695Y]; Preet Bharara & Christine Todd Whitman, *How to Prevent Corruption, Protect the Rule of Law and Protect Democracy*, USA TODAY (Oct. 2, 2018, 10:00 AM EST), https://www.usatoday.com/story/opinion/2018/10/02/prevent-corruption-protect-rule-law-restore-faith-america-column/1491771002 [https://perma.cc/B6Z8-GWMG].

335. Bharara et al., *Proposals for Reform, supra* note 334.

336. Jacqueline Thomsen, *Sally Yates: Trump Is "Tearing Down the Legitimacy" of Justice Department*, HILL (May 15, 2018, 2:16 PM EST), https://thehill.com/blogs/blog-briefing-room/news/387793-sally-yates-trump-is-tearing-down-the-legitimacy-of-justice [https://perma.cc/3229-SCWP].

337. Jennifer Rubin, *Sally Yates: Don't "Normalize" Attacks on the Rule of Law*, WASH. POST (May 15, 2018), https://www.washingtonpost.com/blogs/right-turn/wp/2018/05/15/sally-yates-dont-normalize-attacks-on-the-rule-of-law [https://perma.cc/VAY2-DKMC].

338. Sally Yates, The Rule of Law Under Siege (Nov. 22, 2017), https://www.youtube.com/watch?v=VIoM8Xc_eDI [https://perma.cc/2RUU-DTR5]; *see also* Sally Q. Yates, *Don't Let Trump's Use of Celebrities Distract You from His Criminal-Justice Failures*, WASH. POST (Oct. 16, 2018), https://www.washingtonpost.com/opinions/dont-let-trumps-use-of-celebrities-distract-you-from-his-criminal-justice-failures/2018/10/16/2bfd7b14-d096-11e8-a275-81c671a50422 [https://perma.cc/DWZ4-U4RT].

339. *See* Eric Holder, Address to the 2008 American Constitutional Society National Convention (June 14, 2008), https://www.acslaw.org/video/eric-holder-on-the-rule-of-law-2008-acs-national-convention [https://perma.cc/7LRZ-WH9C].

340. Kamala Harris, Address upon Inauguration to the Office of California Attorney General 1 (2011), https://oag.ca.gov/system/files/attachments/press_releases/n2021_final_speech.pdf [https://perma.cc/6ALD-B7XJ].

341. *Id.* at 2.

342. *Id.* at 3.

343. Maurice Merleau-Ponty, Humanism and Terror xxiv (John O'Neill trans., Beacon Press 1969) (1947).

344. A new prosecutor, Rachel Rollins, was recently elected in Boston, taking office in the weeks prior to publication of this piece. Her campaign rhetoric more closely mirrors, and in some way exceeds in ambition, the progressive discourse of Krasner, although it is too early to evaluate what policy changes she will oversee.

345. See Bruce Western & Becky Pettit, Mass Imprisonment, in Bruce Western, Punishment and Inequality in America 11, 14–15 (2006).

346. Krasner recently unveiled what he called significant impacts of his signature bail policy change, in which his office requests cash bail in fewer cases. Samantha Melamed, Philly DA Larry Krasner Stopped Seeking Bail for Low-Level Crimes. Here's What Happened Next., Phila. Inquirer (Feb. 19, 2019), https://www.philly.com/news/philly-district-attorney-larry-krasner-money-bail-criminal-justice-reform-incarceration-20190219.html [https://perma.cc/89X2-YFXQ] (quoting Krasner as declaring at a press conference, "[w]e do not, we should not, imprison people for poverty"). But even the study that Krasner cited found that his policy was having barely any effect on wealth-based detention in Philadelphia. It had only led to an eight percentage-point decrease in the use of secured cash bail—and even this reduction had almost no effect on pretrial detention, because those individuals were largely being bailed out on low money bonds prior to the policy changes. Aurelie Ouss & Megan T. Stevenson, Evaluating the Impacts of Eliminating Prosecutorial Requests for Cash Bail 11 (George Mason Legal Studies Research Paper No. LS 19-08, 2019), https://papers.ssrn.com/sol3/papers.cfm?abstract_id=3335138; see also id. at 3 ("[T]he main policy impact of the No-Cash-Bail reform was to release more defendants without monetary conditions, with modest effects on pretrial detention.") (emphasis added).

347. See, e.g., Joe Trinacria, Krasner Requests Budget Increase for DA's Office, Phila. Mag. (Apr. 25, 2018, 9:06 AM), https://www.phillymag.com/news/2018/04/25/krasner-budget-increase-da-office [https://perma.cc/BS38-3RAQ].

348. Foxx has arguably been the best of the new prosecutors about sharing her data. In her first year, felony prosecutions decreased only 6.4 percent, which was not a significant decrease given the steady decline that started with her predecessor. And the trend reversed in her second year, with overall felony prosecutions going up 1.3 percent. Foxx's office also has a policy of allowing the police to file drug felonies in Chicago without exercising her own discretion. A Step in the Right Direction: An Analysis of Felony Prosecution Data in

Cook County, RECLAIM CHI. ET AL. 3 (2018), https://www.thepeopleslobbyusa
.org/wp-content/uploads/2018/06/05-2018-Report-Kim-Foxx_FINAL_Print
.pdf [https://perma.cc/EW9C-VSLP]; *Exercising Full Powers: Recommendations
to Kim Foxx on Addressing Systemic Racism in the Cook County Criminal Justice
System*, RECLAIM CHI. ET. AL. 2 (Jan. 2019), https://www.thepeopleslobbyusa
.org/wp-content/uploads/2019/01/2019-Report-Kim-Foxx_ForWeb.pdf
[https://perma.cc/664T-QJRT].

349.   *Exercising Full Powers, supra* note 348, at 2–3.

350.   *See* Ronald Brownstein, *Will Texas Follow Houston's Lead on Drug-Policy
Reform?*, ATLANTIC (May 24, 2018), https://www.theatlantic.com/politics
/archive/2018/05/will-texas-follow-houstons-lead-on-drug-policy-reform
/561035 [https://perma.cc/FBR5-HC76].

351.   Alex Hannaford, *Harris County DA Ran as a Reformer. So Why Is She
Pushing High Bail for Minor Offenses?*, APPEAL (Aug. 9, 2018), https://theappeal
.org/harris-county-kim-ogg-bail-reform-jail [https://perma.cc/KPA3-YR35].

352.   Greg Groogan, *County Judge, District Attorney Clash over Request for
102 New Prosecutors*, FOX 26 NEWS (Jan. 29, 2019), http://www.fox26houston
.com/news/county-judge-district-attorney-clash-over-request-for-102-new
-prosecutors [https://perma.cc/8DMZ-SXYJ].

353.   Maura Ewing, *Punished for Being Poor*, SLATE (Oct. 20, 2017), http://
www.slate.com/articles/news_and_politics/trials_and_error/2017/10/bail
_reform_is_catching_on_in_san_francisco_but_not_fast_enough_for_some
.html [https://perma.cc/U6KG-2H5L].

354.   George Gascón, *Decision Points: Prosecutors Have Opportunities to
Reduce Incarceration and Disparities Through Risk Assessment*, HUFFPOST: BLOG
(Oct. 14, 2015, 11:23 AM ET), https://www.huffingtonpost.com/george-gasc
/decision-points-prosecuto_b_8288908.html [https://perma.cc/7J5M-ETE3].

355.   *See, e.g.*, Amicus Curiae Brief of Attorney General Xavier Becerra, In re
Kenneth Humphrey, No. S247278 (Cal. Oct. 9, 2018) (arguing for a novel and
expansive re-interpretation of the state's power to detain people without bail
under the California Constitution); Notice of Motion and Motion to Detain
Without Bail, People v. Reynoso, No. 18002330 (Cal. Sup. Ct. Feb. 14, 2018)
(advancing the same argument on behalf of Gascón's office).

356.   *See, e.g.*, People's Response and Opposition to Motion for Order Releasing Defendant on Own Recognizance or Bail Reduction at 4, People v. Sanchez,
No. 17013355 (Cal. Sup. Ct. Oct. 3, 2017) (arguing, on behalf of Gascón's office,
that "the court must presume guilt" at bail hearings).

357. *See generally, e.g.*, PAUL BUTLER, LET'S GET FREE: A HIP-HOP THEORY OF JUSTICE 101–21 (2009) (discussing the constraints facing progressive prosecutors).

358. Safiya Bukhari-Alston, *Notes on the Black Panther Party: Its Basic Working Papers and Policy Statements*, FREEDOM ARCHIVES (1971), https://search .freedomarchives.org/search.php?s=%22notes+on+the+black+panther+party %22 [https://perma.cc/H7RA-LAYQ].

359. *See, e.g.*, Kim Foxx, Opinion, *Commentary: Kim Foxx: The Next Steps Toward Criminal Justice Reform After the Van Dyke Trial*, CHI. TRIB. (Oct. 5, 2018), http://www.chicagotribune.com/news/opinion/commentary/ct-perspec -kim-foxx-van-dyke-criminal-justice-1007-20181005-story.html [https://perma .cc/NGC2-7EN3].

360. Akilah Johnson, *That Was No Typo: The Median Net Worth of Black Bostonians Really Is $8*, BOS. GLOBE (Dec. 11, 2017), https://www.bostonglobe.com /metro/2017/12/11/that-was-typo-the-median-net-worth-black-bostonians -really/ze5kxC1jJelx24M3pugFFN/story.html [https://perma.cc/5YYZ-CVMF].

361. *See* Amna A. Akbar, *Toward a Radical Imagination of Law*, 93 N.Y.U. L. REV. 405, 410–11 (2018).

362. Ferguson, Missouri, is one among many representative examples. Responding to the conversion of a municipal police force into a revenue-generating machine, self-styled reformers from the Obama Administration announced that one of the main priorities in resolving its investigation into Ferguson's systemic civil rights violations was, in practice, to require *more* resources for "law enforcement" through "community policing" and other increased expenditures for police training. CIVIL RIGHTS DIV., U.S. DEP'T JUSTICE, INVESTIGATION OF THE FERGUSON POLICE DEPARTMENT 93 (Mar. 4, 2015), https://www.justice.gov/sites/default/files/opa/press-releases/attach -ments/2015/03/04/ferguson_police_department_report.pdf [https://perma.cc /K35Y-MFWL]. The "community policing" mandate was interpreted by the City and federal court monitor as requiring the City to hire *more* police officers, which became a top priority for Ferguson in implementing the decree. Jim Salter & Eric Tucker, *Ferguson Officials Missed Deadlines in Deal with Justice Department*, ASSOCIATED PRESS (Jan. 27, 2017), https://www.apnews.com /a288f62dbeda4a65bb2f35b35bb51aa1 [https://perma.cc/2Q8N-P5U3]. This was a pattern among Obama's police policies and settlements: to lavish money, weapons, and military equipment on police; to "train" police better; and to make sure that police officers have the funds to attach officer-controlled cameras to their militarized vehicles and vests to observe them as they police

impoverished communities. *See, e.g.*, Glen Ford, *Obama Prepares to Reinforce the Militarized Police Occupation of Black America*, BLACK AGENDA REPORT (July 28, 2016), https://www.blackagendareport.com/obama_reinforces_militarized_police [https://perma.cc/2NS2-CQK2].

363.   *See, e.g.*, Alexander, *supra* note 324; Dewan, *supra* note 194; Shaila Dewan & Andrew W. Lehren, *Alabama Prosecutor Sets the Penalty and Fills the Coffers*, N.Y. TIMES (Dec. 13, 2016), https://www.nytimes.com/2016/12/13/us/alabama-prosecutor-valeska-criminal-justice-reform.html [https://perma.cc/5PNY-GFCJ].

364.   *See, e.g.*, *About*, DETROIT COOPERATIVE, http://detroitcooperatives.nationbuilder.com [https://perma.cc/7D6Y-XXP7]; *Cooperatives*, SUSTAINABLE ECON. LAW CTR., https://www.theselc.org/cooperatives [https://perma.cc/3YHX-X2WU]; Jordan Heller, *One of America's Poorest Cities Has a Radical Plan to Remake Itself*, HUFFINGTON POST (Nov. 27, 2018), https://www.huffingtonpost.com/entry/cleveland-ohio-poorest-cities-regeneration_us_5bf2e9d5e4b0f32bd58c1374[https://perma.cc/MDV4-X2TF]. *See generally* GAR ALPEROVITZ, AMERICA BEYOND CAPITALISM (2d ed. 2011).

365.   Felipe De La Hoz, *Activists Launch #CLOSERikers Campaign to Close Rikers Island*, OBSERVER (Apr. 15, 2016), https://observer.com/2016/04/activists-launch-closerikers-campaign-to-close-rikers-island [https://perma.cc/SS4K-LCPT]; Rachel Sudduth, *Close the Workhouse Campaign Releases Plan to Permanently Close Facility*, KMOV4 (Sept. 13, 2018), https://www.kmov.com/news/close-the-work-house-campaign-releases-plan-to-permanently-close-facility/article_e883a14 2-b763-11e8-b516-a728bc8ef89e.html [https://perma.cc/BW9N-UPG4]; Michaela Winberg, *Advocates: Closing the Dilapidated, Decaying House of Correction Isn't Enough*, BILLY PENN (Apr. 19, 2018), https://billypenn.com/2018/04/19/advocates-closing-the-dilapidated-decaying-house-of-correction-isnt-enough [https://perma.cc/P3QH-QDMV].

366.   JUSTICELA, http://justicelanow.org [https://perma.cc/SJ5X-J2UU].

367.   Max Blau, *Legal Pot Is Notoriously White. Oakland Is Changing That.*, POLITICO (Mar. 27, 2018) https://www.politico.com/magazine/story/2018/03/27/oakland-legal-cannabis-hood-incubator-217657 [https://perma.cc/TNM5-HV3B].

368.   David Schaper, *Chicago Creates Reparations Fund for Victims of Police Torture*, NPR (May 6, 2015), https://www.npr.org/sections/thetwo-way/2015/05/06/404545064/chicago-set-to-create-reparation-fund-for-victims-of-police-torture [https://perma.cc/3UJ5-NYDE].

369. *Community Land Trust*, DETROIT PEOPLE'S PLATFORM, http://detroit peoplesplatform.org/resources/community-land-trusts [https://perma .cc/ECK5-MNME].

370. Shortly before publication of this essay, I spoke with District of Columbia officials who reported to me that the average daily population of committed children incarcerated in the juvenile secure facility was down to fifteen. Interview with Seema Gajwani, Special Counsel for Juvenile Justice Reform, Office of the Attorney General, in Washington, DC (March 1, 2019).

371. *See, e.g.*, Christie Donner, Community Reinvestment as the New Public Safety Model, COLO. JUST. REP. 3 (Winter 2018), https://www.ccjrc.org /wp-content/uploads/2018/11/Winter-2018.pdf [https://perma.cc/3R4E -T83S]; Community Reinvestment in Colorado, CO. CRIM. JUST. REFORM COALITION, https://www.ccjrc.org/wp-content/uploads/2018/10/Oct-2018 -Community-Reinvestment-Overview.pdf [https://perma.cc/S5SE-QZHG] (Oct. 2018).

372. *See, e.g.*, Melissa Harris, *Reality Onstage—How Theater Helps Young Women in Prison*, CHI. TRIB. (Nov. 25, 2012), https://www.chicago tribune.com/entertainment/ct-xpm-2012-11-25-ct-ae-1125-plays-in-prisons -20121125-story.html [https://perma.cc/X3XM-68A2]; Reed Johnson, *A Book -store That's Like a Favorite Aunt*, L.A. TIMES (May 28, 2011), http://articles .latimes.com/2011/may/28/entertainment/la-et-tia-chuchas-20110528 [https://perma.cc/8JT2-8SXQ]; Robert Samuels, *How a Book Club Is Helping to Keep Ex-Offenders from Going Back to Jail*, WASH. POST (Feb. 25, 2015), https:// www.washingtonpost.com/local/how-a-book-club-brought-inmates -together-even-on-the-outside/2015/02/25/0468c8ca-a277-11e4-903f -9f2faf7cd9fe_story.html].

The Human Lawyer

1. The vignettes in this piece are composites based on my personal experiences and observations in law school. The names used have been changed where appropriate to respect privacy. I am grateful above all to my parents, Barbara Blackmond and Costas Karakatsanis. This piece also owes a great deal to the hard work of dozens of colleagues and friends. I am especially indebted intellectually to Derrick Bell, Geoff Brounell, Richard Chen, Greg Dworkowitz, Lani Guinier, Jon Hanson, Shuli Karkowsky, Marco Lopez, Richard Parker, Michal Rosenn, and Nicole Ramos. Although *The Human Lawyer* was first published in

2010 in the NYU Review of Law and Social Change, I wrote the piece mostly in 2008 when I was finishing my third year in law school. In reproducing it here largely unedited, I recognize that it is not as I would write it today. But it is important for me to capture how I felt as a law student about our legal system, and to illustrate the evolution in my thinking by juxtaposing it with the other pieces in this book.

2. See *California Three-Strikes Prisoner Set Free*, FAMMGRAM (Families Against Mandatory Minimums, Washington, D.C.), Summer 2006, at 20, 20. *See also* Dean Kuipers, *Less Than Zero*, L.A. WKLY., July 12, 2001.

3. Kuipers, *supra* note 2.

4. Riggs v. California, 525 U.S. 1114, 1115 (1999) (denying Michael Riggs's pro se petition to declare his sentence unconstitutional).

5. *See* Ewing v. California, 538 U.S. 11, 18, 20 (2003) (plurality opinion); Lockyer v. Andrade, 538 U.S. 63, 66, 68 (2003).

6. The great wealth of empirical evidence suggests that mass incarceration fails even to advance its own stated goals and, perversely, may exacerbate the problems that, at least ostensibly, motivated the laws. *See, e.g.*, DRUG WAR FACTS 227, 232, 235–36 (Douglas A. McVay ed., 6th ed. 2007) (discussing recidivism, as well as the disruption of families), *available at* http://drugwarfacts.org/factbook.pdf; JEFFREY A. MIRON, DRUG WAR CRIMES (2004) (arguing that drug prohibition exacerbates many of the problems it purportedly solves). No robust evidence exists linking increased incarcerative penalties to any gains in deterrence of crime, let alone gains that justify the tremendous costs of incarceration. The overwhelming scientific consensus is that increases in sentence length, such as those seen over the last several decades, have not had a significant effect on deterrence. *See, e.g.*, Michael Tonry, *Purposes and Functions of Sentencing, in* 34 CRIME AND JUSTICE: A REVIEW OF RESEARCH 1, 28–29 (Michael Tonry ed., 2006) ("Three National Academy of Science panels . . . reached that conclusion, as has every major survey of the evidence").

7. Ctrs. for Disease Control & Prevention, Smoking and Tobacco Use, Fact Sheet, Tobacco-Related Mortality, http://www.cdc.gov/tobacco/data_statistics /fact_sheets/health_ effects/tobacco_related_mortality (last visited Sept. 9, 2010). More than 49,000 Americans die from the effects of secondhand smoke each year. *Id.*

8. Ali H. Mokdad, James S. Marks, Donna F. Stroup & Julie L. Gerberding, *Actual Causes of Death in the United States, 2000*, 291 J. AM. MED. ASS'N 1238, 1240, 1242 (2004) (estimating that in 2000, 17,000 Americans died from the

use or the indirect effects of the use of illicit drugs and that 16,653 people were killed in alcohol-related car crashes). *See also* NAT'L HIGHWAY TRAFFIC SAFETY ADMIN., TRAFFIC SAFETY FACTS 111 (2005) (finding that alcohol-related fatalities resulted in 16,885 deaths in 2005), *available at* http://www-nrd.nhtsa.dot .gov/Pubs/TSF2005.pdf.

9. *See, e.g.,* Mark Houser, *Exceptions the Rule for DUI Sentences,* PITT. TRIB.-REV., June 8, 2003 (discussing a Pennsylvania law that allows a special exception to mandatory sentences permitting drunk drivers with multiple convictions to spend most of their "incarceration" at home or in halfway houses). *See also* NHTSA, ON DWI LAWS IN OTHER COUNTRIES (2000) (reporting that most countries, as well as most states in the United States, have established fines and licensing sanctions for impaired driving offenses), *available at* http://www.nhtsa.dot.gov/people/injury/research/pub/dwiothercountries /dwi othercountries.html.

As a result of drug-sentencing policy, more than fifty-three percent of those in federal prisons in the United States were sentenced because of a drug offense. *See* HEATHER C. WEST & WILLIAM J. SABOL, U.S. DEP'T OF JUSTICE, PRISON-ERS IN 2007, at 22 tbl.11 (2008) (reporting that 95,446 of 179,204 federal prisoners were incarcerated for drug offenses in 2007), *available at* http://www.ojp.usdoj .gov/bjs/pub/pdf/p07.pdf. The number of drug prisoners increased 1,100 percent between 1980 and 2003. MARC MAUER & RYAN S. KING, THE SENTENC-ING PROJECT, A 25-YEAR QUAGMIRE: THE WAR ON DRUGS AND ITS IMPACT ON AMERICAN SOCIETY 10 (2007), *available at* http://www.sentencingproject. org/doc/publications/dp_25yearquagmire.pdf. This harsh sentencing persists even though alcohol use is much more highly correlated to violent crime than drug use. *See* JENNIFER C. KARBERG & DORIS J. JAMES, U.S. DEP'T OF JUS-TICE, SUBSTANCE DEPENDENCE, ABUSE, AND TREATMENT OF JAIL INMATES, 2002, at 6 tbl.7 (reporting that among jailed individuals in 2002, 37.6 percent of those imprisoned for an offense labeled "violent" used alcohol at the time of their offense and only 21.8 percent used drugs), *available at* http://bjs.ojp.usdoj .gov/content/pub/pdf/sdatji02.pdf. The United States Code requires lengthy, mandatory minimum sentences for possessing and distributing illegal drugs. *See, e.g.,* 21 U.S.C.A. § 841 (West 2010).

10. Bruce Western & Becky Pettit, *Mass Imprisonment, in* BRUCE WESTERN, PUNISHMENT AND INEQUALITY IN AMERICA 11, 14–15 (2006).

11. *See* PRISON POLICY INITIATIVE, U.S. INCARCERATION RATES BY RACE AND ETHNICITY (2010), available at https://www.prisonpolicy. org/graphs/raceinc.html; *see also* LANI GUINIER & GERALD TORRES,

THE MINER'S CANARY 263 (2002) (The U.S. imprisons black people at a rate six times that of South Africa at the height of apartheid). Black people constitute only fourteen percent of the nation's drug users. MAUER & KING, *supra* note 9, at 20. Incredibly though, black people constitute thirty-seven percent of those arrested for drug offenses, fifty-nine percent of those convicted for drug offenses, and seventy-four percent of those *sentenced to prison* for a drug offense. AM. CIVIL LIBERTIES UNION, CRACKS IN THE SYSTEM: TWENTY YEARS OF THE UNJUST FEDERAL CRACK COCAINE LAW 3 (2006), *available at* http://www.aclu.org/files/pdfs/drugpolic y/cracksinsystem_20061025.pdf.

12.   Although American intervention is more frequently accomplished through proxies, a few of the most overt uses of American force in the twentieth century include Hawaii, the Philippines, Nicaragua, Guatemala, Cuba, Puerto Rico, Iran, Iraq, South Vietnam, Chile, Grenada, Panama, Korea, Laos, and Cambodia. *See generally* HOWARD ZINN, A PEOPLE'S HISTORY OF THE UNITED STATES: 1492–PRESENT (new ed. 2003).

13.   CHRISTOPHER HELLMAN & TRAVIS SHARP, CTR. FOR ARMS CONTROL & NON-PROLIFERATION, THE FY 2009 PENTAGON SPENDING REQUEST—GLOBAL MILITARY SPENDING 1 (2008), *available at* http://www.armscontrolcenter.org/policy/securityspending/articles/fy09_dod_request_global.

The human lawyer asks herself simple but mind-altering and life-changing questions. For example, what would the world look like if the approximately $700 billion spent on the military this year were spent instead on the Peace Corps?

14.   *California Three-Strikes Prisoner Set Free, supra* note 2, at 20.

15.   McCleskey v. Kemp, 481 U.S. 279 (1987) (rejecting an equal protection challenge to the racially disparate application of the death penalty in Georgia and upholding Warren McCleskey's death sentence).

16.   *Id.* at 339 (Brennan, J., dissenting) (responding to the majority's contention that granting McCleskey's claim in the death penalty context would open the door to racial discrimination claims throughout the criminal system and accusing the majority of fearing a criminal legal system truly free of racial bias). Just like the Supreme Court justices, *Harvard Law Review* editors and other law students—worried about prestigious clerkships and successful careers—are often very risk averse. We are hesitant to live principled lives in accordance with our own values, and we are scared of the logical conclusions of our own views. As a result, just like the majority in *McCleskey*, we are afraid of what living up to our own stated values would mean in a world so full of genuine suffering and need.

17. *See* Strickland v. Washington, 466 U.S. 668 (1984) (establishing a two-pronged test for "ineffective assistance of counsel," including a "performance" prong that has been interpreted to have very little bite and a "prejudice" prong that forces those with ineffective lawyers to prove, amid complex litigation, exactly how a constitutionally defective lawyer might have affected their case).

18. *See* LA. CODE CRIM. PROC. ANN. art. 701B(1)(a) (Supp. 2009) (allowing forty-five days of custody before charging document must be filed for a misdemeanor and sixty days for a felony).

19. The median American household earned an estimated $50,303 in 2008. CARMEN DENAVAS-WALT, BERNADETTE D. PROCTOR, JASON C. SMITH, U.S. CENSUS BUREAU, INCOME, POVERTY, AND HEALTH INSURANCE COVERAGE IN THE UNITED STATES: 2008, at 6 (2009), *available at* http://www.census.gov/prod/2009pubs/p60-236.pdf. The median first-year salary at a large corporate law firm in New York City was $160,000 in 2009, not including potentially lucrative bonuses. Ass'n for Legal Career Prof'ls (NALP), NALP Bulletin, How Much Do Law Firms Pay New Associates? A 14-Year Retrospective as Reported by Firms (Sept. 2009), http://www.nalp.org/2009septnew assocsalaries?s=first%20 year%20 associate%20salary.

20. *See, e.g.,* United States v. Philip Morris USA, Inc., 449 F. Supp. 2d 1, 28–29 (D.D.C. 2006) (explaining and criticizing the role of corporate lawyers in strategizing for and covering up the tobacco industry's misconduct for decades and averring that the role of lawyers in deceiving the American public was "a sad and disquiet chapter" in the history of the legal profession), *aff'd in relevant part,* 566 F.3d 1095 (D.C. Cir. 2009). The deceptive actions of those corporate lawyers are all the more egregious when you consider that approximately 443,000 Americans die each year as a result of tobacco. *See* Ctrs. for Disease Control & Prevention, Smoking & Tobacco Use, Fast Facts, http://www.cdc.gov/tobacco/data_statistics /fact_sheets/fast_facts/index.htm (last visited Jan. 18, 2010).

In addition to some of the more high-profile endeavors of corporate lawyers—such as the tobacco litigation, cases concerning the murder and mistreatment of union workers in developing countries, and cases involving the use of chemicals like Agent Orange—large corporate law firms spend each day defending corporations against discrimination suits, protecting companies from paying for the damage their products cause to health and the environment, designing executive compensation systems, and structuring complicated financial deals and intricate contract provisions that help banks and other large financial institutions extract significant rents from the rest of society. Corporate lawyers represent large agriculture businesses using resource-driven litigation to threaten small farmers; credit card companies and mortgage lenders looking to extract ever-increasing interest rates from borrowers experiencing difficult financial conditions; corporate banks foreclosing on homeowners; private prison corporations looking to create and perpetuate unsound and unjust criminal laws; and numerous corporations, shell corporations, and wealthy individuals seeking to shelter their income and assets from government taxation and therefore deprive society of significant revenue each year; and a host of other interests that, with the help of corporate lawyers, have come to dominate American social policy and law.

21.   *See* Supreme Court of the U.S., Members of the Supreme Court of the United States, http://www.supremecourt.gov/about/members_text.aspx (last visited Sept. 9, 2010).

22.   Approximately 664,414 people are homeless on any given night in the United States. U.S. DEP'T OF HOUS. & URBAN DEV., THE 2008 ANNUAL HOMELESS ASSESSMENT REPORT TO CONGRESS 21 (2009), *available at* http://www.hudhre.info/documents/4thHomelessAssessmentReport.pdf. About twenty percent of those homeless in shelters are children. *Id.* at iii.

23.   No matter who you are—whether you are someone like George Bush, Antonin Scalia, and Barack Obama or someone like Paul Robeson, Mahatma Gandhi, and Simone de Beauvoir—the incredible thing about human life is that there is always a next moment in which you must make a new decision about what is right.

24.   For more information on the publication and its past issues, see its website, Project Hope to Abolish the Death Penalty, On Wings of Hope, http://virgilturtle.com/phadp/index.php?option=com_content&task=view&id=114&Itemid=87 (last visited Sept. 9, 2010).

25.   *See* C.C. LANGDELL, A SELECTION OF CASES ON THE LAW OF CONTRACTS, at viii–ix (2d ed. 1879). *See also* Duncan Kennedy, *Legal Education and the Reproduction of Hierarchy*, 32 J. LEGAL EDUC. 591, 596 (1982) (discussing the tendency of law schools to teach the law as separate from policy precisely because of this mystical scientific attribution known as "legal reasoning").

26.   For an excellent introduction to the topic of unconscious bias and its potential connection to various areas of law, see generally Kristin A. Lane, Jerry Kang & Mahzarin Banaji, *Implicit Social Cognition and Law*, 3 ANN. REV. L. & SOC. SCI. 427 (2007) (discussing how experimental psychology has provided substantial evidence that the human mind can operate without conscious awareness of the sources of influences on it and summarizing recent efforts of legal scholarship to consider how the law can and should adopt such findings). *See also*

Anthony G. Greenwald & Linda Hamilton Krieger, *Implicit Bias: Scientific Foundations*, 94 CAL. L. REV. 945 (2006) (discussing the pervasiveness of implicit bias and potential implications for human behavior and law); Jon Hanson & Kathleen Hanson, *The Blame Frame: Justifying (Racial) Injustice in America*, 41 HARV. C.R.-C.L. L. REV. 413 (2006) (describing the complicated social psychological phenomena and pervasive biases that allow us to tolerate a world that is inconsistent with the values we purport to hold); Jon Hanson & David Yosifon, *The Situational Character: A Critical Realist Perspective on the Human Animal*, 93 GEO. L.J. 1 (2004) (arguing that the dominant "rational actor" model of human agency should be replaced with a new conception that incorporates the influences of situation).

27.   An enormous body of research is beginning to catalog the extent to which human behavior is influenced by unconscious biases. For a meta-analysis of this literature, see Anthony G. Greenwald, T. Andrew Poehlman, Eric Luis Uhlmann & Mahzarin R. Banaji, *Understanding and Using the Implicit Association Test: III. Meta-analysis of Predictive Validity*, 97 J. PERSONALITY & SOC. PSYCHOL. 17 (2009) (recommending the use of both an implicit association test and self-report measures jointly as predictors of behavior). Other research has produced startling results in real-world analysis of legal cases. *See, e.g.*, Jennifer L. Eberhardt, Paul G. Davies, Valerie J. Purdie-Vaughns & Sheri Lynn Johnson, *Looking Deathworthy: Perceived Stereotypicality of Black Defendants Predicts Capital-Sentencing Outcomes*, 17 PSYCHOL. SCI. 383 (2006) (finding that, in cases involving a white victim, the more stereotypically black a defendant is perceived to be, the more likely that person is to be sentenced to death).

28.   This phenomenon is so pervasive that it can be found in nearly every debate on law and policy. For example, "trickle-down economics" is fairly obviously a gimmick that wealthy groups invented and employ (perhaps even in good faith) to justify massive economic inequality. But the workings of the economy are complicated enough and most conversations short enough that it is hard to prove the "theory" wrong completely or casually explain its irrelevance to nearly every argument in which it is invoked, so people are allowed to maintain and articulate in public a culturally credible belief in the hypothesis.

Or, for example, take any of the cases in which courts have upheld harsh prison sentences by superficially invoking the idea of deterrence. Although most evidence discredits the simplistic view of "deterrence" offered by courts without serious reflection, *see supra* note 6, it is the kind of empirical question that is very difficult conclusively to prove. So, the courts are permitted casually to invoke the concept and to maintain the clean hands of perceived intellectual credibility. *See* Harmelin v. Michigan, 501 U.S. 957, 1007–08 (1991) (Kennedy, J., concurring in part) (noting the "clarity" of the mandatory life sentence for cocaine possession and its connection to deterrence, one of the "first purposes of criminal law"). The same concept animates the Supreme Court's entire jurisprudence surrounding police interrogation. The Court apparently assumes that reciting a few quick "warnings" has some meaningful role in making less coercive police interactions with those who are largely frightened and unsophisticated. The Court similarly assumes that, during a police encounter, a person can freely consent to being searched. Anyone who works in the criminal punishment system knows that these "warnings" and this "knowing and voluntary" "consent" are utterly insufficient to protect those subjected to custodial interrogations and complete fictions given the actual psychological dynamics at work during those interactions. The Supreme Court is making empirical assumptions about how coercive those interactions are and what it would take to diffuse them without a sufficient understanding of what it is like to be in that situation and how police interactions are experienced by those who live in certain communities. Instead of crafting meaningful rules, the Court allows police to exploit people so long as they follow a few hollow procedures that, in the empirical view of the judges, magically transform inherently coercive situations into free and intelligent dialogues. *See generally* Davis v. United States, 512 U.S. 452 (1994) (demonstrating the unsupported assumption of both the majority and the dissent that simply giving *Miranda* warnings is sufficient to render an interaction knowing, voluntary, and intelligent).

29. Laws, beliefs, policies, and other results consistent with common flaws in decision-making should be viewed with even greater skepticism than outcomes that are inconsistent with the operation of those biases.

30. Strong evidence suggests that corporations and wealthy individuals have fared better in court than others. *See, e.g.*, Stephen Breyer, *The Federal Sentencing Guidelines and the Key Compromises upon Which They Rest*, 17 HOFSTRA L. REV. 1, 20–21 (1988) (noting that prior to the imposition of the Federal Sentencing Guidelines, courts were far more lenient on white-collar criminals (typically wealthier offenders) than on those convicted of similar common law crimes). *See generally* D. Michael Risinger, *Navigating Expert Reliability: Are Criminal Standards of Certainty Being Left on the Dock?*, 64 ALB. L. REV. 99 (2000) (noting that civil defendants—usually corporations—fare much better than criminal defendants—usually the indigent—in judicial opinions concerning expert testimony, even though the expert-evidence analysis is meant to be doctrinally identical); Alec Karakatsanis, A Tale of Two Doctrines (May 2008) (unpublished

manuscript, on file with author) (analyzing the doctrinal divergence in the Supreme Court's proportionality jurisprudence between the civil punitive damages and criminal punishment contexts and discussing the similar divergence in the Supreme Court's statutory interpretation of substantive criminal law in cases involving white-collar criminals as opposed to cases typically involving indigent defendants). *Cf. The Supreme Court, 2006 Term—Leading Cases*, 121 HARV. L. REV. 185, 275 (2007) (discussing how courts have used the Fourteenth Amendment to perpetuate dominant notions of class and culture).

Evidence also shows that other marginalized groups consistently fare poorly in court. *See, e.g.*, U.S. SENTENCING COMM'N, FINAL REPORT ON THE IMPACT OF *UNITED STATES V. BOOKER* ON FEDERAL SENTENCING 106 (2006) (noting that, when controlling for other factors, immigrants receive federal prison sentences almost 36 percent longer than U.S. citizens do), *available at* http://www.ussc.gov/booker_report/booker_report.pdf. These kinds of trends repeat themselves in myriad ways throughout our culture and our law. *See, e.g.*, N.Y. CIVIL LIBERTIES UNION, THE ROCKEFELLER DRUG LAWS: UNJUST, IRRATIONAL, INEFFECTIVE (2009) (noting that while whites constitute the vast majority of drug users and dealers in New York, blacks and Latinos constitute the vast majority of those sent to jail for drug-related offenses), *available at* http://www.nyclu.org/files/publications/nyclu_pub_ rockefeller.pdf. *See also supra* note 11.

We must always be sensitive to these outcomes, whether we are examining salary differences based on gender or trends concerning which charitable causes people of certain classes choose to support. The potential for bias and other flaws is simply too great, in both our laws and in our lives, to proceed without vigilance.

31.   To view the image and to learn more about the photographer, see *A Pulitzer-Winning Photographer's Suicide* (NPR broadcast, Mar. 2, 2006), *available at* http://www. npr.org/templates/story/story.php?storyId=5241442.

32.   One child dies every five seconds from starvation. FOOD & AGRIC. ORG. OF THE UNITED NATIONS, THE STATE OF FOOD INSECURITY IN THE WORLD 4 (2004), *available at* ftp://ftp.fao.org/docrep/fao/007/y5650e/y5650e00.pdf.125.

Policing, Mass Imprisonment, and the Failure of American Lawyers

1.   The term "jumpout" is slang in the DC area for infamous squads of armed police officers who conduct surprise "stop-and-frisk" maneuvers. *See* Nicole Flatow, *If You Thought Stop-and-Frisk Was Bad, You Should Know About*

Jump-Outs, THINKPROGRESS (Dec. 11, 2014, 11:00 AM), http://thinkprogress
.org/justice/2014/12/10/3468340/jump-outs [http://perma.cc/F374-VL8L].

2. The United States has 5 percent of the world's population but 25 percent of the world's prisoners. *See* Adam Liptak, *Inmate Count in U.S. Dwarfs
Other Nations'*, N.Y. TIMES (Apr. 23, 2008), http://www.nytimes.com/2008
/04/23/us/23prison.html. Its current rate of incarceration is about five to ten
times that of other comparably wealthy countries and five times its own steady
historical average prior to 1980. *See generally* Bruce Western & Becky Pettit,
Mass Imprisonment, in BRUCE WESTERN, PUNISHMENT AND INEQUALITY IN
AMERICA 11, 14–15 (2006); *Highest to Lowest—Prison Population Rate*, INT'L
CTR. FOR PRISON STUDIES, http://www.prisonstudies.org/highest-to-lowest
/prison_population_rate?field_region_taxonomy_tid=All (last visited Apr. 8,
2015) [http://perma.cc/L79X-MRQB].

3. Of the more than 13 million arrests in 2010, only 4 percent were arrests
for "violent crimes." *See* FED. BUREAU OF INVESTIGATION, *Arrests, in* UNIFORM
CRIME REPORT: CRIME IN THE UNITED STATES, 2010 (2011), http://www.fbi
.gov/about-us/cjis/ucr/crime-in-the-u.s/2010/crime-in-the-u.s.-2010/persons
-arrested/arrestmain.pdf [http://perma.cc/KD68-6ATE].

4. LANI GUINIER & GERALD TORRES, THE MINER'S CANARY: ENLISTING
RACE, RESISTING POWER, TRANSFORMING DEMOCRACY 263 (2002).

5. *See* ALLEN J. BECK & CANDACE JOHNSON, BUREAU OF JUSTICE STA-
TISTICS, U.S. DEP'T OF JUSTICE, NCJ NO. 237363, SEXUAL VICTIMIZATION
REPORTED BY FORMER STATE PRISONERS, 2008, at 5 (2012), http://www.bjs.gov
/content/pub/pdf/svrfsp08.pdf [http://perma.cc/JW94-4GQF] (finding that
9.6 percent of former state prisoners reported at least one instance of sexual victimization during their most recent period of incarceration).

6. It is worth all lawyers contemplating George Bernard Shaw's brilliant
"smallpox" analogy to explain the "thoughtless wickedness with which we scat-
ter sentences of imprisonment." GEORGE BERNARD SHAW, *Preface* to MAJOR
BARBARA (1907).

7. *See, e.g.*, Foucha v. Louisiana, 504 U.S. 71, 80 (1992) ("Freedom from
bodily restraint has always been at the core of the liberty protected by the
Due Process Clause from arbitrary governmental action." (quoting Shapiro v.
Thompson, 394 U.S. 618, 638 (1969)))); United States v. Salerno, 481 U.S. 739,
750 (1987) (recognizing the "fundamental nature of th[e] right" of freedom
from confinement); Schilb v. Kuebel, 404 U.S. 357, 365 (1971) ("[A] statutory
classification based upon suspect criteria or affecting 'fundamental rights' will

encounter equal protection difficulties unless justified by a *'compelling* governmental interest'"). Federal statutory law similarly provides that each sentence issued by a federal court must be "not greater than necessary" to accomplish legitimate enumerated goals. 18 U.S.C. § 3553(a) (2012). The federal courts have abandoned any serious intellectual inquiry of demonstrating that the particular prison terms that they impose, let alone the rampant imposition of mandatory minimum sentences for nonviolent drug offenses, are "necessary."

8. *See, e.g.,* Noam Chomsky, *International Terrorism: Image and Reality, in* WESTERN STATE TERRORISM (Alexander George ed., 1991), http://www.chomsky.info/articles/199112--02.htm [http://perma.cc/ST3R-4LSX]; Noam Chomsky, *Who Are the Global Terrorists?, in* WORLDS IN COLLISION: TERROR AND THE FUTURE OF THE GLOBAL ORDER (Ken Booth & Tim Dunne eds., 2002), http://www.chomsky.info/articles/200205--02.htm [http://perma.cc/R3HQ-SDWN]; Glenn Greenwald, *Salon Radio: Manipulative Use of the Term "Terrorism,"* SALON (Mar. 14, 2010, 8:16 AM), http://www.salon.com/2010/03/14/terrorism_20 [http://perma.cc/3Z62-MVB6]; Glenn Greenwald, *Terrorism in the Israeli Attack on Gaza,* THE INTERCEPT (July 29, 2014), https://firstlook.org/theintercept/2014/07/29/terrorism-israelgaza-context [https://perma.cc/G6AV-C5LQ]; Tomis Kapitan, *The Reign of "Terror,"* N.Y. TIMES OPINIONATOR (Oct. 19, 2014, 8:00 PM), http://opinionator.blogs.nytimes.com/2014/10/19/the-reign-of-terror. If we define terrorism as acts of violence against civilians to achieve political goals, perhaps the greatest perpetrator of terrorist violence in the modern era has been the American government. *See, e.g.,* WILLIAM BLUM, KILLING HOPE: U.S. MILITARY AND CIA INTERVENTIONS SINCE WORLD WAR II (2004); STEPHEN KINZER, OVERTHROW: AMERICA'S CENTURY OF REGIME CHANGE FROM HAWAII TO IRAQ (2006).

9. "Cigarette smoking is the leading cause of preventable disease and death in the United States, accounting for more than 480,000 deaths every year, or 1 of every 5 deaths." *Current Cigarette Smoking Among Adults in the United States,* CTRS. FOR DISEASE CONTROL & PREVENTION, http://www.cdc.gov/tobacco/data_statistics/fact_sheets/adult_data/cig_smoking (last updated Jan. 23, 2015) [http://perma.cc/FJQ8-FVGW]. Globally, over *five million* human beings die every year from tobacco, *see Tobacco,* WORLD HEALTH ORG., http://www.who.int/mediacentre/factsheets/fs339/en (last updated May 2014) [http://perma.cc/UP9N-W7MU], manufacturers of which threaten countries with debilitating litigation should they attempt to enact public health policies to protect their populations, *see* Sabrina Tavernise, *Tobacco Firms' Strategy Limits Poorer Nations' Smoking Laws,* N.Y. TIMES (Dec. 13, 2013), http://www.nytimes.com/2013/12/13/health/tobacco-industry-tactics-limit-poorer-nations-smoking-laws.html.

10. Unsafe water and sanitation kill over 700,000 children under age five every single year from diarrhea. *Global Water, Sanitation, & Hygiene*, CTRS. FOR DISEASE CONTROL & PREVENTION, http://www.cdc.gov/healthywater /global/wash_statistics.html (last updated Nov. 8, 2013) [http://perma.cc/AGF2 -T82N].

11. Excessive salt consumption, much of it from processed foods and chain restaurants, kills 2.3 million people worldwide and is responsible for one in every ten American deaths. Katie Moisse, *1 in 10 U.S. Deaths Blamed on Salt*, ABC NEWS (Mar. 21, 2013, 4:24 PM), http://abcnews.go.com/blogs/health/2013/03 /21/1-in-10-u-s-deaths-blamed-on-salt [http://perma.cc/6UZ4-AXPU].

12. Almost 10,000 Americans die every year from speeding alone. *Speed Management Safety*, FED. HIGHWAY ADMIN., U.S. DEP'T OF TRANSP., http:// safety.fhwa.dot.gov/speedmgt (last updated Oct. 15, 2014) [http://perma.cc /H43W-X4CR].

13. As of 2009, lack of adequate health insurance killed 45,000 Americans every year. David Cecere, *New Study Finds 45,000 Deaths Annually Linked to Lack of Health Coverage*, HARVARD GAZETTE (Sept. 17, 2009), http://news.harvard .edu/gazette/story/2009/09/new-study-finds-45000-deaths-annually-linked-to -lack-of-health-coverage [http://perma.cc/E4UQ-ULYX].

14. Polluted air causes seven million deaths every year. *7 Million Premature Deaths Annually Linked to Air Pollution*, WORLD HEALTH ORG. (Mar. 25, 2014), http://www.who.int/mediacentre/news/releases/2014/air-pollution/en [http:// perma.cc/4F37-2R9C].

15. Thirty-four thousand nonsmoking Americans die every year from heart disease caused by secondhand smoke. *Health Effects of Secondhand Smoke*, CTRS. FOR DISEASE CONTROL & PREVENTION, http://www.cdc.gov/tobacco /data_statistics/fact_sheets/secondhand_smoke/health_effects (last updated Mar. 5, 2014) [http://perma.cc/SJ2G-QF93].

16. Malnutrition is an underlying cause of forty-five percent of the 6.3 million child deaths that occur globally each year. *Children: Reducing Mortality*, WORLD HEALTH ORG., http://www.who.int/mediacentre/factsheets/fs178/en (last updated Sept. 2014) [http://perma.cc/3Q9V-N458].

17. "The victimization rate was 27.7 rapes per 1,000 female [college] students." BONNIE S. FISHER ET AL., BUREAU OF JUSTICE STATISTICS, U.S. DEP'T OF JUSTICE, NCJ NO. 182369, THE SEXUAL VICTIMIZATION OF COLLEGE WOMEN 10 (2000), https://www.ncjrs.gov/pdffiles1/nij/182369.pdf [http:// perma.cc/9LGW-MGPD].

18. *See* FED. BUREAU OF INVESTIGATION, *supra* note 3.

19. *See* Robert Kuttner, *America Should Send More People to Prison*, HUFF-INGTON POST (Feb. 1, 2015, 10:59 PM), http://www.huffingtonpost.com/robert-kuttner/america-should-send-more-_b_6591730.html [http://perma.cc/TLC7 -45VT]. The number of American "law enforcement" agents investigating white-collar crime and public corruption is a tiny fraction of the number patrolling communities and investigating street crime. *See infra* note 20.

20. It is difficult to quantify the suffering and death caused by large-scale financial fraud and tax evasion, but estimates of the costs of poverty are staggering and approach 1 million deaths annually in America alone. *See, e.g.*, Nicholas Bakalar, *Researchers Link Deaths to Social Ills*, N.Y. TIMES (July 4, 2011), http: //www.nytimes.com/2011/07/05/health/05social.html (citing a study led by Columbia University researchers and based on data from 2000, when many fewer Americans were living in poverty). In any case, such devastating crimes constitute a miniscule and *decreasing* percentage of domestic policing resources. *See, e.g.*, OFFICE OF THE INSPECTOR GEN., U.S. DEP'T OF JUSTICE, FOLLOW-UP AUDIT OF FEDERAL BUREAU OF INVESTIGATION PERSONNEL RESOURCE MANAGEMENT AND CASEWORK ii–iii (2010) (finding that fewer resources were devoted to investigating white-collar crime), http://www.justice.gov/oig /reports/FBI/a1024.pdf [http://perma.cc/S6JM-ZURU]; William K. Black, *Mueller: I Crippled FBI Effort v. White-Collar Crime, My Successor Will Make It Worse*, NEW ECON. PERSPS. (Aug. 26, 2013), http://neweconomicperspectives .org/2013/08/mueller-i-crippled-fbi-effort-v-white-collar-crime-my-successor -will-make-it-worse.html [http://perma.cc/5U2F-E6MR]; Mike Masnick, *FBI Admits It's Not Really About Law Enforcement Any More; Ignores Lots of Crimes to Focus on Creating Fake Terror Plots*, TECHDIRT (Jan. 6, 2014, 11:09 AM), https://www.techdirt.com/articles/20140106/00442525768/fbi-admits-its-not -really-about-law-enforcement-any-more-ignores-lots-crimes-to-focus-creating -fake-terror-plots.shtml [http://perma.cc/R8AN-DLYQ] (discussing the dwindling resources devoted to investigating and policing white-collar crimes).

21. Matt Ferner, *One Marijuana Arrest Occurs Every 42 Seconds in U.S.: FBI Report*, HUFFINGTON POST (Apr. 15, 2014, 7:59 AM), http://www.huffingtonpost .com/2012/10/29/one-marijuana-arrest-occu_n_2041236.html   [http://perma .cc/QF5K-9ZM8].

22. For a discussion of the profit motive in modern policing, see *Developments in the Law—Policing*, 128 HARV. L. REV. 1706, 1723–46 (2015). *See also* Sarah Stillman, *Taken*, NEW YORKER, Aug. 12, 2013, http://www.newyorker.com /magazine/2013/08/12/taken [http://perma.cc/2CQE-75P4]; *Drug Task Force*

Scandals: A National Look, PBS INDEP. LENS (Feb. 23, 2009), http://www.pbs.org/independentlens/tuliatexas/scandals.html [http://perma.cc/35Z4-9Q4W].

23.   *See* Caitlin Dickson, *How the U.S. Ended Up with 400,000 Untested Rape Kits*, THE DAILY BEAST (Sept. 23, 2014), http://www.thedailybeast.com/articles/2014/09/23/how-the-u-s-ended-up-with-400-000-untested-rape-kits.html [http://perma.cc/HGD4-ZRSP].

24.   Max Ehrenfreund, *Charted: The 20 Deadliest Jobs in America*, WASH. POST WONKBLOG (Jan. 28, 2015), http://www.washingtonpost.com/blogs/wonkblog/wp/2015/01/28/charted-the-20-deadliest-jobs-in-america [http://perma.cc/JG3S-FAC7]; *see also* Daniel Bier, *By the Numbers: How Dangerous Is It to Be a Cop?*, FOUND. FOR ECON. EDUC. (Aug. 19, 2014), http://fee.org/blog/detail/by-the-numbers-how-dangerous-is-it-to-be-a-cop [http://perma.cc/87KW-GH5P].

25.   The scientific consensus is that increases in sentence length, such as those seen in American criminal practice over the last several decades, have not had any significant effect on deterrence. *See, e.g.*, Michael Tonry, *Purposes and Functions of Sentencing*, *in* 34 CRIME AND JUSTICE: A REVIEW OF RESEARCH 1, 28–29 (Michael Tonry ed., 2006) ("Three National Academy of Science panels . . . reached that conclusion, as has every major survey of the evidence" (citations omitted)). And yet only after decades of brutal imprisonment are we starting to consider "alternatives" to incarceration, such as drug treatment, which has been proven for many years to be far more cost-effective than caging people. *See, e.g.*, JUSTICE POLICY INST., SUBSTANCE ABUSE TREATMENT AND PUBLIC SAFETY (2008), http://www.justicepolicy.org/images/upload/08_01_rep_drugtx_ac-ps.pdf [http://perma.cc/9EXJ-XSA9].

To put the point slightly differently, consider the growing body of evidence that violent crime rates may actually be determined in significant part by lead exposure in children. *See* Kevin Drum, *America's Real Criminal Element: Lead*, MOTHER JONES, Jan.–Feb. 2013, http://www.motherjones.com/environment/2013/01/lead-crime-link-gasoline [http://perma.cc/2EBM-VFPW]. On a broader level, poverty alleviation, access to healthy food, education that stimulates intellectual and artistic passions, gender equality, and a number of other factors play a role in creating flourishing, safe communities. Our current legal system instead thoughtlessly uses police and prisons as a first resort to control the manifestations of social problems in these other areas rather than reducing the need for policing and prisons by addressing those problems.

26. *See generally* ANGELA Y. DAVIS, ARE PRISONS OBSOLETE? (2003), http:
//www.feministes-radicales.org/wp-content/uploads/2010/11/Angela-Davis
-Are_Prisons_Obsolete.pdf [http://perma.cc/D6EQ-6EAA].

Again, here, the juxtaposition of modern policing tactics with "terrorism" discourse is instructive. We have used the threat of "terrorism" to justify torture,
targeted murder, bloody wars, an all-encompassing global surveillance apparatus that alters the nature of free thought, and trillions of dollars in spending
that could otherwise have transformed the lives of every single American by
ending poverty, saving our environment, and revitalizing our entire domestic
infrastructure. We have done all of this without any evidence that those actions
actually create fewer "terrorists" and despite very real evidence that they only
exacerbate the problem. *See, e.g.*, Mark Mazzetti, *Use of Drones for Killings Risks
a War Without End, Panel Concludes in Report*, N.Y. TIMES (June 26, 2014), http:
//www.nytimes.com/2014/06/26/world/use-of-drones-for-killings-risks-a-war
-without-end-panel-concludes-in-report.html (discussing bipartisan panel's
criticism of government for failing to rigorously weight costs and benefits of
drone strikes). *See generally Data Rivers 2.0*, GLOBAL TERRORISM DATABASE,
UNIV. OF MD., http://www.start.umd.edu/gtd/features/GTD-Data-Rivers.aspx
(last visited Apr. 8, 2015) [http://perma.cc/K4CK-EHH4] (charting patterns in
rise of terrorism-related incidents by country and region since the United States
announced its "War on Terror").

If courts and lawyers justify assassinations, indefinite detention, and dragnet
global surveillance to counter a threat not nearly as significant as the threat of
speeding or drunk driving, what will happen when we are asked to apply these
principles to perceived domestic problems? The creeping adoption of the language and logic of military battles against "terrorists" into domestic policing
reflects a slow march toward fascism that I fear we will not perceive until it is
too late.

27. *See* Troxel v. Granville, 530 U.S. 57, 65–66 (2000) (plurality opinion).

28. Illinois v. Allen, 397 U.S. 337, 346 (1970).

29. *See* MO. SUPREME COURT, 2013 MISSOURI JUDICIAL REPORT SUP-
PLEMENT: FISCAL YEAR 2013, at 302, 303, http://www.courts.mo.gov/file
.jsp?id=68905 [https://perma.cc/Y99G-4YGM]; U.S. CENSUS BUREAU, *Ferguson (City), Missouri*, U.S. CENSUS BUREAU: ST. & COUNTY QUICKFACTS, http:
//quickfacts.census.gov/qfd/states/29/2923986.html (last visited Apr. 8, 2015)
[http://perma.cc/N4E3-TFJN].

30. *See, e.g.*, Class Action Complaint, Fant v. City of Ferguson, No. 4:15-cv-253 (E.D. Mo. Feb. 8, 2015), http://www.civilrightscorps.org/work/criminalization-of-poverty/ferguson-mo-debtors-prisons (I represent the plaintiffs in this case); First Amended Class Action Complaint, Mitchell v. City of Montgomery, No. 2:14-cv-186 (M.D. Ala. May 23, 2014), (same); Chris Albin-Lackey, HUMAN RIGHTS WATCH, PROFITING FROM PROBATION (2014), http://www.hrw.org/reports/2014/02/05/profiting-probation.

31. *See* Grits for Breakfast, *Class C Misdemeanor Arrests and Incarceration in Texas, By the Numbers* (March 30, 2019), available at http://gritsforbreakfast .blogspot.com/2019/03/class-c-misdemeanor-arrests-and.html.

32. *See, e.g.*, Atul Gawande, *Hellhole*, NEW YORKER, Mar. 30, 2009, http://www.newyorker.com/magazine/2009/03/30/hellhole [http://perma.cc/6ZN2 -GEPS]; Jennifer Gonnerman, *Before the Law*, NEW YORKER, Oct. 6, 2014, http://www.newyorker.com/magazine/2014/10/06/law-3 [http://perma.cc /NQU8-VP77]; Julie K. Brown, *In Miami Gardens, Store Video Catches Cops in the Act*, MIAMI HERALD (Sep. 8, 2014, 6:58 PM), http://www.miamiherald .com/news/local/community/miami-dade/article1957716.html [http://perma .cc/9ESM-69MW]; Julie K. Brown, *Prisoner: I Cleaned Up Skin of Inmate Scalded in Shower; Human-Rights Groups Call for Federal Intervention*, MIAMI HERALD (June 25, 2014, 10:28 PM), http://www.miamiherald.com/news/local /community/miami-dade/article1972693.html [http://perma.cc/K6G7-SR4A]; Shaun King, *One Small Town's Police Have Killed More People Than Police in Germany and the UK Combined*, DAILY KOS (Feb. 12, 2015, 7:22 AM), http:// www.dailykos.com/story/2015/02/12/1363996/-Pasco-Washington-police -have-killed-more-people-than-police-in-Germany-the-UK-combined [http: //perma.cc/462T-YP2D]; Ross Tuttle & Erin Schneider, *Stopped-and-Frisked: "For Being a F**king Mutt,"* THE NATION (Oct. 8, 2012), http://www.thenation .com/article/170413/stopped-and-frisked-being-fking-mutt-video [http:// perma.cc/3FVN-ABUD].

33. *See, e.g.*, David Carroll, *Gideon's Despair*, MARSHALL PROJECT (Jan. 2, 2015, 7:15 AM), https://www.themarshallproject.org/2015/01/02/four-things -the-next-attorney-general-needs-to-know-about-america-s-indigent-defense -crisis [https://perma.cc/55KG-JL2M?type=source].

34. Andrew E. Taslitz, *The Guilty Plea State*, CRIM. JUST., Fall 2008, at 4, http://www.americanbar.org/content/dam/aba/publishing/criminal_justice _section_newsletter/crimjust_cjmag_23_3_taslitz.authcheckdam.pdf [http:// perma.cc/V8PN-GU3C].

35. United States v. Salerno, 481 U.S. 739, 755 (1987).

36. *See, e.g.*, Laura Sullivan, *Bail Burden Keeps U.S. Jails Stuffed with Inmates*, NPR (Jan 21, 2010, 2:00 PM), http://www.npr.org/2010/01/21/122725771/Bail -Burden-Keeps-U-S-Jails-Stuffed-With-Inmates [http://perma.cc/YC64 -4PMZ].

37. *See, e.g.*, U.S. DEP'T OF JUSTICE, INVESTIGATION OF THE NEW- ARK POLICE DEPARTMENT 9 n.7 (2014), http://big.assets.huffingtonpost.com /NPDFindingsReport.pdf [http://perma.cc/PE2D-2LBG] (finding up to ninety- three percent of police stops in Newark to be unjustified); A.C. Thompson, *Feds Find "Systemic Violations of Civil Rights" by New Orleans Police Department*, PRO- PUBLICA (Mar. 17, 2011, 3:40 PM), http://www.propublica.org/nola/story/feds -find-systemic-violations-of-civil-rights-by-new-orleans-police-departm [http: //perma.cc/A8CZ-PQWP]; *see also, e.g.*, Spencer Ackerman, *Inside Chicago's Leg- acy of Police Abuse: Violence "as Routine as Traffic Lights,"* THE GUARDIAN (Mar. 3, 2015, 12:39 PM), http://www.theguardian.com/us-news/2015/mar/03/chicago -police-violence-homan-square [http://perma.cc/6MEP-ULCH]; Alice Brennan & Dan Lieberman, *Florida City's "Stop and Frisk" Nabs Thousands of Kids, Finds 5-Year-Olds "Suspicious,"* FUSION (May 9, 2014), http://fusion.net/justice/story /miami-gardens-stop-frisk-nabs-thousands-kids-finds-667430 [http://perma.cc /QE64-PE75] ; John Conroy, *Police Torture in Chicago*, CHI. READER, Oct. 8, 2009, http://www.chicagoreader.com/chicago/police-torture-in-chicago-jon-burge -scandal-articles-by-john-conroy/Content?oid=1210030 [http://perma.cc/XP5P -2K3V]; Nick Pinto, *When Cops Break Bad: Inside a Police Force Gone Wild*, ROLL- ING STONE (Jan. 29, 2015), http://www.rollingstone.com/culture/features/when -cops-break-bad-albuquerque-police-force-gone-wild-20150129 [http://perma.cc /7CHH-EWHC]; Catherine E. Shoichet, Eliott C. McLaughlin & Kyung Lah, *Justice Dept.: Cleveland Police Has Pattern of Excessive Force*, CNN (Dec. 4, 2014, 8:59 PM), http://www.cnn.com/2014/12/04/us/cleveland-justice-department -police-excessive-force [http://perma.cc/TV5J-ATV3].

Unlawful policing tactics have also spawned a pandemic of perjury, popu- larly called "testilying" by police officers and others. *See, e.g.*, Radley Balko, *How Do We Fix the Police "Testilying" Problem?*, WASH. POST (Apr. 16, 2014), http://www.washingtonpost.com/news/the-watch/wp/2014/04/16/how-do -we-fix-the-police-testilying-problem [http://perma.cc/7V3Y-CFPM]; Nick Malinowski, *Testilying: Cops Are Liars Who Get Away with Perjury*, VICE (Feb. 3, 2013), http://www.vice.com/read/testilying-cops-are-liars-who-get-away -with-perjury [http://perma.cc/TR2U-WFEL]. Although quantification of this problem is difficult, my interviews of public defenders, criminal defendants, and police officers around the country support the conclusion that the vast majority of criminal cases concerning guns and drugs include some kind of false or misleading statements in order to conceal a constitutional violation. Just as we are irrationally drawn to focus on "bad criminals," many people look at these stories and seek to blame "bad cops." This is a serious mistake. Part of the system's success is its ability to get people to focus on criticizing "bad apples" rather than on challenging deeper structural problems.

38. NAT'L RESEARCH COUNCIL, STRENGTHENING FORENSIC SCIENCE IN THE UNITED STATES 7 (2009), https://www.ncjrs.gov/pdffiles1/nij/grants /228091.pdf [https://perma.cc/NY2W-3H67] (concluding that, except for DNA evidence, every other area of forensic testimony offered for decades in American courts lacked a reliable scientific basis that supported many conclusions offered by so-called forensic "experts"); see also, e.g., David Grann, Trial by Fire, NEW YORKER, Sept. 7, 2009, http://www.newyorker.com/magazine/2009 /09/07/trial-by-fire[http://perma.cc/F9DH-6WLW]; Spencer S. Hsu, Convicted Defendants Left Uninformed of Forensic Flaws Found by Justice Dept., WASH. POST (Apr. 16, 2012), http://www.washingtonpost.com/local/crime/convicted -defendants-left-uninformed-of-forensic-flaws-found-by-justice-dept/2012/04 /16/gIQAWTcgMT_story.html [http://perma.cc/EE2Y-DPW5].

39. See, e.g., Joseph Shapiro, As Court Fees Rise, the Poor Are Paying the Price, NPR (May 19, 2014, 4:02 PM), http://www.npr.org/2014/05/19/312158516 /increasing-court-fees-punish-the-poor.

40. See, e.g., Eyewitness Misidentification, INNOCENCE PROJECT, http:// www.innocenceproject.org/causes-wrongful-conviction/eyewitness -misidentification (last visited Apr. 8, 2015) [http://perma.cc/7BCG-KHKS].

41. For example, although courts created a doctrine that a person cannot be convicted of perjury based only on the testimony of a single other witness, see Weiler v. United States, 323 U.S. 606, 607 (1945) ("The general rule in prosecutions for perjury is that the uncorroborated oath of one witness is not enough to establish the falsity of the testimony of the accused set forth in the indictment" (quoting Hammer v. United States, 271 U.S. 620, 626 (1926)) (internal quotation marks omitted)), American courts nonetheless allow such convictions for much more serious crimes, like murder, and routinely allow police officers to secure convictions for entirely victimless crimes that may not even have occurred.

42. See, e.g., COMM'N ON SAFETY AND ABUSE IN AMERICA'S PRISONS, VERA

INST. OF JUSTICE, CONFRONTING CONFINEMENT 13 (2006), http://www.vera .org/sites/default/files/resources/downloads/Confronting_Confinement.pdf [http://perma.cc/8UK8-USMJ] ("Every year, more than 1.5 million people are released from jail and prison carrying a life-threatening contagious disease.").

43. *See, e.g.*, ALLEN J. BECK ET AL., BUREAU OF JUSTICE STATISTICS, NCJ NO. 241399, SEXUAL VICTIMIZATION IN PRISONS AND JAILS REPORTED BY INMATES, 2011–12, at 6 (2013), http://www.bjs.gov/content/pub/pdf/svpjri1112 .pdf [http://perma.cc/N2R5-VV8W] (finding that 3.2 percent of jail inmates reported being sexually abused during their current stay in jail).

44. Indeed, these fundamental flaws and the need for new collective forms of legal practice exist in the civil context as well, where people and families need lawyers to help them with housing, medical benefits, protection from predatory financial products, child custody, immigration, illegal employment practices, and a variety of other issues central to living a flourishing life. And the revenues of the two hundred largest corporate law firms were $96.3 billion in 2013, more than sixty-nine times the total funding spent on civil legal aid for low-income people in the U.S. *See* Pete Davis (@PeteDDavis), TWITTER (Apr. 18, 2018, 9:49 AM), https://twitter.com/PeteDDavis/status/1118874275027587073; *see also generally, e.g.*, PETE DAVIS, OUR BICENTENNIAL CRISIS: A CALL TO ACTION FOR HARVARD LAW SCHOOL'S PUBLIC INTEREST MISSION (2017), http://hlrecord.org/wp-content/uploads/2017/10/OurBicentennialCrisis.pdf.

ABOUT THE AUTHOR

Alec Karakatsanis is the founder of Civil Rights Corps, a nonprofit organization that uses innovative litigation, advocacy, and storytelling to challenge the systemic injustice of the criminal punishment bureaucracy. Before founding Civil Rights Corps, Alec was a public defender in Alabama and Washington, DC, representing people accused of crimes who were unable to pay for an attorney.

Alec was awarded the 2016 Trial Lawyer of the Year for his role in bringing constitutional civil rights cases to challenge widespread wealth-based jailing across the United States and the 2016 Stephen B. Bright Award for contributions to indigent defense in the South. Alec's work with Civil Rights Corps challenging the money bail system in California was recently honored with the 2018 Champion of Public Defense Award by the National Association of Criminal Defense Lawyers.

Alec is interested in ending human caging, surveillance, the death penalty, police, immigration laws, war, hierarchy, and inequality. He also likes playing the piano, soccer, and making weird paintings. Alec graduated from Yale College in 2005 with a degree in Ethics, Politics & Economics and Harvard Law School in 2008, where he was a Supreme Court Chair of the *Harvard Law Review*. He lives in Washington, DC.

PUBLISHING IN THE PUBLIC INTEREST

Thank you for reading this book published by The New Press. The New Press is a nonprofit, public interest publisher. New Press books and authors play a crucial role in sparking conversations about the key political and social issues of our day.

We hope you enjoyed this book and that you will stay in touch with The New Press. Here are a few ways to stay up to date with our books, events, and the issues we cover:

- Sign up at www.thenewpress.com/subscribe to receive updates on New Press authors and issues and to be notified about local events
- Like us on Facebook: www.facebook.com/newpress -books
- Follow us on Twitter: www.twitter.com/thenewpress

Please consider buying New Press books for yourself; for friends and family; or to donate to schools, libraries, community centers, prison libraries, and other organizations involved with the issues our authors write about.

The New Press is a 501(c)(3) nonprofit organization. You can also support our work with a tax-deductible gift by visiting www.thenewpress.com/donate.